ON THIS DAY

DK Delhi

Senior Editors Virien Chopra, Shatarupa Chaudhuri
Project Art Editors Heena Sharma, Sanjay Chauhan
Editorial Team Arushi Mathur, Bipasha Roy, Mark Silas
Art Editors Sifat Fatima, Ankita Sharma
Assistant Art Editor Bhavnoor Kaur
Illustrators Aparajita Sen, Mohd. Zishan, Priyal Mote
Senior Picture Researcher Sumedha Chopra
Picture Researcher Rituraj Singh
Managing Editor Kingshuk Ghoshal
Managing Art Editor Govind Mittal
DTP Designers Nityanand Kumar, Pawan Kumar Singh, Satish Chandra Gaur
Senior DTP Designer Harish Aggarwal
Pre-Production Manager Balwant Singh
Production Manager Pankaj Sharma
DK India Editorial Head Glenda Fernandes
DK India Design Head Malavika Talukder
Jacket Designer Tanya Mehrotra

DK London

Senior Editor Sam Atkinson
Senior Designer Michelle Staples
Project Editor Amanda Wyatt
Editorial Assistant Zaina Budaly
Managing Editor Rachel Fox
Managing Art Editor Owen Peyton Jones
Senior Production Editor Andy Hilliard
Senior Production Controller Meskerem Berhane
Jacket Design Development Manager Sophia MTT

Publisher Andrew Macintyre
Associate Publishing Director Liz Wheeler
Art Director Karen Self
Publishing Director Jonathan Metcalf

Written By Andrea Mills, Meghaa Gupta, Upamanyu Das, Zaina Budaly, Amanda Wyatt

First published in Great Britain in 2021 by
Dorling Kindersley Limited
DK, One Embassy Gardens, 8 Viaduct Gardens,
London, SW11 7BW

The authorised representative in the EEA is Dorling Kindersley Verlag GmbH. Arnulfstr. 124, 80636 Munich, Germany

10 9 8 7 6 5 4 3 2 1
001–322077–Oct/2021

A CIP catalogue record for this book is available from the British Library.
ISBN: 978-0-2414-7120-3

Printed and bound in China

For the curious
www.dk.com

This book was made with Forest Stewardship Council™ certified paper – one small step in DK's commitment to a sustainable future. For more information go to www.dk.com/our-green-pledge

CONTENTS

INTRODUCTION

How did different cultures around the world come up with ways to organize days into months and years? The most common approaches were a lunar calendar, based on the approximately 30-day cycle of the Moon, and a solar calendar that uses one cycle of Earth's rotation around the Sun – a little bit more than 365 days.

A global calendar

The vast majority of countries around the world now use the same solar calendar in everyday life. This calendar is called the Gregorian calendar. However, many religious and traditional festivals are worked out using a lunar calendar, which is why celebrations such as Diwali, Easter, Ramadan, and Rosh Hashanah do not fall on the same days each year.

The calendar we use today had its origins in ancient Rome. In 46 BCE, Julius Caesar ordered the creation of a more accurate calendar that reflected the solar year. This new calendar, which came into effect on 1st January 45 BCE, was made up of 365 days, with an extra day added every fourth year (0.25 days for each year). The Julian calendar became widely used throughout the Roman Empire, which stretched across Europe and into north Africa, and parts of Asia.

Julius Caesar added a month named after himself to the Julian calendar, the month we know today as July.

This Aztec Sun stone served an unknown purpose, but shows the symbols for the months as well as other periods of time in the Mesoamerican calendar.

29th February was not originally a leap day – the Julian calendar added the extra day after 24th February.

Gregory's reforms

By the 16th century, the difference between an actual solar year and the Julian calendar had drifted by about 10 days. This happened because the length of a year is not exactly 365.25 days – it's closer to 365.24 days. The Roman Catholic pope, Gregory XIII, introduced the Gregorian calendar in 1582. Among other adjustments, ten days were cut from the calendar to bring the date back into line with a solar year. So in 1582 the day after Thursday 4th October was Friday 15th October.

Over the next couple of centuries, most nations using the Julian calendar converted to the Gregorian system, though Russia and Greece didn't switch until the 20th century. The difference between the dates of the Julian and Gregorian calendars means that a day may have had one date in one country, and a date ten or more days later in another. For the purposes of this book, we have given the dates that were being used in the relevant country at the time – whether that was the Julian or Gregorian calendar.

Forgotten histories

Keeping track of different calendars can be an issue, but is not the only problem facing a day-by-day history. Traditionally, history has been written by those in power, so the stories of people from marginalized groups are not well documented. However, in recent years, there has been an enthusiastic interest in reclaiming these lost histories, bringing the stories of women, Black people, and other groups to a wider audience. We have included as many of these stories in this book as we can.

Black history month highlights the stories of Black people throughout history, such as civil rights activist Sojourner Truth.

Ada Lovelace Day was set up in 2009 to celebrate the achievements of this computing pioneer, and all women in STEM (Science, Technology, Engineering, and Mathematics) careers.

January 1

45 BCE

Julian calendar

In ancient Rome, a new calendar named after ruler Julius Caesar came into use. In this calendar, the length of a year became the number of days we know it today – 365, increasing to 366 every fourth year.

Born this day

1894 Satyendra Nath Bose, mathematician and physicist from British-occupied India. German-born US physicist Albert Einstein was a friend of Bose, and built on Bose's theories in some of his own work.

1959

Cuban Revolution

Nearly six years of civil war between the Cuban government and communist rebels came to an end. Revolutionary leader Fidel Castro overthrew president Fulgencio Batista, who fled to the Dominican Republic at dawn. Castro seized power and remained in charge of Cuba for 49 years until 2008.

Also on this day

1801 Italian astronomer Giuseppe Piazzi spotted the dwarf planet Ceres – the biggest object ever discovered in the asteroid belt.

1863 US president Abraham Lincoln issued the Emancipation Proclamation during the US Civil War, freeing millions of enslaved people.

1892 Ellis Island Immigration Station in New York Harbor, USA, started processing European immigrants. The first was Irish teenager Annie Moore.

2002 The Euro

With the new Euro currency entering circulation, 12 countries in the European Union (EU) replaced their national currencies with Euro banknotes and coins.

1975

Mysterious monarchs

US biologist Kenneth C Brugger first documented the winter location of the monarch butterfly in the mountains of Mexico. He found forested slopes covered with millions of butterflies that had travelled south from the USA and Canada for more than 4,800 km (3,000 miles).

Also on this day

1492 The surrender of the Spanish city of Granada to Christian forces marked the end of more than 700 years of Islamic rule in Spain.

1929 Canada and the USA agreed to redirect the Niagara River to reduce erosion and protect the Niagara Falls.

1963 The Viet Cong won its first major victory at the Battle of Ap Bac during the Vietnam War.

2004

Stardust sample

Flying close to Comet Wild 2, NASA's *Stardust* space probe grabbed samples of dust left in the comet's wake. It became the first-ever spacecraft to take a sample from a comet and bring it back to Earth.

1879

Cricket hat-trick

Nicknamed the Demon Bowler, Australian cricketer Fred Spofforth bowled out three English batsmen with three balls in a row. This was the first-ever hat-trick in test cricket, at a match held at the Melbourne Cricket Ground in Australia.

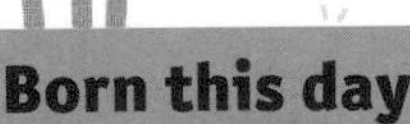

Born this day

1920 Isaac Asimov, US author and biochemist. He was a celebrated science-fiction writer and editor of around 500 books about space, science, and robots. His most famous works are the *Foundation* and *Robot* series.

1868

The Meiji Restoration

Emperor Meiji announced that Japan was back under the direct rule of the emperor, after almost seven centuries of control by warlords known as shoguns.

1888

Drinking straw

US inventor Marvin Stone received a patent for his invention of an artificial straw made by twisting paper into the shape of a tube. He was fed up with ryegrass straws spoiling the taste of his drinks.

The rights of women

1792

British writer and early champion of women's rights Mary Wollstonecraft finished *A Vindication of the Rights of Woman*, a book in which she argued that women are equal to men, and deserve the same rights to a full education.

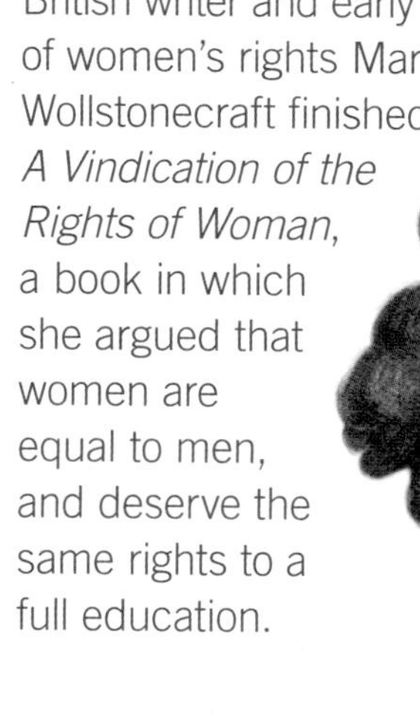

Born this day

1892 J R R Tolkien, British author. His most popular books, *The Hobbit* and *The Lord of the Rings*, are set in Middle-earth, a fantasy world of his own creation.

Also on this day

1925 Political leader Benito Mussolini became dictator of Italy, announcing that he would rule by force if necessary.

1957 The first electric watch, the Hamilton Electric 500, was launched in the USA. It was unreliable, constantly requiring new batteries.

2019 A lander successfully touched down on the far side of the Moon for the first time, as part of the Chinese mission Chang'e 4.

1944

Operation Carpetbagger

Allied forces carried out the first of more than 3,000 air missions to drop essential supplies and weapons. These items were delivered by parachute to resistance fighters across large parts of Nazi-occupied Europe.

1936

Topping the charts

US magazine *Billboard* published the first music hit parade – a list of the week's bestselling songs. More than 80 years later, it still releases weekly charts of the most popular songs and albums, as well as charts split by different types of music.

Born this day

1809 Louis Braille, French teacher. Totally blinded by a childhood accident, he designed the writing system named after him. Braille consists of raised dots on paper that visually impaired people can read with their fingers. Louis Braille's birthday is now celebrated as World Braille Day.

2010 Tower in the desert

The Burj Khalifa officially opened in Dubai in the United Arab Emirates. It stands about 828 m (2,717 ft) tall and has more than 160 floors.

Also on this day

1853 Solomon Northup was freed from slavery in Louisiana, USA. The memoir of his experiences, *Twelve Years a Slave*, was made into an award-winning film in 2013.

1906 South Africa's cricket team scored their first international test match win in a four-day game against England.

2007 Nancy Pelosi became the first woman Speaker of the House of Representatives in the USA.

January 5

1709

The Great Frost

Temperatures across Europe plummeted overnight and stayed icy for three months during the coldest winter for 500 years. Rivers and lakes were covered in ice and thousands of people froze to death.

1886

Jekyll and Hyde

Published on this day, the book *Strange Case of Dr Jekyll and Mr Hyde* by Scottish writer Robert Louis Stevenson tells the story of a respected doctor with a split personality.

Also on this day

1769 Scottish inventor James Watt patented improvements to the steam engine, kickstarting the Industrial Revolution.

1941 Troops from Australia and the UK defeated Italy in the Battle of Bardia in Libya during World War II.

2005 US scientists identified a new planet in the Solar System. Smaller than the Moon, Eris is now known as a dwarf planet.

Born this day

1941 Hayao Miyazaki, Japanese animation director. He co-founded Studio Ghibli, a Japanese animation studio, and wrote and directed animated feature films such as *Spirited Away* and *My Neighbor Totoro*.

Festival of ice

1985

The first Harbin Ice and Snow Festival opened in China. Each year millions of people come to Harbin to see carved ice sculptures as big as buildings at the two-month-long festival.

January 6

1942 Around the world

The *Pacific Clipper* seaplane landed in New York in the USA, completing the first commercial plane flight round the world. The flight had covered 32,000 km (20,000 miles) in just over a month of flying.

Born this day

1967 A R Rahman, Indian film score composer. He has sold more than 200 million albums worldwide.

Butler vs butcher 1681

The first-ever boxing match recorded in the newspapers was fought between the Duke of Albemarle's butler and butcher in England. There weren't many rules, but the beefy butcher was declared the winner.

2018 A giant hot drink

Mexicans celebrated Three Kings' Day with the largest-ever cup of hot chocolate. It contained 4,817 litres (1,272 gallons) of hot cocoa made from locally grown chocolate.

Also on this day

1863 US inventor James Plimpton launched a new fashion for roller skating when he patented his four-wheeled "rocker skates".

1929 Mother Teresa, a Roman Catholic nun, arrived in Kolkata, India, where she devoted her life to caring for the poor.

1987 US astronomers reported that they had detected light from the birth of a faraway galaxy, 12 billion years after it happened.

January

7

1785

Up, up, and away!

French inventor John-Pierre Blanchard and US scientist John Jeffries became the first people to fly between countries, when they travelled from the UK to France in a hot-air balloon.

1990

Dangerous angle

Tilting more than 5 m (16 ft), the Leaning Tower of Pisa in Italy was closed for the first time in its 800-year history for urgent restoration work to stop it from toppling over.

1958

The Flying V

US guitar makers Gibson patented the futuristic Flying V electric guitar. Sales were slow at first, but rock stars like Jimi Hendrix turned this V-shaped instrument into a music icon.

Also on this day

1914 French boat *Alexandre La Valley* was the first to sail along the Panama Canal, which connects the Atlantic and Pacific oceans.

1939 In a lab in Paris, French physicist Marguerite Perey discovered Francium, an extremely rare radioactive element.

1985 Japan launched *Sakigake*, its first interplanetary spacecraft.

Born this day

1985 Lewis Hamilton, British Formula 1 driver. He has broken the record for Formula 1 wins, but he is also an avid campaigner against racism, championing diversity in motor sports.

January

8

1297

Monk of Monaco

Francesco Grimaldi disguised himself as a monk to gain access to the Rock of Monaco. He then seized Monaco's fortress in an event commemorated on the country's coat of arms.

Also on this day

1493 Italian explorer Christopher Columbus reported spotting mermaids off the coast of modern-day Dominican Republic. They turned out to be large, grey, ocean-dwelling mammals called manatees.

1877 Lakota warrior Crazy Horse fought his last battle against US soldiers at Wolf Mountain in Montana, USA. Crazy Horse was forced to surrender due to harsh weather.

2007

What's that smell?

A pungent smell of rotting eggs filled the streets of New York City, USA, on this day, alarming citizens. Fire trucks scrambled to detect the source without success, but fortunately the mystery odour faded that same day.

1912

African National Congress

The South African Native National Congress (SANNC), the forerunner of the African National Congress (ANC) was formed in South Africa. Its mission was to fight against the unjust and oppressive treatment of Black people.

Born this day

1935 Elvis Presley, US singer. The biggest star of the rock 'n' roll era, the King – as he was known – made the new sound popular with his unique dance moves and soulful voice.

1947 David Bowie, British singer and songwriter. A master performer and a genius at reinventing himself, Bowie was a leading voice in glam rock.

1768

Roll up, roll up!

The world's first modern circus opened in London, UK, organized by horse rider Philip Astley. The show began with tricks on horseback around the circus ring and grew to include acrobats and jugglers.

2007

First iPhone

US entrepreneur Steve Jobs presented the first iPhone to the public. With a camera and internet browser built in, this mobile phone was called the "invention of the year" by *Time* magazine.

Born this day

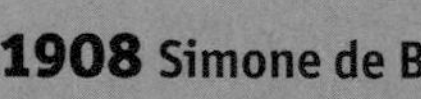

1908 Simone de Beauvoir, French thinker, writer, and women's rights advocate. In her books, she argued that women should have the same opportunities as men.

1816

Safety lamp

British chemist Sir Humphry Davy trialled his new safety lamp featuring an enclosed flame to protect miners. Previous lamps had open flames, which triggered explosions with the flammable gases in coal mines.

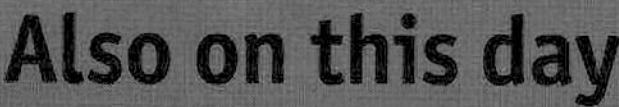

Also on this day

1918 The Battle of Bear Valley, a clash between a band of Yaqui people and US Army soldiers, marked the final conflict of the American Frontier Wars.

1960 The foundation stone was laid in the construction of Aswan High Dam – the world's largest embankment dam – across the Nile River in Egypt.

1992 The first exoplanets – planets orbiting stars beyond the Solar System – were found by two astronomers, Aleksander Wolszczan of Poland and Dale Frail of Canada.

1863 Underground opening

The world's first underground railway network opened in London, UK. About 30,000 passengers travelled by steam locomotive on the Metropolitan line on the first day.

1901 Striking oil

The US oil industry began when crude oil started gushing from a drill at Spindletop Hill in Texas, USA. The gusher produced 100,000 barrels of oil a day at first, and was only capped after nine days.

1985 Electric vehicle

British inventor Clive Sinclair launched the Sinclair C5 battery-powered electric vehicle. Although the pedal car was widely criticized for being impractical and unsafe, its environmentally friendly electric design was ahead of its time.

Also on this day

1929 The famous *Tintin* comic strip by Belgian cartoonist Hergé was first published in the weekly supplement *Le Petit Vingtième.*

1946 The first General Assembly of the United Nations (UN) organization was held in London, UK, with 51 countries represented.

1946 To test the strength of radar, the US Army Signal Corps bounced radio signals off the Moon in an experiment known as Project Diana.

Born this day

1924 Max Roach, Black American jazz artist and music composer. He became one of the most influential jazz drummers in history.

January 11

Also on this day

532 A week-long riot began at a chariot race in Constantinople in the Byzantine Empire. The rioters destroyed around half the city.

1851 The Taiping Rebellion in China started a 14-year civil war between the Qing rulers and breakaway group Taiping Heavenly Kingdom.

1964 A report by US Surgeon General Luther Terry linked smoking cigarettes to lung cancer for the first time.

1922 Insulin injection

The hormone insulin was first used to treat a condition called diabetes. A 14-year-old Canadian boy named Leonard Thompson received the first insulin injection.

Born this day

1885 Alice Paul, US women's rights campaigner. She was best known for championing the 19th Amendment to the US Constitution, which ensured equal voting rights for everyone, regardless of gender.

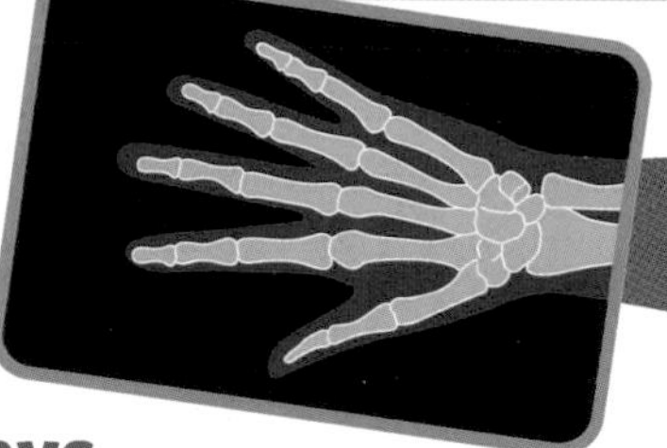

1896 Using X-rays

British doctor John Hall-Edwards made the first-ever medical use of X-rays, to examine a patient's hand with a needle inside it. Doctors now routinely use X-rays to look inside the human body.

2020 Top tortoise

After helping to save his species through a breeding programme, the giant tortoise Diego retired to the Galápagos Islands in the Pacific Ocean. Thanks to him and two other male tortoises, the giant tortoise population increased from just 15 to more than 2,000.

January 12

2014 Record-breaking rap

A freestyle rap performance with improvised lyrics by the KJ52 Freestyle Team in Florida, USA, lasted a record-breaking 12 hours and two minutes.

Also on this day

1528 Gustav I was crowned King of Sweden. He ruled for the next 37 years, laying the foundations for modern Sweden.

1962 US Army helicopters transported hundreds of paratroopers to their target in Operation Chopper. This was the first US military operation of the Vietnam War.

2010 A devastating earthquake in Haiti killed more than 230,000 people.

Born this day

1863 Swami Vivekananda, Hindu monk. He promoted religious tolerance and world peace, especially among young people. His birthday is celebrated as National Youth Day in India.

1995 Wolf revival

Eight grey wolves from Jasper National Park in Canada were reintroduced to Yellowstone National Park, USA, to revive the US population of the species. Hunting had wiped out grey wolf populations 70 years before.

1967 Cryonics

After US psychology teacher Dr James Bedford died of cancer, his body became the first to be deep-frozen through cryonics, a process that preserves a human body for possible revival in future.

1871

Drilling down

The patent for the first electric dental drill was filed by US dentist and inventor George Green. This major advancement allowed for continuous, high-speed dental work.

Born this day

1596 Jan Van Goyen, Dutch painter. He created more than 1,200 paintings and 1,000 drawings in his lifetime. Most were scenic landscapes of his native Netherlands.

2008 Kayaking adventure

Australians James Castrission and Justin Jones set a record for the longest ocean voyage on a double kayak when they arrived in New Zealand after paddling 3,200 km (2,000 miles) from Australia. Their journey lasted 62 days.

1942 A quick exit

An ejector seat was used for the first time in history during World War II. Helmut Schenk, a German jet fighter pilot, escaped successfully from his faulty aircraft by activating the system.

Also on this day

1910 In the first public radio broadcast, an opera performance was transmitted live from New York City's Metropolitan Opera House, USA.

2018 A message sent in error warning of an imminent ballistic missile strike on the Pacific islands of Hawaii, USA, caused public panic.

2020 The Murchison meteorite, which landed in Australia in 1969, was confirmed to be the oldest material on Earth, at 7 billion years old.

January

14

Summer of Love

1967

The Human Be-In was a festival held at a park in San Francisco, USA. Poets, musicians, activists, and students all gathered to celebrate alternative lifestyles, which led to the city's famous Summer of Love.

Born this day

1943 Shannon Lucid, US astronaut. She spent 188 days on the Russian space station *Mir* studying the effects of space travel on the human body.

Also on this day

1761 At a place called Panipat in what is now northern India, Afghan forces clashed with the Maratha Empire in the Third Battle of Panipat. Thousands of soldiers died.

2005 *Huygens* became the first probe to land on a moon in the outer Solar System. It arrived by parachute on Titan, the largest moon of Saturn, to take pictures and carry out tests.

1897

Aconcagua ascent

Argentina's Cerro Aconcagua, the highest peak in the Americas, was climbed for the first time when Swiss mountaineer Matthias Zurbriggen reached its summit at 6,960 m (22,834 ft).

1997

Ancient Lyceum

Greek archaeologists found an ancient site in Athens, Greece, that they believed to be the Lyceum. This was an exceptional school run by the great thinker Aristotle, who taught his students philosophy, science, and poetry.

January 15

1797

Top hat

According to stories told later, the hatter John Heatherington caused chaos when he paraded in a new hat through the streets of London, UK. Women fainted and the crowds shoved each other to get a look at the new design, the "top hat".

Good Queen Bess

1559

The coronation of 25-year-old Elizabeth I was held at Westminster Abbey in London. Her 45-year reign as Queen of England was considered to be a golden era of peace, progress, and prosperity.

Born this day

1929 Martin Luther King, Jr, Black American minister and activist. He was awarded the Nobel Peace Prize for his work as a leader of the Civil Rights Movement in the USA.

Sully's landing

2009

When his plane experienced engine trouble soon after take-off, US pilot Chesley Sullenberger managed to land it safely in the Hudson River, USA, saving the lives of all 155 people on board.

Also on this day

1919 Disaster struck when a tank of liquid molasses burst open and flooded the streets of Boston, USA, killing 21 people.

1962 The Derveni papyrus was discovered in Greece. It was later dated to 340 BCE, making it the oldest manuscript ever found in Europe.

1967 The first Super Bowl took place in Los Angeles. This American football championship game became the biggest annual sporting event in the USA.

January

16

2006 Africa's first female president

When Ellen Johnson Sirleaf was sworn in as the new president of Liberia, she became the first woman to be elected head of state of an African country.

Also on this day

1913 Indian mathematician Srinivasa Ramanujan wrote to Cambridge University in the UK outlining his solutions to many maths problems, some of which remained unsolved by experts at the time. He was invited to Cambridge, where he made important contributions to mathematics.

1979 The shah of Iran, Mohammad Pahlavi, was forced into exile after protests and violent demonstrations by Islamic rebels.

1547 Ivan the Terrible

Teenager Ivan IV was crowned the first tsar of Russia. He ruled through terror and was prone to murderous rages, becoming known as Ivan the Terrible.

Born this day

1932 Dian Fossey, US conservationist. She spent two decades in the forests of Rwanda studying mountain gorillas, and later wrote the book *Gorillas in the Mist* about her experiences.

378 CE Tikal takeover

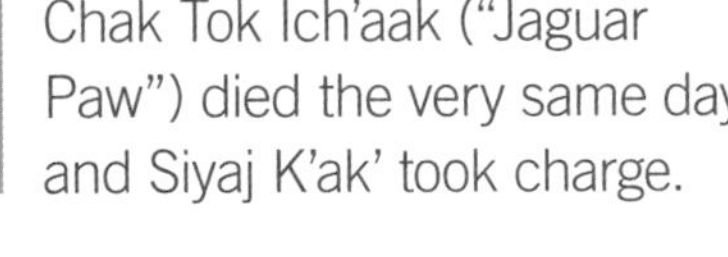

According to records etched in stone, a warrior named Siyaj K'ak' ("Fire is born") marched into the Mayan city of Tikal (now in modern-day Guatemala). The ruler Chak Tok Ich'aak ("Jaguar Paw") died the very same day and Siyaj K'ak' took charge.

January

17

Sawn in half

1921

British magician PT Selbit became the first person to perform the illusion of sawing someone in half. His assistant Betty Barker survived the trick at his London show to the relief of the audience.

Born this day

1964 Michelle Obama, Black American lawyer and writer. She became the first Black woman to serve as the USA's first lady when her husband Barack Obama became the country's president.

1987

Caught on camera

The coelacanth was filmed for the first time in the Indian Ocean off the east coast of Africa. This rare bony fish had been discovered in 1938.

1893

Hawaiian queen

A US coup forced Queen Liliuokalani of Hawaii, its final monarch, to step down. Hawaii later became the 50th state of the USA. The US government has since apologized for its part in the coup.

Also on this day

1920 The 18th Amendment of the US Constitution banned the sale of alcohol in the USA. It was only repealed 13 years later.

1991 After Iraqi troops invaded Kuwait, the Gulf War began with bombing raids against Iraq by a US-led alliance of nations.

1997 Norwegian explorer Børge Ousland became the first person to make a solo crossing of Antarctica on foot. It had taken him 64 days.

Also on this day

1871 The second German Empire was proclaimed following the unification of German states during the Franco-Prussian War.

1912 The ill-fated expedition of British explorer Robert Falcon Scott reached the South Pole only to find that Norwegian adventurer Roald Amundsen had arrived a month earlier. Scott's entire team perished on the return journey to base camp.

2002 The civil war in Sierra Leone officially ended after 11 years of conflict.

1593

The Battle of Nong Sa Rai

King Naresuan of Siam killed Crown Prince Minchit Sra of Burma in an elephant battle that ended the Burmese invasion. The day is now celebrated as Royal Thai Armed Forces Day.

1943

Bread ban

Sliced bread was banned in the USA to reduce the costs for additional labour and equipment during World War II. However, the new measure only lasted two months.

Born this day

1884 Elena Arizmendi Mejia, Mexican women's rights activist. She set up the Neutral White Cross Organization to nurse the injured during the Mexican Revolution.

1911

Landing at sea

An aircraft landed on a ship for the first time. The risky manoeuvre was carried out successfully by pilot Eugene Ely on the flight deck of the battleship USS *Pennsylvania*, which was anchored in San Francisco Bay, USA.

January

19

Also on this day

1817 To liberate Chile, Argentinian soldiers and Chilean patriots invaded the country by crossing the Andes mountains.

1981 The Algiers Accords ended the Iran hostage crisis, in which 52 US citizens were held hostage by Iran. The hostages returned home the next day.

1991 Invading Iraqi forces in Kuwait opened oil wells and pipelines, causing massive environmental damage.

1966

Indian icon

Indira Gandhi became the first female prime minister of India. She reduced India's reliance on other countries for food by increasing grain production. Gandhi served two terms before she was assassinated in 1984.

Zeppelin raid

1915

Germany used a Zeppelin L3 airship in a bombing mission for the first time. The attack on Great Yarmouth in England resulted in two deaths. Further Zeppelin raids killed about 500 people in the UK during World War I.

1986

Virus attack

An early computer virus, called BRAIN, was created by the Pakistani brothers Basit and Amjad Farooq Alvi to discourage software piracy.

Born this day

1839 Paul Cézanne, French artist. He produced more than 200 still-life paintings, 900 oil paintings, and 400 watercolours during four decades of work.

1946 Dolly Parton, US singer. She is celebrated for making country music popular and writing more than 3,000 songs.

January 20

2009

Obama presidency

Barack Obama was sworn in as the 44th president of the USA. He was the first Black person in history to be elected to the role. A lawyer and community organizer, he served as president for eight years.

1885

Roller-coaster ride

The first US patent for a roller-coaster design was given to La Marcus Thompson of Coney Island, USA. His switchback railway reached speeds of just 9 kph (6 mph).

1892

Basketball beginnings

Two teams at the YMCA school in Springfield, Massachusetts, USA, played the first official basketball match. The game had been thought up by their gym teacher.

Also on this day

1788 The first fleet of 736 British convicts and their jailers sailed into Botany Bay in Australia, where they established a penal colony.

1942 Nazi officials met to discuss the "Final Solution" – their plan to kill Europe's Jews by sending them to extermination camps in Poland.

2014 Half of South Korea's population fell victim to computer hacking when credit card details of around 20 million citizens were stolen.

Born this day

1910 Joy Adamson, Austrian naturalist. She carried out wildlife conservation work in Kenya, and raised an orphan lioness cub named Elsa, who was eventually released back into the wild.

January 21

1793

Off with his head

Louis XVI, the king of France, was executed by guillotine after he was found guilty of high treason by the French National Convention. Thousands gathered in the Place de la Révolution in Paris to witness their former ruler meet his fate.

1976

Going supersonic

Seven years after its first flight, the supersonic airliner Concorde started regular passenger service from London, UK, and Paris, France. The Concorde travelled at up to 2,179 kph (1,354 mph), twice the speed of sound.

1911

Monte Carlo Rally

In the first-ever Monte Carlo Automobile Rally, 23 cars starting from 11 different locations drove across Europe to meet up at the finish line in Monaco. The event was an opportunity to showcase the latest car technology.

Born this day

1920 Errol Barrow, first prime minister of Barbados. He led the Caribbean island to independence from the UK in 1966. His birthday is now a national holiday.

Also on this day

1924 Vladimir Lenin, leader of the Soviet Union, died. His embalmed body remains on public display in a mausoleum in Red Square in Moscow, Russia.

2017 Four million people across 160 cities in the USA and many other countries took part in the Women's March, a protest against US president Donald Trump.

2020 Scientists dated an asteroid found in the Australian village of Yarrabubba at 2.2 billion years old, making it the oldest asteroid discovered on Earth.

Born this day

1912 August Strindberg, Swedish author. He is best known as a playwright – he wrote more than 60 dramas in his lifetime.

Also on this day

1517 At the Battle of Ridaniya, Sultan Selim I of the Ottoman Empire conquered the Mamluk forces and seized control of Egypt.

1824 In a rare African victory against colonial powers, the Ashanti defeated British forces along the Gold Coast in Ghana.

1997 A metal piece from a disintegrating rocket fell from the sky in Oklahoma, USA, and harmlessly hit Lottie Williams – the only person to be struck by space debris.

Pope's bodyguards

Switzerland sent 150 soldiers known as Swiss Guards to protect Pope Julius II at the Vatican, the headquarters of the Roman Catholic Church. Today, Switzerland still sends guards to the Vatican, where they patrol in their brightly coloured uniforms.

2006 Bolivian president

Evo Morales took office as the first Indigenous president of Bolivia. He belongs to the Aymara, a South American Indigenous group based in the central Andes mountains.

Anglo–Zulu face-off

Britain waged war against the Zulus to expand its control over southern Africa. On the same day during the Anglo–Zulu War, Zulu warriors were victorious at the Battle of Isandlwana, while British forces triumphed at the Battle of Rorke's Drift.

January

23

Born this day

1910 Django Reinhardt, jazz musician of Romani origin. Although he lost two fingers in a fire, Django was a guitarist and composer who found fame throughout Europe.

1939 Ed Roberts, US activist. Paralysed due to polio, he was the first wheelchair-bound student at the University of California, USA, and led multiple campaigns for the disability rights movement.

1960 Challenger Deep

The deepest point in Earth's oceans, named Challenger Deep, was visited by humans for the first time. Jacques Piccard of Switzerland and Don Walsh of the USA took five hours to descend 10,912 m (35,800 ft) in their submersible *Trieste*.

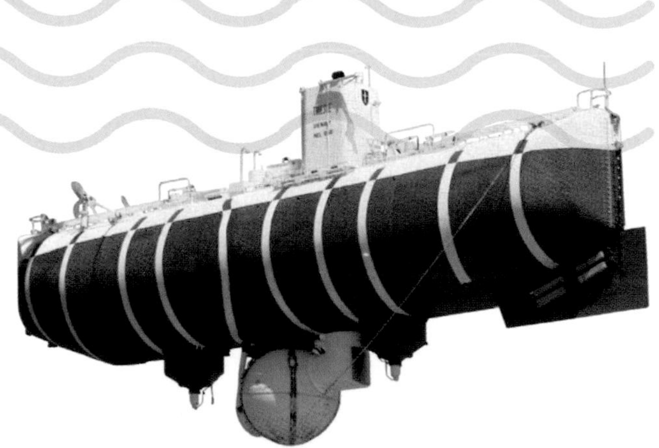

1957 Flying frisbee

US inventor Walter Frederick Morrison sold the rights to his new invention – a flying disc – to the Wham-O toy company, which would call it the "Frisbee". It became one of the world's most popular toys.

Also on this day

1556 The Shaanxi earthquake in China was the deadliest earthquake in recorded history. It killed around 830,000 people.

1719 Holy Roman Emperor Charles VI merged two independent territories to create the nation of Liechtenstein.

2020 An ancient Egyptian voice was heard for the first time when British scientists made a 3D print of a mummified priest's vocal tract.

1368 The Ming Dynasty

The coronation of General Zhu Yuanzhang as emperor of China marked the start of the Ming Dynasty, who ruled the country for the next three centuries.

January 24

41 CE

Emperor Claudius

Disgusted at the tyranny of the Roman emperor Caligula, the imperial bodyguards assassinated him and proclaimed his uncle Claudius the new emperor. Claudius was an effective leader, and under his rule Rome finally conquered Britain.

Born this day

1864 Marguerite Durand, French women's rights activist. She founded a newspaper run exclusively by women and helped to create organizations for working women.

1984 Macintosh on sale

With a price tag of US $2,500 (around US $5,000 today), the first generation Apple Macintosh personal computer went on sale in the USA.

1848 California Gold Rush

Mill worker James W Marshall found flakes of gold at Sutter's Mill, along the Sacramento River in California, USA. Following his discovery, prospectors flocked to the area in search of gold.

Also on this day

1859 Moldavia and Wallachia in central Europe were united by Alexandru Ioan Cuza. This region eventually became the country of Romania.

1986 Spacecraft *Voyager 2* came within 81,800 km (50,600 miles) of Uranus and discovered five new moons in its orbit.

2006 The Walt Disney Company took over Pixar, the pioneering computer animation studio behind *Toy Story*.

1995

Missile scare

Mistaking Norwegian research rocket Black Brant XII for a US Trident missile, Russia prepared to launch a nuclear attack in retaliation. Thankfully, action was halted and procedures were reviewed to avoid similar incidents in the future.

1921

Robot world

The word "robot" was heard for the first time in *Rossumovi Univerzální Roboti*, a science-fiction play by Czech writer Karel Čapek, which featured a robotic humanoid. This originated from the Czech word *robota*, meaning "forced labour".

Born this day

1759 Robert Burns, Scotland's national poet. He wrote about 300 poems, including *Auld Lang Syne*. His birthday is celebrated every year as Burns Night.

2004

Life on Mars

NASA's space rover *Opportunity* landed on Mars, where it spent 14 years gathering information. The most exciting revelation of its mission was historical evidence of water, making it possible that life may once have existed on Mars.

Also on this day

1890 Nellie Bly, a US journalist, completed a trip around the world in a record-breaking 72 days.

1971 General Idi Amin seized power in Uganda. His eight-year rule was one of the most brutal leaderships in history.

2011 Protests against corruption and oppression erupted in Egypt as part of the Arab Spring, a series of uprisings that spread across many Arab countries.

January 26

1926

Television trial

Scottish inventor John Logie Baird made the first public demonstration of television to 50 scientists at his laboratory in London, UK. The TV would later become the centre of home entertainment for millions all over the world.

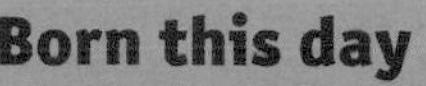

Born this day

1944 Angela Davis, Black American activist and author. She took charge of the Communist Party USA and stood up for civil rights, racial equality, and women's rights.

1924

Winter gold

The first gold medal at the Olympic Winter Games was won by US skater Charles Jewtraw at the 500 m speed skating event held in Chamonix, France. The medal remains on display at the Smithsonian Institution in Washington, DC, USA.

1905

Cullinan Diamond

The world's largest gem-quality rough diamond, weighing a whopping 3,106.75 carats, was unearthed at a mine in Cullinan, South Africa. It was later cut into nine big pieces – the largest of which was the Great Star of Africa, now embedded in the Royal Sceptre of the British Crown.

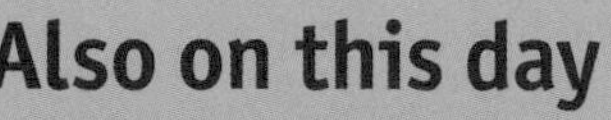

Also on this day

1564 At the Council of Trent, Pope Pius IV and key members of the Catholic Church agreed on reforms to religious doctrines.

1950 India became a republic when the Constitution of India came into effect. This day is celebrated as India's Republic Day.

1972 Serbian flight attendant Vesna Vulović fell 10,160 m (33,330 ft) from an exploded aircraft and miraculously survived.

January 27

1945

Liberation of Auschwitz

The Nazi concentration camp called Auschwitz was liberated by Soviet forces, who found more than 7,000 survivors and hundreds of corpses. This date is now remembered as International Holocaust Remembrance Day.

2010

Apple iPad

Apple's first tablet computer was announced by CEO Steve Jobs at a press conference in San Francisco, USA. The large screen made it easier to play games, read ebooks, and watch videos.

Also on this day

1868 The Battle of Toba-Fushimi started in Japan, resulting in the downfall of the Tokugawa Shogunate and the beginning of the Meiji era.

1967 The Outer Space Treaty, which banned nuclear weapons and military activities in space, was signed by the USA, UK, and Soviet Union.

1973 The Paris Peace Accords was signed by the USA, South Vietnam, Viet Cong, and North Vietnam to end the long-running Vietnam War.

Born this day

1756 Wolfgang Amadeus Mozart, Austrian composer. He wrote more than 600 pieces of music in his lifetime, becoming one of the world's most influential composers.

1944

Siege of Leningrad

Soviet soldiers successfully forced German troops out of Leningrad, ending the nearly 900-day-long siege of the city. One million Soviet civilians died of hunger or illness during this siege – the longest of World War II.

January

28

1896

Speed demon

The first person convicted of a speeding offence was Walter Arnold from Kent, UK. A police officer chased him down on a bicycle and gave him a one shilling fine (around £4 in today's money) for breaking the speed limit of 3.2 kph (2 mph). He was driving at 13 kph (8 mph).

1951

Seabird sighting

Previously thought extinct, the cahow seabird was spotted on the Pacific island of Bermuda by local teenager David Wingate, who later became a conservationist.

Build with bricks

1958

The Danish LEGO® Group submitted the patent for its "toy building element". Interlocking LEGO® bricks are still based on this original patent, with about 75 billion pieces sold every year.

Also on this day

1671 Plundering pirate Henry Morgan and his army of 1,500 men raided Panama, seized its capital city, and stole its national treasures.

1871 The German states led by the Kingdom of Prussia finally defeated France at Paris, ending the Franco-Prussian War.

1986 Space Shuttle *Challenger* broke apart 73 seconds into its flight when a booster engine failed. All seven crew members died.

Born this day

1608 Giovanni Alfonso Borelli, Italian scientist. He is known as a pioneer of biomechanics – the study of the structure, function, and movement of a living organism.

1912 Jackson Pollock, US abstract expressionist artist. He created paintings by pouring or splattering paint from above.

January 29

1845
The Raven
A mysterious narrative poem by US poet Edgar Allan Poe called "The Raven" was first published in *The Evening Mirror*, bringing him instant fame.

1978
Aerosol ban
Sweden became the first country to ban the use of aerosol sprays containing chlorofluorocarbons (CFCs). These compounds damage the ozone layer, a part of Earth's atmosphere that protects us from harmful radiation from the Sun.

1886
Birth of the automobile
German engineer Karl Benz applied for a patent for his invention of a three-wheeled, petrol-powered automobile in Berlin, Germany. Patent number 37435 marked the start of the automobile industry.

Born this day
1881 Alice Evans, US scientist. Her research on bacteria in milk and cheese helped to promote pasteurization, a process that destroys microorganisms in dairy products.

1954 Oprah Winfrey, Black American TV personality. Born into poverty, she is now a billionaire thanks to her hugely popular talk show, and has donated millions to charity.

Also on this day
1892 The Coca Cola Company was formed in the USA. It created one of the world's bestselling soft drinks.

2002 US president George W Bush described Iran, Iraq, and North Korea as an "axis of evil" in his State of the Union address.

2018 With its LA premiere, *Black Panther* became the first Marvel film to have a mainly Black cast and Black director.

January 30

Tet Offensive

1968

North Vietnamese soldiers began to launch surprise military attacks on multiple sites in South Vietnam, including a US embassy. Their aim was to incite rebellion among the South Vietnamese against US intervention in the Vietnam War.

Also on this day

1649 King Charles I of England was executed in front of crowds gathered in Whitehall, London, after being found guilty of treason.

1933 Adolf Hitler was sworn in as chancellor of Germany, marking the start of his dictatorship.

1948 Mahatma Gandhi, leader of the Indian independence movement, was assassinated at the age of 78 in New Delhi by a Hindu extremist.

Born this day

1913 Amrita Sher-Gil, Hungarian-born Indian painter. She studied art in Paris, France, before returning to India, and fused elements of Eastern and Western styles in her modern Indian art.

1959

Unsinkable ship

Danish liner MS *Hans Hedtoft*, which had been called unsinkable and safe, hit an iceberg and sank during its first voyage. None of the 95 people aboard survived. Only a lifebelt was ever recovered.

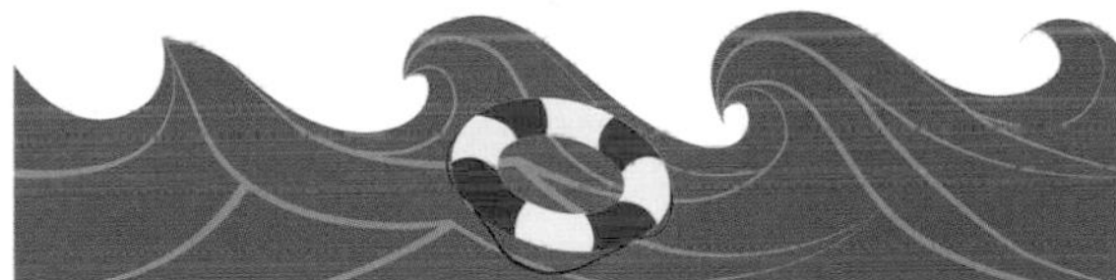

First modern suspension bridge

1826

The Menai Suspension Bridge was opened to take vehicles from the island of Anglesey to the northwest coast of Wales. This was the world's first modern suspension bridge.

January 31

2015 Golfing glory

Although 17-year-old Lydia Ko of New Zealand finished the Coates Gold Championship in Florida, USA, in second place, the tournament pushed her overall status up to the top spot. This made her the youngest player ever to be ranked world number one.

Also on this day

1865 The 13th Amendment to the US Constitution abolishing slavery across the country was passed by Congress.

1990 The first McDonald's in the Soviet Union opened, drawing hungry crowds to the fast food restaurant in Pushkin Square, Moscow.

2020 The UK ceased to be part of the European Union (EU), following 47 years as a member state.

Born this day

1797 Franz Schubert, Austrian classical composer. He wrote around 1,500 pieces of music, mostly piano and solo songs.

1981 Justin Timberlake, US singer and entertainer. He found fame as a child star before becoming a bestselling music artist.

The return of the Arabian oryx 1982

Ten Arabian oryx were reintroduced to the deserts of Oman after decades of conservation efforts and captive breeding programmes to bring them back from extinction in the wild.

February 1

1985 Searching for aliens

The Search for Extraterrestrial Intelligence (SETI) Institute started looking for alien life in the Universe. It remains the only US research organization focused on finding evidence of extraterrestrial activity.

Born this day

1878 Alfréd Hajós, Hungarian swimmer. He was the first modern Olympic swimming champion to win two gold medals and one silver medal over his career.

1902 Langston Hughes, Black American poet and novelist. As a founder of the Harlem Renaissance movement, he wrote about the lives of working-class Black people.

1960 Greensboro protests

When four Black students were refused service in a Woolworth store in Greensboro, North Carolina, USA, they stayed put and staged a protest against racial segregation in the country. This marked the first of many Greensboro protests against inequality.

Also on this day

1895 Fountains Valley in Pretoria was declared the first protected nature reserve on the African continent by Paul Kruger, president of the South African Republic.

2003 Disaster struck when Space Shuttle *Columbia* exploded over Texas, USA, shortly before landing, killing the seven astronauts on board.

2009 Jóhanna Sigurðardóttir spent her first day as prime minister of Iceland. She became the first national head of government from the LGBTQ+ community.

February 2

1709

Island castaway

After being marooned alone on a deserted island for more than four years, Scottish naval officer Alexander Selkirk was finally rescued.

Born this day

1977 Shakira, Colombian singer and songwriter. She has received hundreds of music awards for her memorable pop songs and unique Latin American style.

1925

Heroic huskies

Teams of husky dogs travelled more than 1,000 km (620 miles) across winter snow to the remote Alaskan town of Nome in the USA. They were carrying life-saving diphtheria serum, which prevented an outbreak of the deadly disease.

Also on this day

1887 Groundhog Day got underway in Pennsylvania, USA, when a groundhog named Punxsutawney Phil was first given the job of "predicting" a longer winter or an early spring.

1943 The Battle of Stalingrad, the bloodiest battle of World War II, ended in Soviet victory.

2004 Swiss tennis ace Roger Federer took the world number one ranking and maintained it for a record-breaking 237 weeks.

1912

Spectacular stunt

US daredevil Frederick Rodman Law performed the first stunt for a film when he parachuted from the torch of the Statue of Liberty in New York Harbor, USA.

February

3

1982 Heavy lifting

The Russian heavy-transport helicopter Mil Mi-26, piloted by a crew of two, lifted a mass of 56,770 kg (125,156 lb) up to a height of 2,000 m (6,560 ft) in Moscow. This was the heaviest load ever lifted by helicopter.

Also on this day

1870 The 15th Amendment to the US Constitution was ratified (formally approved), ensuring that Black men had the right to vote.

1966 The Soviet Union's *Luna 9* touched down on the Moon. It was the first spacecraft to survive landing on the lunar surface.

1972 The deadliest blizzard in recorded history began in Iran, killing 4,000 people and destroying about 200 villages.

1931 Earthquake in Hawke's Bay

The worst natural disaster in New Zealand's history, the Hawke's Bay earthquake, shook the east coast of North Island, killing 258 people.

Born this day

1790 Gideon Mantell, British palaeontologist. While reconstructing a fossil, he realized it belonged to an enormous extinct animal, which he named *Iguanodon.*

1970 Warwick Davis, British actor. He has appeared in various roles in the *Star Wars* films. Born with a rare form of dwarfism, he co-founded the Little People UK charity.

1995 Piloting in space

US astronaut Eileen Collins became the first female Space Shuttle pilot when she flew the *Discovery* close to Russia's Mir space station. The mission lasted eight days.

February 4

1945

Yalta Conference

Three leaders – British prime minister Winston Churchill, US president Franklin D Roosevelt, and Soviet leader Joseph Stalin – met at the Yalta Conference in the Soviet Union to decide the future of Europe after World War II.

1993

Znamya satellite

Russian scientists reflected a brief flash of sunlight over the night skies of Europe using a mirror on the Znamya satellite. This was a test to see whether they could increase daylight hours on Earth.

Born this day

1868 Constance Georgine Markievicz, Irish countess. She was the first woman elected as a member of the British parliament.

1918 Ida Lupino, British film actor. She played many inspiring roles in Hollywood before becoming one of the first women to direct a film.

Also on this day

960 Zhao Kuangyin was crowned Taizu, the first emperor of the Song Dynasty. This marked the start of three centuries of Song rule in southern China.

1938 Disney's *Snow White and the Seven Dwarfs* – the first full-length animated feature film – was released, and went on to become a huge box-office hit.

2004 Mark Zuckerberg launched a social networking site for Harvard University students. This was Facebook, now a social media giant.

1936

Synthetic radium

Radium, the radioactive metal found in some rocks, was produced artificially by US scientist John J Livingood – the first time an element had been created synthetically.

February 5

1869 Striking gold

The world's biggest gold nugget was discovered in the Australian town of Moliagul. Two British miners struck gold when they unearthed the so-called "Welcome Stranger", which weighed an astonishing 72 kg (158 lb).

1661 Qing ruler

Emperor Kangxi of the Qing Dynasty began his reign in China. His rule lasted a record-breaking 61 years, making him the longest-reigning emperor in Chinese history.

Also on this day

1885 King Leopold II of Belgium set up the Congo Free State. He exploited the wild rubber growing on the land for his own personal gain.

1953 Children in Britain could finally eat as much chocolate as they wanted when sweet rationing ended eight years after the end of World War II.

Born this day

1985 Cristiano Ronaldo, Portuguese footballer. The winner of 31 major trophies, he has been awarded the *Ballon d'Or* for the world's best player five times, and has scored more than 700 goals.

1852 Museum of art

The State Hermitage Museum in Saint Petersburg, Russia, opened to the public. It contained a collection of paintings belonging to Empress Catherine the Great, and is now one of the world's most spectacular art museums.

February 6

1921

Chaplin the director

The silent comedy film *The Kid* was released, starring Charlie Chaplin as a kindly tramp who found an abandoned baby and took care of him. This was the first time Chaplin directed a feature film.

Round the world trip

2018

SpaceX's Falcon Heavy rocket carried a Tesla car into space. The automobile is still floating around Earth, with a dummy dressed in a spacesuit in the driver's seat and items in the glove box.

2019

Brainy bees

Scientists proved that honeybees can do basic maths by solving arithmetic problems, according to a study published by RMIT University in Australia. Despite their small brains, the bees seemed to have understood how to add and subtract in an experiment involving a maze.

Born this day

1945 Bob Marley, Jamaican singer and songwriter. This legendary artist brought reggae music to the masses with his influential and inspiring songs calling for social justice and equality.

Also on this day

1778 The Treaty of Alliance was signed by the USA and France in Paris during the American Revolutionary War. It was the first time the USA was recognized as a free country.

1840 The Treaty of Waitangi was signed by British officials and Māori chiefs in the Bay of Islands. The British later used the treaty to claim rulership over New Zealand.

1993 The Indigenous Sámi people of Scandinavia celebrated their national day for the first time with hundreds of festivities, including flying the Sámi flag.

February

7

1959

Record flight

A flight endurance world record was set when two young pilots, Robert Timm and John Cook, flew an aircraft over the Great Basin Desert in Nevada, USA, for 64 days, 22 hours, and 19 minutes without stopping. Their plane was refuelled in the air.

Walking in space

1984

US astronaut Bruce McCandless performed the first untethered spacewalk when he left NASA's Space Shuttle *Challenger* in Earth's orbit and moved freely for 90 minutes, enjoying the views from 273 km (170 miles) above the planet.

Born this day

1978 Omotola Jalade Ekeinde, Nigerian actor, singer, business leader, and activist. She has featured in around 300 Nollywood films.

1979 Tawakkol Karman, Yemeni human rights activist. She received the Nobel Peace Prize in 2011 for her leading role in a pro-democracy protest movement.

Smashed to pieces

1845

The ancient Roman Portland Vase, which dates back to the 1st century BCE, was broken by a visitor to the British Museum in an act of vandalism. In the late 1980s, the glass vase was restored to its original state.

Also on this day

1992 The Maastricht Treaty was signed by 12 western European nations, laying the foundations for the European Union (EU).

2008 South African Ram Barkai set a record by swimming in the most southerly part of the world – off Antarctica's Queen Maud Land.

2014 Scientists dated the Happisburgh footprints of Norfolk, UK, to be at least 800,000 years old – the oldest outside Africa.

February 8

1974

Stay in space

NASA's longest space mission was recorded when three US astronauts completed 84 days on the US space station Skylab. The mission demonstrated that humans could live and work in space for extended periods of time.

1865

Genetics

Austrian monk Gregor Mendel presented his research on the inherited characteristics of pea plants to the Brünn Society for Natural Science in modern-day Czech Republic. His work led to a better understanding of human genetics.

Also on this day

1587 After 19 years in captivity, Mary, Queen of Scots, was beheaded for her part in a plot to kill Queen Elizabeth I of England.

1841 British inventor Henry Fox Talbot patented his calotype process, the first photographic process to produce a positive image from a negative.

1904 Japan launched a torpedo attack on Port Arthur, a Russian naval base in China, triggering the Russo–Japanese War.

Born this day

1828 Jules Verne, French author. He wrote many bestsellers, including *20,000 Leagues Under the Sea* and *Around the World in 80 Days*.

1672

Optics experiment

English scientist Isaac Newton showed the Royal Society in London how a prism could be used to bend sunlight and reveal its spectrum of colours. This led to the development of modern optics, the study of the behaviour of light.

Also on this day

1969 The Boeing 747 Jumbo Jet took off from Everett in Washington, USA, on its first flight, transforming the aviation industry.

2009 Egyptian archaeologists found around 30 mummies in a burial chamber at Saqqara dating back more than 2,600 years.

2019 The South Korean film *Parasite*, by Bong Joon Hoo, became the first non-English-language film to win a Best Picture Oscar.

1971

Baseball icon

Black American baseball player Leroy "Satchel" Paige was the first Black player to be nominated for the Baseball Hall of Fame, for an illustrious career spanning 50 years.

1995

Navajo tribute

Bernard Harris tested spacesuits in subzero temperatures in Earth's orbit, becoming the first Black astronaut to carry out a spacewalk. He dedicated his walk to the Navajo Nation and carried their flag on his adventure.

Born this day

1854 Aletta Henriëtte Jacobs, Dutch doctor and activist. She was the first official female university student in the Netherlands, and one of the first Dutch women to become a doctor.

1932 Gerhard Richter, German artist. He mixed together a wide range of styles and subjects in his paintings and photography.

Beatlemania begins

1964

An appearance by British band The Beatles on the US TV programme *The Ed Sullivan Show* drew 73 million viewers. Also known as the Fab Four, the band experienced frenzied Beatlemania wherever they went, leading to more British stars finding fame in the USA.

February 10

1942
Going gold

The first gold record was given to US big band leader Glenn Miller for *Chattanooga Choo Choo*. Miller's record label presented him with a copy of the single sprayed in gold to celebrate 1.2 million sales. Today, gold records are awarded to singles that sell 500,000 copies in the USA or 400,000 copies in the UK.

1996
Man versus machine

IBM's Deep Blue became the first computer to beat a world chess champion when it defeated Garry Kasparov in the first game of a match held in Philadelphia, USA.

Born this day

1835 Christian Andreas Victor Hensen, German zoologist. He discovered the important part played by minute aquatic organisms, which he called "plankton", in marine food chains.

1842 Agnes Mary Clerke, Irish astronomer. Her book *A Popular History of Astronomy During the Nineteenth Century* simplified the science of astronomy for Victorian readers.

Also on this day

1763 The Treaty of Paris ended the Seven Years' War, the first truly global conflict, which had spread from Europe to the Americas.

1863 The patent for the first artificial leg was granted to US inventor Dubois D Parmelee.

2013 Pope Benedict XVI declared his intention to retire. He was the first pope to resign since Gregory XII in 1415.

1722
A pirate's end

Swashbuckling pirate Bartholomew "Black Bart" Roberts died in battle. During his life he had plundered about 400 ships in the Caribbean and off the coasts of the Americas and Africa. After the British Royal Navy shot him, his body was buried at sea and never found.

2014

Olympic first

German Carina Vogt became the first-ever women's ski jumping champion when she won the gold medal at the Sochi Winter Olympics in Russia.

Born this day

1930 Barbara Mary Quant, British fashion designer. Her mini-skirts and hot pants became fashion necessities in the 1960s.

1972 Kelly Slater, US surfer. He won a record-breaking 11 world surfing championships.

660 BCE

National Foundation Day

According to tradition, Japan was founded on this day by Jimmu, the first Japanese emperor. This date is now celebrated every year in Japan as a public holiday, known as National Foundation Day.

1990

Mandela freed

South African activist Nelson Mandela, who fought against apartheid (a system of racial discrimination), was released after 27 years in prison. He had been arrested on charges of conspiracy against the government.

Also on this day

1576 The king of Denmark gave Tycho Brahe the island of Hven, where the astronomer built his own observatory to study the skies.

1929 With the signing of the Lateran Treaty, the Vatican City in Rome became a country – the smallest in the world to this day.

2011 President Hosni Mubarak of Egypt resigned after 30 years in power, following protests against his rule across the country.

February 12

1947 Dior's New Look

French fashion designer Christian Dior presented his "New Look" collection in Paris. Models wore elegant jackets and stylish, form-fitting dresses, which became a fashion sensation all around the world.

Born this day

1809 Charles Darwin, British naturalist. His theory of natural selection changed the course of science and our view of history.

1881 Anna Pavlova, Russian ballet dancer. She was the first ballerina to tour the world, and is famous for her solo role in *The Dying Swan*.

Also on this day

1818 Chile officially declared its independence from Spain, after nearly 300 years of colonial rule.

1909 The National Association for the Advancement of Colored People (NAACP) was founded to bring an end to racial discrimination in the USA.

2001 ***NEAR Shoemaker*** became the first space probe to orbit and land on an asteroid, 433 Eros.

1994 Stealing The Scream

Two thieves broke into the National Gallery in Oslo, Norway. They sneaked out with Norwegian artist Edvard Munch's most famous painting, *The Scream*. Almost three months later, it was safely recovered and returned.

1912 The last emperor

Nearly 2,000 years of imperial rule ended in China when six-year-old Emperor Puyi was forced to abdicate (give up the throne) after three years in power.

February 13

1258 Siege of Baghdad

After a 13-day siege, the city of Baghdad surrendered to Mongol ruler Hulagu Khan and his army. Thousands were killed in the bloodshed that followed, and the Islamic Golden Age came to a devastating end.

Born this day

1879 Sarojini Naidu, Indian poet and activist. She was the first female president of the Indian National Congress.

1908 Pauline Frederick, US journalist. The first woman to be employed as a network news correspondent, she inspired other women to work in the media industry.

Also on this day

1945 During World War II, the UK and USA began three days of bombing raids on the city of Dresden, Germany. The resulting firestorm destroyed more than 6.5 sq km (2.5 sq miles) of the city centre.

2004 The largest known diamond in the Universe – a white dwarf star – was discovered by astronomers. They named it Lucy, after a song by The Beatles.

2008 Australian prime minister Kevin Rudd formally apologized to the First Australians for the suffering caused by previous governments.

1866 Daylight robbery

US outlaw Jesse James carried out his first bank robbery, stealing US $15,000 from the Clay County Savings Association in Missouri, USA. This was one of the first bank robberies carried out in broad daylight.

1988 Bobsleigh heroes

With no history in winter sports and limited training, four Jamaicans competed in the four-person bobsleigh event at the Winter Olympics in Calgary, Canada. They finished last, but were celebrated as heroes for their sportsmanship and team spirit.

February

14

1946

ENIAC announced

The first electronic, general-purpose computer, called Electronic Numerical Integrator And Computer (ENIAC), was revealed to the public at the University of Pennsylvania, USA. An all-women team programmed the computer.

2016

Revolutionary robot

Sophia – the first artificial intelligence (AI) humanoid robot – was switched on during her first public appearance in Austin, USA. She made speeches, told jokes, and appeared to show empathy.

Also on this day

1779 British explorer James Cook was killed in a fight with locals in Hawaii during his third voyage of discovery.

1928 Scottish scientist Alexander Fleming discovered penicillin, the world's first antibiotic.

1949 The Israeli Parliament, called Knesset, met for the first time in the capital city of Jerusalem following national elections.

269 CE

Valentine's Day

Saint Valentine was martyred in Rome. Many centuries later, his saint's day came to be associated with love letters and romance.

Akbar the Great

1556

The third Mughal emperor, Akbar, came to the throne at the age of 13. For the next five decades, he expanded Mughal rule across much of the Indian subcontinent.

Born this day

1914 Margaret E Knight, US inventor. She had 27 patents in her name, but is best known for creating flat-bottomed paper bags.

February

15

1932

Going for gold

US athlete Eddie Eagan won Olympic gold with the bobsleigh team at Lake Placid, USA. As he had won gold for boxing at the Olympics in 1920, he became the only person to win golds at the summer and winter games in different sports.

1943

Wartime women

A poster of a female worker saying "We Can Do It!" was put up on the walls of Westinghouse factories in the USA during World War II. Originally a call for employees to work harder, the poster later became a symbol for empowered women.

Also on this day

1942 Thousands of Allied soldiers became prisoners of war after the key Pacific base of Singapore fell to Japanese forces in World War II.

2001 The first draft of the complete human genome – the set of instructions that make up our genetic code – was published by scientists.

2013 A meteor blew up with the force of a nuclear explosion over Chelyabinsk, Russia, destroying buildings and injuring 1,500 people.

Born this day

1820 Susan B Anthony, US women's rights activist. She was an influential social reformer and the president of the National American Woman Suffrage Association.

1965

The Canadian flag

Canada's official national flag was raised for the first time on Parliament Hill in Ottawa. The maple leaf at its centre has been a national symbol for centuries.

February

16

2003

Infamous heist

Thieves broke into the Antwerp Diamond Centre in Belgium, sneaked past 10 different types of security measure, and made off with US $100 million of diamonds, gold, and jewellery.

Also on this day

1857 US Congress approved funding for the Columbia Institution for the Instruction of the Deaf and Dumb and the Blind. It was the first school for students with hearing, speech, and sight difficulties.

1933 The existence of a type of invisible material called dark matter was suggested by US astronomer Fritz Zwicky.

1945 The Alaska Equal Rights Act was signed in the USA to prevent discrimination against the Indigenous peoples of Alaska.

Tomb discovery

1923

When British archaeologist Howard Carter entered the burial chamber of Pharaoh Tutankhamun in Thebes, Egypt, he found ancient treasures, undisturbed since 1324 BCE. As well as the mummy of the boy king inside a gold coffin, there were clothes, jewellery, games, and food for the afterlife.

1946

Chopper takes flight

The Sikorsky S-51 took off on its first test flight. It was used as a communication and evacuation helicopter by the US Air Force, and was also the first helicopter to be used by private companies.

Born this day

1973 Cathy Freeman, Indigenous Australian sprinter. Among the First Australians, she was the first to win gold at the Commonwealth Games and gold in an Olympic solo event.

February 17

1454 Unique feast

At an extravagant banquet known as the Feast of the Pheasant in Lille in modern-day France, guests were treated to spectacular entertainment, such as an enormous pie with musicians playing inside.

Born this day

1917 Whang-od, traditional Filipino tattooist. She is the last and oldest person to perform her craft.

1963 Michael Jordan, Black American basketball player. He led the Chicago Bulls to six National Basketball Association (NBA) championships and is considered one of the greatest basketball players of all time.

1972 Volkswagen Beetle

When the 15,007,034th VW Beetle rolled off the production line, the Beetle overtook Henry Ford's Model T as the world's bestselling car. Its compact design and affordable price made it a hit with drivers around the globe.

Red cross 1863

A group of Swiss citizens in Geneva set up the International Committee for Relief to the Wounded, later renamed the International Committee of the Red Cross, to help people injured in conflicts.

Also on this day

1936 The Phantom, a crime-fighting cartoon character created by US writer Lee Falk, first appeared in comics. Although he had no special powers, his heroic actions, colourful costume, and mask made him the world's first superhero.

1869 The periodic table of elements was first written down by Russian chemist Dmitri Mendeleev.

2008 Kosovo declared independence from Serbia, following years of conflict between the Serbians and the Kosovans, who have Albanian heritage.

February

18

1911

First airmail

The world's first official airmail was sent from Allahabad in India. French pilot Henri Pequet delivered 6,500 letters, sealed with a special stamp, to the city of Naini 10 km (6 miles) away.

Also on this day

1852 A giant glass fish tank was ordered by the London Zoo. This "Fish House" opened a year later as the world's first public aquarium.

1930 The distant planet Pluto (classified as a dwarf planet in 2006) was spotted by US astronomer Clyde Tombaugh in a photograph.

1978 The first Ironman Triathlon was held in Hawaii to settle a debate about whether runners, swimmers, or cyclists were the fittest athletes.

2015

Seadragon species

The rare ruby seadragon was reported in the journal *Royal Society Open Science*. It was the first new seadragon species to be discovered in 150 years. This 25 cm (9.8 in) long fish lives off Western Australia and is named for its red colour.

Born this day

1898 Enzo Ferrari, Italian racing driver. He founded the famous sports car company Ferrari, known for its fast luxury cars.

1930

Flying cow

Elm Farm Ollie was the first cow to fly in a plane and be milked in the air. She flew 115 km (72 miles) in an aircraft over Missouri, USA, so scientists could study whether altitude had any effect on how much milk she produced.

2002 Mapping Mars

NASA's *Mars Odyssey* spacecraft began mapping the surface of the Red Planet. It has since sent back thousands of images and located ice on the Martian surface. It remains the longest active spacecraft around a planet other than Earth.

Also on this day

1600 The Huaynaputina volcano erupted in the Andes mountains of Peru, killing about 1,500 people and destroying surrounding villages.

1942 Executive Order 9066 was issued by US president Franklin D Roosevelt for Japanese-Americans to be locked up in concentration camps during World War II.

2008 The world's longest-serving political leader, Cuban president Fidel Castro, resigned after 31 years in power.

1914 Special delivery

Taking advantage of the inexpensive US postal system, the parents of four-year-old Charlotte May Pierstorff sent her in the mail to her grandparents more than 117 km (73 miles) away. Her train journey was chronicled in the book *Mailing May*.

Born this day

1473 Nicolaus Copernicus, Polish genius. He was not only an accomplished astronomer, but also a mathematician, physician, economist, translator, and diplomat.

1977 Seafloor discovery

Hydrothermal deep-sea vents, found on the seafloor, were seen for the first time by scientists on board the US submersible *Alvin* in the Galápagos Rift in the Pacific Ocean. The nutrient-rich hot springs provide a unique habitat for clams and crabs.

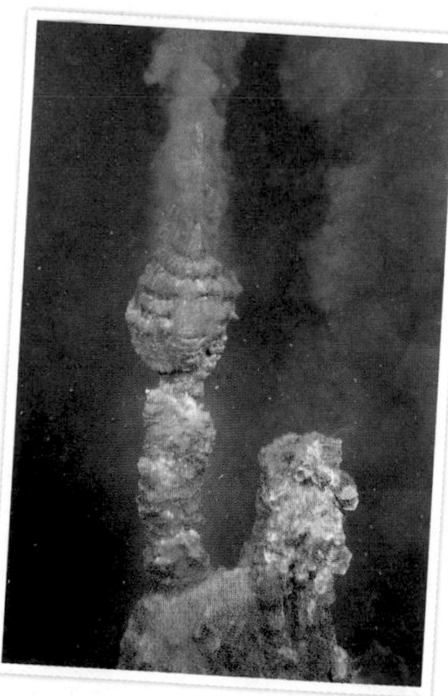

February 20

1877 Ballet premiere

At the Bolshoi Theatre in Moscow, Russia, Pyotr Ilyich Tchaikovsky's *Swan Lake*, about a princess who transforms into a swan, was first performed in public. Despite poor reviews at the time, *Swan Lake* has since become one of the world's most popular ballets.

Born this day

1927 Sidney Poitier, Bahamian-American actor and film director. He was the first Black man to win an Academy Award for Best Actor.

1988 Rihanna, Barbadian singer and songwriter. She has launched multiple global companies.

1986 A home in space

The Soviet Union launched the first module of the space station Mir. It would take 10 years to build fully, with six more modules being added.

Also on this day

1913 Construction started on Canberra, Australia's capital city.

1965 NASA's Ranger 8 lunar probe took close-up pictures of the Moon's surface for the first time.

2012 Seeds buried by squirrels 30,000 years ago were used to grow plants by scientists in Russia.

1707

Decline of a dynasty

Mughal emperor Aurangzeb died after 49 years in power. He was the last effective ruler of the Mughal Empire, which was at its biggest during his reign. His territory covered most of the Indian subcontinent.

February 21

1804 First steam locomotive

British engineer Richard Trevithick's steam-powered railway locomotive made its first journey. In just over four hours, the steam engine hauled five wagons, 10 tonnes of iron, and 70 people almost 16 km (10 miles).

Born this day

1933 Nina Simone, Black American singer and songwriter. She was a campaigner for racial justice.

Also on this day

1848 German thinkers Karl Marx and Friedrich Engels published their influential political ideas in *The Communist Manifesto.*

1974 Josip Broz Tito was declared Yugoslavia's "president for life" by the country's new constitution.

1995 US adventurer Steve Fossett landed in Canada after four days of flying solo across the Pacific Ocean in a hot-air balloon.

1858 Alarm raised

US inventor Edwin Holmes installed the first electric burglar alarm in a home in Boston, USA. Within a few years, he'd sold more than 1,200 alarms to safety-conscious customers, thwarting would-be burglars.

1965 Malcolm X shot

Malcolm X, a Black American Muslim activist, was killed in New York City. He had fought for racial justice for Black Americans.

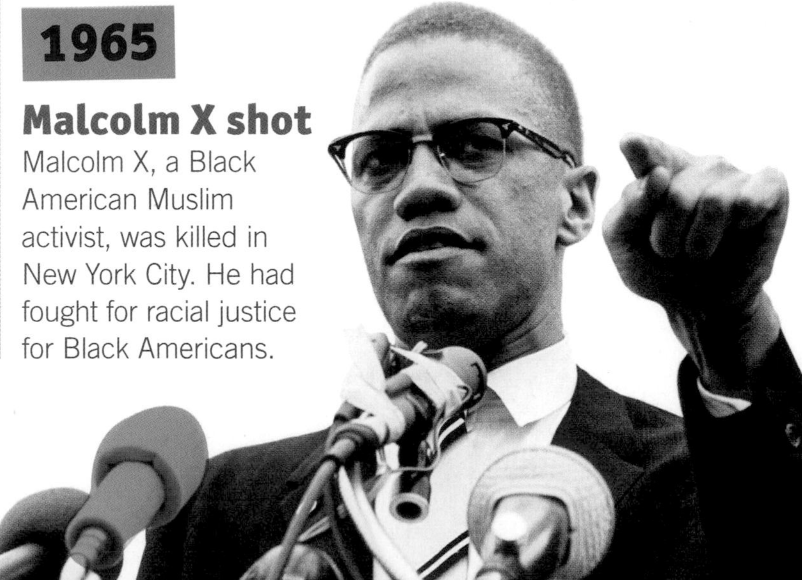

February

22

1997

Dolly the sheep

Scottish scientists announced the existence of Dolly the sheep, the world's first successfully cloned adult mammal. She was grown from a cell taken from an adult sheep, making her an identical genetic copy (a clone) of that sheep.

Also on this day

1848 The February Revolution started in France, with large crowds gathering in Paris to rebel against the monarchy.

1924 The story of "Bobbie the Wonder Dog", who found his way back home to Silverton, Oregon, USA, from 4,800 km (3,000 miles) away, was published in the town newspaper.

1959 US racing car legend Lee Petty won the first Daytona 500 race in Florida, USA.

1935

Hollywood's first interracial dance duo

The American comedy movie *The Little Colonel* premiered in the USA. Child star Shirley Temple and entertainer Bill "Bojangles" Robinson danced together on the stairs, in what was the first mixed-race dance partnership in a Hollywood film.

Born this day

1876 Zitkala-Sa, Yankton Dakota activist. She founded the National Council of American Indians to protect the rights, citizenship, and culture of Indigenous Americans.

2011

Football fury

Tempers boiled over during a football match between Argentinian teams Claypole and Victoriano Arenas. The referee gave a record-breaking 36 red cards after a brawl erupted on the pitch. The players, substitutes, and coaches of both teams were sent off.

Also on this day

1807 The Slave Trade Act, proposed by William Wilberforce to abolish the slave trade in the British Empire, was approved by Parliament.

1987 Astronomers spotted light from Supernova 1987A, an exploding star. This was the first supernova to be studied in detail.

2019 Argentinian footballer Lionel Messi scored his 50th hat-trick for FC Barcelona as they beat Sevilla 4–2 to top the Spanish League.

1954 Polio vaccine

The first injections of the polio vaccine were given to children at Arsenal Elementary School in Pittsburgh, USA. Developed by US doctor Jonas Salk, the vaccine was used to protect millions from the disease.

1945 Marines on Mount Suribachi

During the Battle of Iwo Jima, US marines raised their national flag on Mount Suribachi on the Pacific island of Iwo Jima after reaching the summit of the mountain. US forces later took control of the Japanese island.

Born this day

1868 W E B Du Bois, Black American civil rights activist. He co-founded the National Association for the Advancement of Colored People (NAACP).

532 Hagia Sophia

Byzantine emperor Justinian I ordered the construction of a grand Christian church that would become the centre of the Eastern Orthodox faith for almost 1,000 years. Hagia Sophia still stands today in Istanbul, Turkey, but it is now a mosque.

February

24

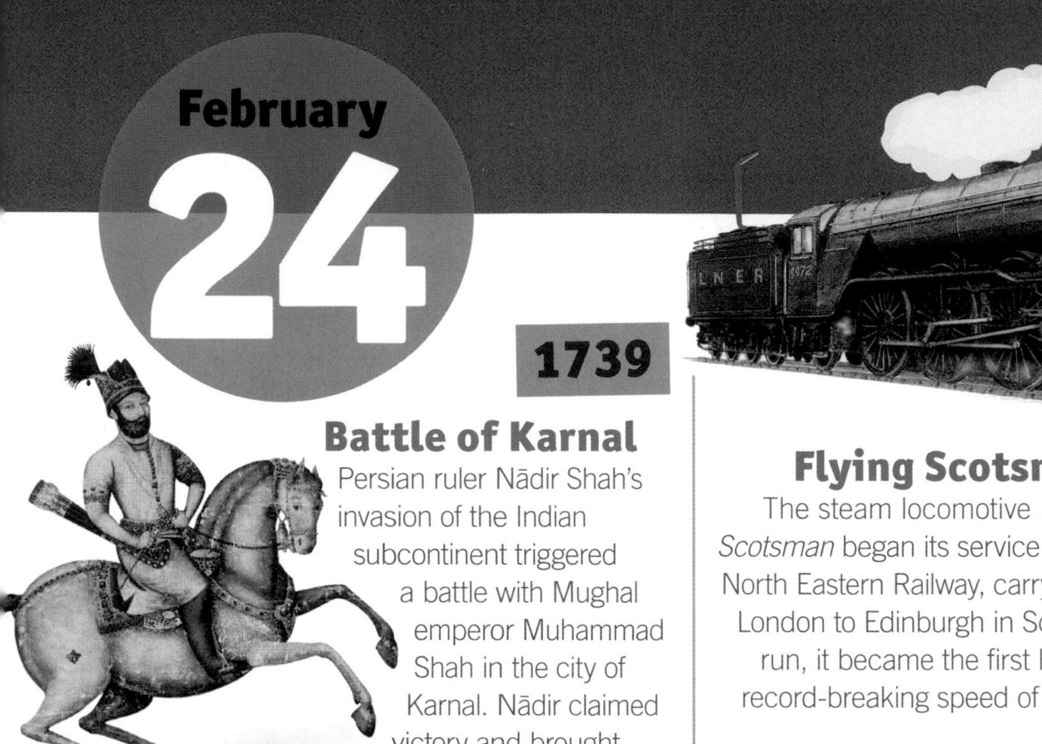

1739

Battle of Karnal

Persian ruler Nādir Shah's invasion of the Indian subcontinent triggered a battle with Mughal emperor Muhammad Shah in the city of Karnal. Nādir claimed victory and brought about the end of the Mughal Empire.

Also on this day

1848 King Louis Philippe I was removed from power during the February Revolution, and later made his escape by disguising himself as an ordinary man named "Mr Smith" and catching a cab out of Paris, France.

1920 At a meeting of about 2,000 people in Munich, Germany, politician Adolf Hitler founded the Nazi Party on his path to taking control of Germany.

Flying Scotsman

1923

The steam locomotive *Flying Scotsman* began its service with the London and North Eastern Railway, carrying passengers from London to Edinburgh in Scotland. During a test run, it became the first locomotive to reach a record-breaking speed of 160 kph (100 mph).

Born this day

1304 Ibn Battuta, Moroccan globetrotter. He travelled 120,000 km (75,000 miles) across Asia and Africa, and recorded his epic adventures in a travel book.

2018

Biggest art class

At the annual MassKara Festival in Quezon City in the Philippines, 16,692 art enthusiasts gathered for the world's largest art lesson ever. Those taking part learned how to draw colourful carnival masks in a class that ran for 45 minutes.

1951

Continental competition

The first Pan American Games began in Argentina with an opening ceremony in Buenos Aires. More than 25,000 athletes from across the nations of the Americas competed in various sporting events.

Also on this day

1570 Pope Pius V removed England's Queen Elizabeth I from the Catholic Church when she re-established the separate Church of England as the nation's faith.

1870 Overcoming fierce opposition, Hiram Rhodes Revels became the first Black person to take a seat in the US Congress.

1992 The Russian space agency Roscosmos was founded to replace the Soviet space programme.

1986

New leader

After the People Power Revolution led to the end of dictatorship in the Philippines, a new democratic era began when Corazon Aquino was sworn in as the country's first female president. She ruled for six years, during which time she strengthened civil rights.

Born this day

1841 Pierre-Auguste Renoir, French painter. He was an artist of the Impressionism school, which used light, colour, and texture to capture "impressions" of the world.

Heavyweight champion

1964

Black American boxer Cassius Clay, later known as Muhammad Ali, took the title of world heavyweight champion after his rival Sonny Liston retired after their sixth round in the ring at Miami Beach, USA. He went on to become the first boxer to win the world championship three times.

February

26

1909

Kinemacolor

Motion pictures created using the first successful colour film process, Kinemacolor, were shown for the first time at the Palace Theatre in London, UK. Kinemacolor was invented by British filmmaker George Albert Smith.

1616

Galileo silenced

The Roman Catholic Church banned Italian astronomer Galileo Galilei from teaching and sharing his theory that Earth orbits the Sun. At the time it was believed that Earth was at the centre of the Solar System.

Born this day

1829 Levi Strauss, German-born US entrepreneur. He set up the first jeans company to mass-produce the casual trousers made from denim, and patented the design of blue jeans.

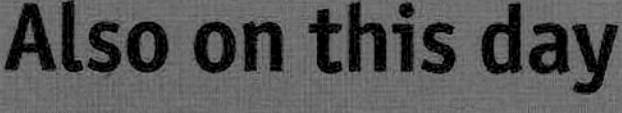

Also on this day

1606 Dutch navigator Willem Jansz became the first European to land in Australia.

1935 Radio Detection And Ranging (RADAR) was first demonstrated by Scottish physicist Robert Alexander Watson-Watt, to detect aircraft.

2008 The Svalbard Global Seed Vault, which stores seeds of food crops from around the world, was opened. It was built inside a mountain on the remote Norwegian island of Spitsbergen.

1919

Grand Canyon

US president Woodrow Wilson signed an Act of Congress to make the Grand Canyon in Arizona an official national park. Today, this giant canyon, carved out by the Colorado River, receives about 6 million visitors a year.

February 27

1594

Henry of Bourbon

Henry IV became the first noble from the House of Bourbon to be crowned king of France. His coronation marked the beginning of one of the most influential dynasties in Europe. The monarch brought peace and progress to France, earning him the nickname "Good King Henry".

Born this day

1956 Meena Keshwar Kamal, Afghan activist. She established the Revolutionary Association of the Women of Afghanistan to promote the rights and education of women. She founded schools for refugee women and their children.

1998

Costly cake

The most expensive slice of wedding cake sold for US $29,900 at a Sotheby's auction in New York, USA, more than 60 years after it was baked. It was made in 1937 for the wedding reception of the Duke and Duchess of Windsor. The money raised at this sale was given to charity.

Also on this day

1844 The Dominican Republic began a 12-year struggle for independence from Haiti on the Caribbean island of Hispaniola.

1947 British physicist James Stanley Hey discovered that the Sun emits radio waves.

1999 Millions queued at polling stations in Nigeria to elect a civilian president and replace 15 years of military rule with a democratic government.

1933

Burning of Parliament

The German Parliament building, known as the Reichstag, was set on fire in a deliberate attack. Nazi leader Adolf Hitler blamed the fire on his communist opponents and used it as an opportunity to increase his own power.

February

28

DNA structure

1953

Using images of deoxyribonucleic acid (DNA) taken by British scientist Rosalind Franklin, fellow scientists James Watson and Francis Crick revealed the double helix structure of DNA, announcing their discovery on this day. Their mapping of the DNA molecule helped scientists understand how genes pass between generations of families.

Born this day

1890 Vaslav Nijinsky, Russian ballet dancer and choreographer. Known as the God of Dance, he used his creative ideas and athletic physique to transform the role of men in ballet.

202 BCE Han Dynasty

Four centuries of the Han Dynasty started with the coronation of Liu Bang as Emperor Gaozu of Han. Born a peasant, Liu Bang became an influential leader who brought peace and prosperity to China.

2012 Prehistoric penguins

Fossils found in New Zealand turned out to be *Kairuku grebneffi*, an extinct species of giant penguin, which stood almost as tall as humans. This bird lived 27 million years ago when much of the country was underwater.

Also on this day

1897 Queen Ranavalona III was forcibly removed as the last monarch of Madagascar by French troops who took over the island in the Indian Ocean.

1935 US chemist Wallace Carothers invented nylon. This strong synthetic fabric was used to make stockings, as well as ropes and parachutes during World War II.

1991 The Gulf War ceasefire was declared by US president George H W Bush after Iraq withdrew from Kuwait.

February

29

1964

Blackbird unveiled

US president Lyndon B Johnson revealed the Lockheed SR-71 Blackbird, a spy plane that could reach record-breaking speeds of up to 3,200 kph (2,000 mph) and an altitude of 21,000 m (70,000 ft).

Born this day

1960, 1964, 1968 The Henriksen children, Norwegian leap-day siblings. All three Henriksen siblings, Heidi, Olav, and Leif-Martin, celebrate their birthday once every four years on this day.

Also on this day

1692 Three women were accused of witchcraft in Salem, USA, leading to public hysteria and the famous Salem witch trials.

1940 With her win for Best Supporting Actress in *Gone with the Wind*, Hattie McDaniel became the first Black actor to win an Oscar.

1996 The Siege of Sarajevo ended after nearly four years of fighting in the capital of Bosnia and Herzegovina, and the loss of 13,000 lives.

1912

Moving stone

The *Piedra Movediza* or "Moving Stone" of Tandil in Argentina mysteriously fell and broke into pieces. Delicately balanced at the top of a hill, this ancient rock had been a symbol of the city of Tandil since it was founded in 1823.

2012

Tallest tower

Following nearly four years of construction, the Tokyo Skytree in Japan was completed. Soaring 634 m (2,080 ft) into the sky, the building remains the world's tallest tower.

March 1

1896 Battle of Adwa

A well-equipped Ethiopian army defeated a smaller force of Italian invaders near the town of Adwa during the First Italo–Ethiopian War. This landmark victory proved that an African country could triumph over European colonists.

1954 Hydrogen bomb

The largest-ever nuclear test was carried out by the USA on the Marshall Islands in the Pacific Ocean. The 15 megaton explosion of a hydrogen bomb code-named Castle Bravo left a giant crater and damaged the health of nearby communities.

Also on this day

589 David, a Welsh bishop, is believed to have died on this day. Now the patron saint of Wales, St David is celebrated on this day every year.

1872 Yellowstone National Park, USA, became the world's first national park, preserving its natural beauty and wildlife for future generations.

1896 French scientist Henri Becquerel accidentally discovered radioactivity, a release of radiation by small particles inside objects.

Born this day

1868 Alaska Packard Davidson, US law enforcement officer. She joined the FBI as the first female special agent.

1994 Justin Bieber, Canadian pop star. He rose to international fame after posting videos of himself singing online.

1873 New typewriter

E Remington and Sons, a typewriter manufacturer from New York City, USA, began producing the first modern typewriter. Their machine used the QWERTY keyboard layout designed by inventor Christopher Sholes.

2014 12 Years a Slave

The acclaimed film *12 Years a Slave* was the first movie with a Black director to win the Oscar for Best Picture. British filmmaker Steve McQueen (left) adapted the 1853 memoirs of Solomon Northup, which described his experiences as an enslaved Black man.

Born this day

1904 Theodor Seuss Geisel, US writer and illustrator. Using the pseudonym Dr Seuss, he wrote popular children's stories, including *The Cat in the Hat.*

2018 Penguin population

The discovery of a huge penguin colony in the Danger Islands, off the coast of western Antarctica, was announced. About 1.5 million Adélie penguins had been hiding in plain sight and were only found thanks to satellite images and a survey on the ground.

1791 Semaphore system

French inventor Claude Chappe invented a system of visual symbols that could be understood over long distances. He used towers topped with moving mechanical arms to send the first messages but hand-held flags have also been used.

L

Also on this day

1657 The Great Fire of Meireki raged through the city of Edo, killing thousands and destroying more than half of the Japanese capital.

1955 Black teenager Claudette Colvin refused to give up her seat to a white woman on a segregated bus in the USA, months before Rosa Parks famously protested in the same way.

1972 NASA's space probe *Pioneer 10* was launched with a metal plaque on board that gave information about Earth's location.

March 3

1875

Battle on the ice

The first game of indoor ice hockey was played at the Victoria Skating Rink in Quebec, Canada. Two teams of nine players used skates, sticks, and a wooden puck. This fast-paced game is now Canada's national winter sport.

Born this day

1882 Elisabeth Abegg, German teacher. During World War II, she helped Jewish people hide or escape from the Nazi regime.

1917 Sameera Moussa, Egypt's first woman nuclear physicist. She devoted her life to finding peaceful uses for nuclear energy.

1887

Miracle worker

In the USA, six-year-old Helen Keller, who had lost her sight and hearing after an illness, met teacher Anne Sullivan. The educator taught Keller how to communicate through touch, helping her go on to become a campaigner for disabled people and a celebrated author.

2017

Nintendo Switch

Gaming fans were delighted with the release of this Japanese handheld device that could also be used as a home console. Eighty million units were sold worldwide in its first four years.

Also on this day

2005 US pilot Steve Fossett became the first person to fly around the world non-stop without refuelling their aircraft. His journey lasted 67 hours.

2014 The largest virus ever found was announced by scientists. They had discovered *Pithovirus sibericum* buried in a 30,000-year-old block of Siberian ice.

2014 The annual World Wildlife Day was celebrated for the first time to raise awareness and encourage conservation of Earth's diverse animal and plant species.

March 4

1351 King U-Thong

Ramathibodhi I, crowned King U-Thong, became the ruler of a vast kingdom in the Chao Praya Valley, in present-day Thailand. During his reign, U-Thong formed alliances, expanded trade, created a legal system, and built a capital city.

Born this day

1877 Garrett Morgan, Black American entrepreneur. Despite a limited education, he invented a breathing apparatus, discovered a way of straightening hair, and improved traffic signals.

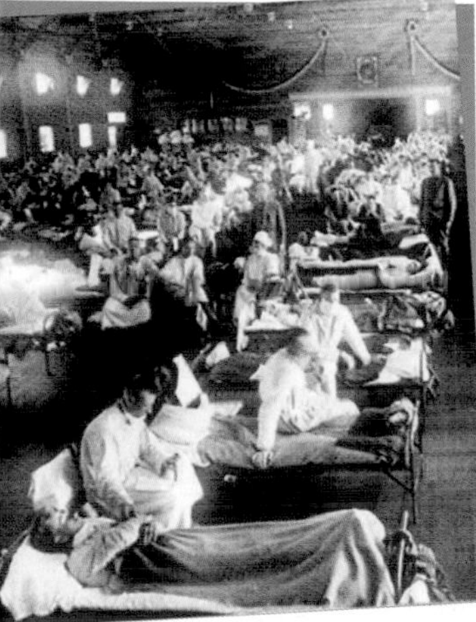

1918 Spanish flu

The first recorded cases of Spanish flu were found in about 100 soldiers suffering similar cold-like symptoms at the US army base of Fort Riley in Kansas. This highly contagious disease claimed millions of lives worldwide.

2020 Tightrope stunt

When he walked on a tightrope over the Masaya volcano in Nicaragua, US daredevil Nik Wallenda became the first person to cross an active volcano. He wore a mask to avoid inhaling fumes during the nail-biting feat, shown live on television.

Also on this day

1789 The US Constitution went into effect as the supreme governing law of the USA.

1951 The first Asian Games were held in New Delhi, India, with 11 countries taking part.

1980 Nationalist leader Robert Mugabe won the elections in Zimbabwe and took charge as the country's first Black prime minister.

Day for chiefs

First celebrated in 1977, Custom Chief's Day is now an annual public holiday in the island nation of Vanuatu. It honours the chieftain leaders and celebrates local traditions with feasts, festivals, and carnivals.

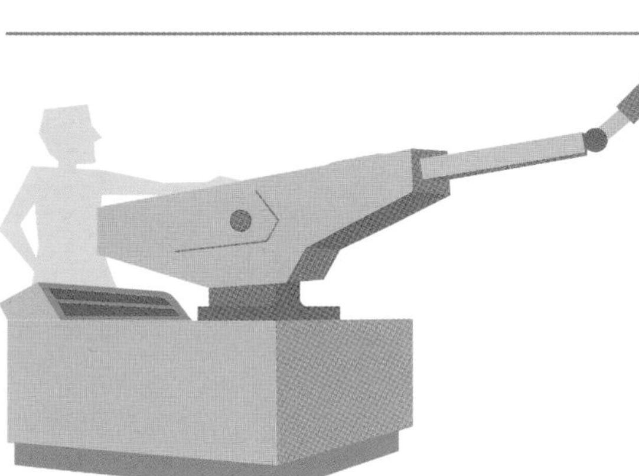

1965 Unimate's robot arm

The company Unimate applied for a patent for the world's first industrial robot. Designed by US inventor George Devol, this robotic arm could carry out repetitive jobs without tiring, and marked the beginning of robots being used in factory production lines.

Spitfire's first flight

Showcasing a sleek design with curved wings, the Spitfire aircraft was flown over Eastleigh airfield, UK, on its first test flight. This aircraft, made famous during World War II, reached high speeds at an altitude of 7,000 m (23,000 ft).

Born this day

1885 Louise Pearce, US scientist. She helped find a cure for a fatal illness called African sleeping sickness, and tested a drug for it in the Belgian Congo.

Also on this day

1616 Polish astronomer Nicolaus Copernicus's book *On the Revolutions of the Heavenly Spheres* was banned by the Pope as it went against religious thinking by suggesting that Earth moved around the Sun.

1770 The Boston Massacre took place on the streets of Boston, USA, when British soldiers opened fire on a group of protesters, killing five people.

1946 Former British prime minister Winston Churchill gave a speech at a college in the USA, likening the spread of Soviet influence to an "Iron Curtain" being drawn across Europe.

March 6

2018 Message in a bottle

The world's oldest message in a bottle was discovered on a beach on Wedge Island, Australia. Dated 12 June, 1886, it had been thrown into the Indian Ocean from a German ship named *Paula*, which was tracking ocean currents.

Born this day

1475 Michelangelo, Italian Renaissance painter and sculptor. He sculpted the marble masterpiece *David* and painted the ceiling of the Sistine Chapel in Vatican City.

Battle of the Alamo 1836

This key battle in the Texas War of Independence ended when thousands of Mexican soldiers overthrew a group of Texans who had spent 13 days defending the Alamo, a Catholic fortress and mission, near modern-day San Antonio, USA.

Independent Ghana 1957

Citizens celebrated all over Ghana as British colonial rule came to an end. Ghana was one of the first African nations to gain independence from colonial powers.

Also on this day

1204 The Siege of Château Gaillard in France ended when French soldiers climbed up a toilet chute to sneak in and conquer the English-owned fortress.

1835 The maid of Scottish author Thomas Carlyle accidentally burned his manuscript for *The French Revolution: A History*. He rewrote the book from memory and it became a bestseller.

1930 The first frozen foods, packaged as Birds Eye Frosted Foods, became available to shoppers in Springfield, Massachusetts, USA.

March

7

2010

Landmark win

US film director Kathryn Bigelow became the first woman to win an Academy Award for Best Director for *The Hurt Locker*, an action film about a bomb disposal team during the Iraq War.

Also on this day

1848 Hawaiian king Kamehameha III signed the Great Māhele, ending the tradition of shared access to land and introducing private ownership. Many Indigenous Hawaiians lost land as a result.

1902 Dutch settlers in South Africa known as Boers utterly defeated British forces at the Battle of Tweebosch, bringing an end to the Second Boer War.

1971 Bangladeshi political leader Sheikh Mujibur Rahman gave his Speech of Bangabandhu – a rallying call to Bangladeshi people to prepare for the impending war of independence.

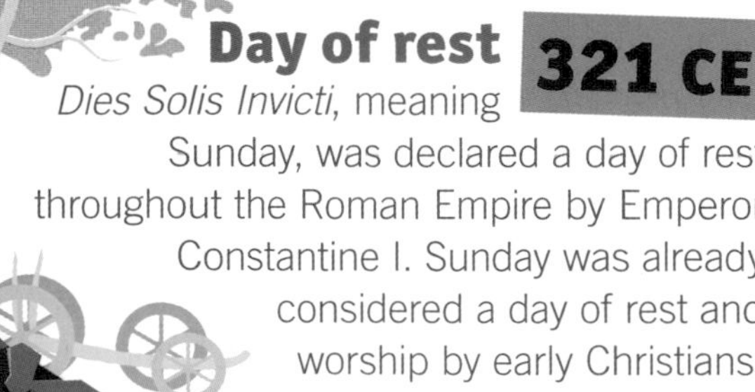

Day of rest

321 CE

Dies Solis Invicti, meaning Sunday, was declared a day of rest throughout the Roman Empire by Emperor Constantine I. Sunday was already considered a day of rest and worship by early Christians.

Born this day

1938 Janet Guthrie, US race-car driver. She was the first woman to race in the Indianapolis 500 and Daytona 500 championships.

1944 Ranulph Fiennes, British explorer. He was the first to cross Antarctica on foot and also climbed Mount Everest.

Rhineland occupation

1936

Without warning, German military forces marched into the Rhineland, reoccupying this strip of land on the border with France. This move broke the agreements of both the Locarno Treaty and the Treaty of Versailles, and increased tensions between European countries in the years before World War II.

March

8

1010 Epic poem

The Persian poet Abul-Qâsem Ferdowsi Tusi, better known as Ferdowsi, finished writing *Shahnameh* ("Book of Kings"). With about 100,000 lines, it ranks among the world's longest epic poems written by one person.

Also on this day

1736 Nader Shah was crowned shah of Iran. He was one of the most important leaders in Iran's history.

1817 The New York Stock Exchange was formed by a group of US stockbrokers renting offices in Wall Street. It evolved into the world's largest stock exchange.

2014 Malaysia Airlines Flight 370 disappeared from radar on the way to Beijing. The most expensive search operation in aviation history followed.

1910 Woman pilot

The first woman in history to receive a pilot's licence was French actor turned aviator Raymonde de Laroche. She received her licence from the Aéro-Club de France, the only organization to issue pilot licences at the time.

International Women's Day 1975

The United Nations (UN) celebrated International Women's Day for the first time on this day. This now annual event celebrates achievements throughout history and highlights issues affecting girls and women.

Born this day

1951 Monica Helms, US transgender activist, author, and US Navy veteran. She created the Transgender Pride Flag, first flown at a Pride Parade in Phoenix, USA.

March

9

1842

Golden dreams

Legend has it that Francisco Lopez fell asleep under a tree in Placerita Canyon and dreamed he was floating in a golden pool. When he woke, he pulled out some wild onions from the ground and found gold flakes on their roots. His find was recorded as the first gold discovery in California, USA.

Born this day

1979 Oscar Isaac, Guatemalan-American actor. He played Poe Dameron in the *Star Wars* films and Apocalypse in the *X-Men* movies.

1959

Barbie doll

Named after the inventor's daughter, the Barbie doll was revealed at the New York toy fair. Based on a German doll called Bild Lilli, Barbie has been updated over the years to match changing fashions.

141 BCE

Teenage emperor

Liu Che became emperor of China at the age of 16, founding the Han Dynasty. He reigned for the next 54 years during a period of great political, military, and cultural progress.

Also on this day

1009 The name Lithuania was first written down in a book by monks at the Quedlinburg Abbey in Germany.

1945 Forty-eight hours of bombing raids on Tokyo by US warplanes began. The city was badly damaged and more than 80,000 people were killed.

2005 A third gender option of "eunuch" was added to Indian passports in recognition of the country's *hijra* community.

1876

Telephone call

The first telephone call was made when Scottish inventor Alexander Graham Bell used his new electric device to summon his assistant Thomas Watson from a neighbouring room with the words, "Mr Watson, come here. I want to see you."

Also on this day

1098 Edessa was established by the Crusaders as their first kingdom and Christian state, located in modern-day Armenia.

1831 The French Foreign Legion was created by King Louis Philippe as a military service to defend and advance the French Empire.

2006 NASA's *Mars Reconnaissance Orbiter* spacecraft entered orbit around Mars, and began mapping the surface of the Red Planet.

1535

Guest on Galápagos

Tomés de Berlanga, Bishop of Panama, discovered the Galápagos Islands when his ship blew off course in the Pacific Ocean. Galápagos is an ancient Spanish word for tortoise – Berlanga found giant tortoises and marine iguanas living on the islands.

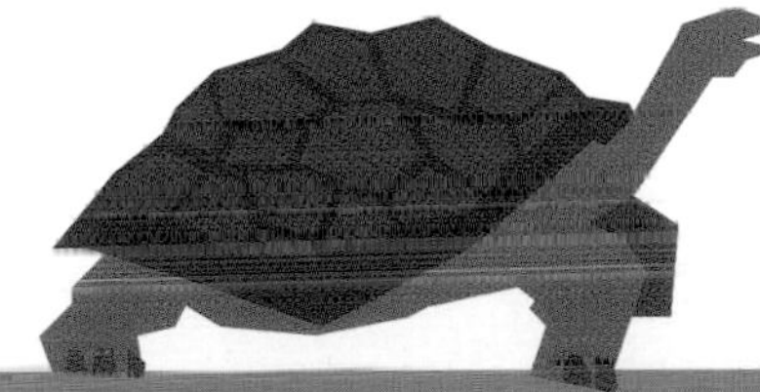

Born this day

1981 Samuel Eto'o, Cameroonian footballer. A star striker, he holds the record for scoring the most goals in the history of the African Cup of Nations, with a total of 18.

241 BCE

Battle of Aegusa

Fought between the Romans and Carthaginians, this battle for control of the western Mediterranean Sea ended with the sinking of about 50 Carthaginian ships. It brought an end to the First Punic War, the first of three wars fought between the rival states.

March 11

COVID-19 pandemic 2020

With the number of cases rapidly increasing worldwide, the World Health Organization (WHO) officially declared the outbreak of new disease COVID-19 a pandemic and advised countries to act urgently. This highly contagious disease would go on to infect millions of people.

Born this day

1926 Ralph David Abernathy, Black American civil rights leader. He worked with Martin Luther King, Jr to end racial segregation on public transport in the USA with the Montgomery bus boycotts.

2011 Fukushima disaster

A devastating earthquake off the coast of Japan triggered a huge tsunami that destroyed or damaged many buildings and killed around 20,000 people. At the Fukushima nuclear reactor, the quake caused radioactive materials to be released into the air and ocean in the worst nuclear disaster since the accident at Chernobyl, Ukraine, in 1986.

Also on this day

1888 A severe blizzard called the Great White Hurricane brought transport systems to a halt and interrupted communication in and around New York City, USA.

1985 Mikhail Gorbachev was chosen as the new leader of the Soviet Union. He made several political and economic reforms that would, in part, lead to the collapse of the communist state.

2004 The Spanish rail network in Madrid was targeted by Islamic extremists who detonated 10 bombs on four trains, killing 191 civilians.

1967 Animals in danger

The first endangered species list was published by the US Department of the Interior, which was tasked with protecting rare wildlife in the country. The list featured 78 species at risk of extinction, including the grizzly bear, Florida manatee, American alligator, and bald eagle.

March 12

SARS outbreak alert

2003

The WHO announced a global health alert warning about a new disease that was infecting people in China, Hong Kong, and Vietnam. The airborne virus was later named severe acute respiratory syndrome (SARS).

Born this day

1929 Lupe Anguiano, Mexican-American civil rights activist. She was an advocate for women's rights. She trained women for job opportunities and advised the government on welfare reforms.

1954 Anish Kapoor, British-Indian artist. He was the first living artist to have a solo show at the Royal Academy of Arts in London, UK.

1930

Salt March

Indian nationalist campaigner Mahatma Gandhi set off with supporters on a 24-day march to collect salt by the Arabian Sea. This peaceful protest against the tax on salt imposed by British authorities covered 386 km (240 miles).

1881

Scottish star

Having moved to Britain from his native Guyana, Andrew Watson (top centre) made his footballing debut for Scotland as the first Black international player and team captain.

Also on this day

1913 Canberra was announced as Australia's capital. It was a new city built midway between Sydney and Melbourne.

1938 German troops crossed the border and invaded Austria, on what became known as the Day of the Anschluss (meaning "connection").

2017 At the age of 50, Kazuyoshi Miura became the oldest professional footballer to score a goal, for Japan's Yokohoma FC.

March

13

Uranus discovered 1781

British astronomer William Herschel discovered the planet Uranus while studying the stars. Although others had spotted light from the remote world before, Herschel recognized it as a new planet – the first to be found since ancient times.

Also on this day

1925 This date was chosen to celebrate 600 years since the city of Tenochtitlán was established on Lake Texcoco as the capital of the Aztec Empire.

1954 The KGB was founded as the security agency for the Soviet Union. It soon became one of the world's most effective organizations for gathering secret information.

1988 The Seikan Tunnel opened to connect the Japanese islands of Honshu and Hokkaido. The undersea section of the 54 km (34 mile) railway tunnel is buried 100 m (328 ft) below the seabed.

Born this day

1733 Joseph Priestley, British chemist. Through his scientific experiments, he discovered many gases, including oxygen. He also invented carbonated (sparkling) water.

1848 March revolution

As revolution spread across Europe, protesters demanding political change rioted in the Austrian city of Vienna. Hoping to calm the people and restore peace, the government forced the unpopular Prince Metternich, chancellor of Austria, to resign.

1997 Phoenix Lights

Sightings of unidentified flying objects (UFOs) in a V-shape formation were reported by many people observing the evening skies over Arizona and Nevada in the USA. The puzzling lights caused much debate, but the mystery was never solved.

1988 First Pi Day

The annual celebration of the mathematical sign Pi (Greek letter π) was first held at a science museum in San Francisco, USA. Maths fans celebrate by reciting the number and eating pie.

1889

Gifted graduate

Indigenous American Susan La Flesche Picotte graduated from medical school top of her class. She went on to become the first Indigenous American doctor in the USA and used her medical knowledge to help her Omaha tribe.

Also on this day

1489 Catherine Cornaro, the last monarch of the Kingdom of Cyprus, abdicated her throne and gave the Mediterranean island to the Republic of Venice.

1931 ***Alam Ara***, the first Indian film with sound, was released. Its soundtrack drew huge audiences.

2020 An aircraft belonging to French airline Air Tahiti Nui flew 15,715 km (9,765 miles) from Tahiti to Paris, a record-breaking distance for a passenger flight.

Born this day

1965 Aamir Khan, Indian actor and director. He has played diverse roles in Bollywood movies, and ranks among the biggest film stars in Asia.

Most wanted 1950

The first list of "Ten Most Wanted Fugitives" was released by the FBI, the US law enforcement agency, after a reporter asked for the names of the country's most dangerous criminals on the run.

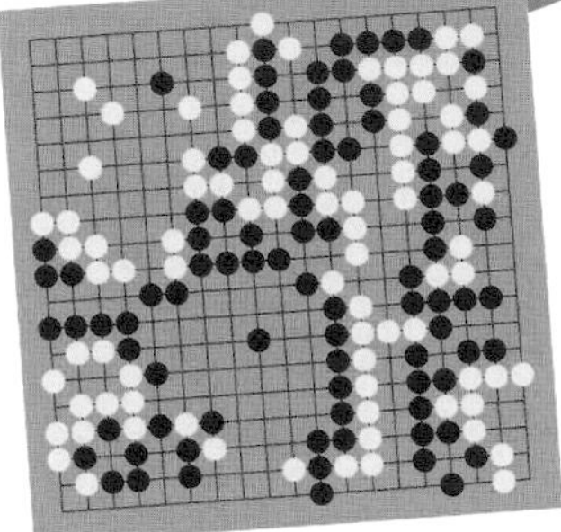

2016

Ready, set, Go

Despite the complexities of the ancient board game Go, Google DeepMind's AlphaGo program beat 18-times world champion Lee Sedol 4–1 at a match in Seoul, South Korea.

1879

Catching criminals

French criminologist Alphonse Bertillon joined the French police force. He went on to make vital contributions to forensic science, and developed anthropometry, a technique using body measurements to help identify suspected criminals.

Van Gogh gallery

1901

A display of 71 paintings by Vincent Van Gogh at the Bernheim-Jeune Gallery in Paris, France, was greatly admired. The Dutch painter had died 11 years earlier, and sold only a few paintings in his lifetime.

Also on this day

44 BCE Ancient Roman leader Julius Caesar was stabbed to death by a group of senators after he declared himself "dictator for life".

1937 The world's first blood bank was opened by US physician Bernard Fantus in Chicago, USA.

2002 Norwegian skier Ragnhild Myklebust won 5 golds at the Winter Paralympics, bringing her total to 22 golds and making her the most successful Winter Paralympian.

Born this day

1933 Ruth Bader Ginsburg, US Supreme Court Justice. The second woman to take this position, she was also the first Jewish female Supreme Court Justice. She was best known for supporting the rights of women and workers.

1872

Playing football

At the first-ever FA Cup final, held at Kennington Oval cricket ground in London, UK, Wanderers FC beat Royal Engineers AFC 1–0. This annual English cup is the world's oldest football competition.

Born this day

1750 Caroline Herschel, German-born British astronomer. She was the first woman to discover a comet, and helped her brother, William Herschel, with astronomical calculations.

1916 Tsutomu Yamaguchi, Japanese naval engineer. He was the only person to have survived both the Hiroshima and Nagasaki atomic bombings of World War II.

2019

Endurance swim

South African swimmer Sarah Ferguson was the first person to swim around Easter Island in the Pacific Ocean, covering a distance of 62 km (39 miles) in 19 hours.

1926

Rocket launch

In a pioneering moment for rocket propulsion, the first liquid-fuel rocket – launched from a field in Auburn, USA, by US scientist Robert H Goddard – flew for two seconds at 96 kph (60 mph).

Also on this day

1815 Prince Willem declared himself king of the Netherlands, becoming the country's first monarch.

1827 The *Freedom's Journal*, the first newspaper owned and run by Black Americans, was published in New York City, USA.

1844 An article about hay fever symptoms was published by British doctor John Bostock, providing the first medical explanation of allergies.

461 CE

St Patrick

Christian bishop St Patrick is thought to have died on this day. Now the patron saint of Ireland, he is known for using the three leaves of the shamrock plant to describe the nature of the Holy Trinity – God, Jesus, and the Holy Spirit. The anniversary of his death is today recognized as St Patrick's Day – an annual celebration of Irish culture.

Also on this day

1861 The Kingdom of Italy was officially proclaimed in Turin after a decade of revolution. Victor Emmanuel was crowned its first king.

1958 ***Vanguard I***, the first solar-powered satellite, was launched by the USA. It is the oldest human-made object orbiting Earth.

1992 A majority of white voters in South Africa voted "Yes" in a public vote to end apartheid.

1969

Israel's Iron Lady

Golda Meir was elected prime minister, becoming the first woman to lead Israel. In power for five years, she led her nation through the 1973 Yom Kippur War and became known as the Iron Lady of Israeli politics.

Born this day

1902 Alice Greenough Orr, first woman professional rodeo performer in the USA. She won four world saddle bronc championships.

1969 Alexander McQueen, British fashion designer. McQueen launched his career as head designer at French fashion house Givenchy and later went on to establish his own luxury brand.

2001

Eden Project

A giant greenhouse of eight connected domes, called the Eden Project, opened to visitors in Cornwall, UK. The domes now house about 5,000 different plant species from around the world.

March

18

Champion pigeon 2019

Armando, a super speedy racing pigeon, was sold for €1.25 million at an auction in Belgium. Most racing pigeons fetch around €2,500, but Armando deserved his extraordinary price tag for winning almost every race he entered.

1967 Tactile blocks

Designed by Seiichi Miyake, Tenji tactile blocks were first used next to a school for blind people in Okayama City, Japan. The blocks were made in bright colours with raised patterns to help blind people find their way more easily.

Born this day

1904 Margaret Tucker, First Australian activist. She was the first female First Australian to join the Ministry of Aboriginal Affairs and the first woman on the Aborigines Welfare Board in Australia.

1970 Queen Latifah, Black American singer, rapper, and actor. She has won both a Grammy Award and a Golden Globe.

Throwaway fashion 1966

Paper dresses for US $1 were advertised by the Scott Paper Company in a fashion article in *Time* magazine in the USA. More than half a million disposable paper dresses were sold in a year, but the fashion trend was short-lived.

Also on this day

1662 The first public buses hit the road in Paris. These horse-drawn carriages stopped at set points on a route to pick up passengers.

1925 The Tri-State Tornado left the longest trail in recorded history. It killed almost 700 people in the USA.

1965 Cosmonaut (Soviet astronaut) Alexei Leonov became the first person to leave a spacecraft and perform a tethered spacewalk.

March 19

1279

Battle of Yamen

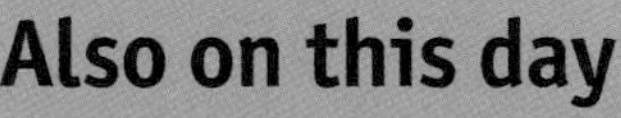

In China, the Song Dynasty ended after the Battle of Yamen, a clash at sea in which the invading Mongol Yuan navy defeated the Song navy. Yuan emperor Kublai Khan took power.

1842

Empty seats

The French play *Les Ressources de Quinola* opened to an almost empty theatre because the writer Honoré de Balzac – in a publicity stunt gone wrong – had declared the show was already a sellout.

Born this day

1848 Wyatt Earp, legendary figure in the Wild West. He blazed his own trail across the USA, working as a gunfighter, gambler, miner, law officer, and saloonkeeper.

Also on this day

1982 Argentinian workers landed on the British-controlled Falkland Islands and raised their national flag, triggering a 10-week war between the two countries.

2018 The last surviving male northern white rhinoceros, called Sudan, died of old age in Kenya.

2019 US mathematician Karen Uhlenbeck became the first woman to win the Norwegian Abel Prize for her pioneering work.

Sagrada Família

1882

Bishop Urquinaona laid the first stone of the Sagrada Família, a huge cathedral in Barcelona, Spain. This unique building designed by the famous Catalan architect Antoni Gaudí is still being built almost 150 years later.

March

20

1916

Theory of relativity

Science genius Albert Einstein published his general theory of relativity. This groundbreaking work explained how time, space, mass, and gravity all work together. Einstein's theory transformed our understanding of physics.

Also on this day

1800 Italian inventor Alessandro Volta wrote to the Royal Society of London to describe his new invention – an electric battery.

1995 Terrorists in Japan released the toxic nerve gas sarin on the Tokyo subway system during rush hour, killing 12 people and injuring more than 5,500 commuters.

2013 Celebrating joy and well-being, the first UN International Day of Happiness took place.

1959

Tight squeeze

A very uncomfortable new world record was set when 25 students crammed into a public phonebox in Durban, South Africa. When the phone rang, no one could reach to answer it!

Born this day

1957 David Foster, Australian athlete. His father taught him woodchopping as a child, and this world champion woodcutter has since won more than 180 world titles.

1966

Stolen trophy

The World Cup football trophy was taken from an exhibition in London, UK. A dog named Pickles saved the day by sniffing out the stolen treasure a week later, ready for the England team to hold it aloft when they won the 1966 World Cup.

March 21

1871

German chancellor

Otto von Bismarck was declared the first chancellor of the German Empire. He united the German states into a powerful nation. Under his rule, Germany retained its dominance in Europe until World War I.

Born this day

1685 Johann Sebastian Bach, German composer. A talented organist and violinist, he wrote music for choirs and orchestras, and is famous for the *Brandenburg Concertos.*

1806 Benito Pablo Juárez García, Mexican politician. He became the first Indigenous president of Mexico in 1858.

1846

All that jazz

Belgian musician and instrument maker Adolphe Sax filed a patent for eight different types of wind instrument, all variations of the saxophone. His invention later became popular with jazz musicians.

Also on this day

1916 US chess champion Frank James Marshall played a record-breaking 105 games at the same time in a tournament in Washington, DC, USA.

1935 Shah of Iran Reza Shah Pahlavi requested that Persia be called Iran by other nations.

2006 The first message was sent using Twitter, when its US founder Jack Dorsey published the tweet, "Just setting up my twttr".

Ballooning record

1999

Swiss explorer Bertrand Piccard and British balloonist Brian Jones became the first people to travel around the world non-stop in a hot-air balloon. Their *Breitling Orbiter 3* landed near Cairo, Egypt, at the end of their 20-day journey.

March

22

1998

Microlight milestone

The first circumnavigation of the globe by microlight took off from Brooklands in the UK. British adventurer Brian Milton flew the microlight around the world and set a new world record on landing four months later.

1993

World Water Day

On the recommendation of the United Nations (UN) Conference in Brazil, World Water Day was first observed. This annual event highlights the plight of 2 billion people around the world who are living without water that is safe to drink.

Born this day

1923 Marcel Marceau, French mime artist. His silent onstage character Bip the Clown sparked a public appreciation of mime.

1929 Yayoi Kusama, Japanese artist. Known as the "princess of polka dots", she is famous for her unique paintings and sculptures.

1635

Peacock Throne

After seven years in the making, the jewelled Peacock Throne was shown to the world in a ceremony at the Red Fort in Delhi, India. Mughal emperor Shah Jahan sat on it as he celebrated the seventh anniversary of his coronation.

Also on this day

1895 French brothers Auguste and Louis Lumière gave the first public demonstration of movie film technology with their camera projector, the cinématographe.

1945 The Arab League was set up in Cairo, Egypt, when six Arab nations came together to create closer bonds between each other.

1995 Cosmonaut (Russian astronaut) Valeri Polyakov returned to Earth after 438 days aboard the *Mir* space station – the longest-ever stay in space.

Also on this day

1983 US president Ronald Reagan announced the Strategic Defense Initiative, nicknamed "Star Wars", to protect the country against nuclear attacks.

2003 The Japanese fantasy film *Spirited Away* became the first non-US animation film to win the Oscar for Best Animated Feature.

2014 The first cases of Ebola virus disease were reported by the World Health Organization (WHO) in Guinea. The epidemic caused at least 11,000 deaths in West Africa.

Born this day

1882 Amalie Emmy Noether, German mathematician. She made a big impact in algebra and physics with her work.

1983 Mo Farah, British-Somalian long-distance runner. He won four Olympic gold medals in the men's 5,000 m and 10,000 m.

1956

Islamic republic

Pakistan was proclaimed the world's first Islamic republic, following the Lahore Resolution of 1940, which proposed an independent state for Muslims. This date is now celebrated in Pakistan as Republic Day.

Going up!

1857

The world's first lift opened to the public in the Haughwout department store in New York City, USA. Inventor Elisha Otis designed and installed this steam-powered invention to carry passengers up and down multiple floors safely.

Sandstorm in Sochi

2018

Fierce winds blew sand from the Sahara desert over the Mediterranean Sea and into Europe. The sand tuned the snowy-white slopes of Sochi, Russia, bright orange, with media reports likening the landscape to the Red Planet, Mars.

March 24

Shōgun

1603

Tokugawa Ieyasu was given the Japanese title of shōgun, meaning military leader, which marked the start of more than 260 years of Tokugawa Shogunate rule. He set up a second capital in the fishing village of Edo, which later expanded to become Tokyo.

Also on this day

1882 German physician Robert Koch announced his discovery of the bacterium that causes the disease tuberculosis (TB).

1944 Seventy-six Allied pilots escaped from the German Stalag Luft III prisoner-of-war camp through a tunnel dug in secret.

2002 US animated comedy *Shrek*, starring a green ogre, won the first Academy Award for Best Animated Feature.

1921

Women's Olympiad

Monte Carlo, Monaco, hosted the Women's Olympiad – the first international women's sports event. For five days, 100 female athletes, including gold-winning shot putter Lucile Ellerbe Godbold, took part in a variety of track and field competitions.

Born this day

1826 Matilda Joslyn Gage, US activist. She founded the National Woman Suffrage Association and campaigned for social reforms to benefit women and Indigenous Americans.

1874 Harry Houdini, Hungarian-born US illusionist. He became famous for his astonishing disappearing tricks and amazing escape acts.

1989

Major oil spill

When US oil tanker *Exxon Valdez* struck a reef in the Gulf of Alaska, about 37,000 tonnes of oil spilled into the sea. The leaked oil poisoned local wildlife, such as sea birds, otters, and seals, and caused environmental damage to 2,400 km (1,500 miles) of Alaskan coastline.

March

25

Also on this day

1306 Robert the Bruce was crowned king when Scotland regained its independence from English rule.

1655 Using his telescope, Dutch astronomer Christiaan Huygens spotted Titan, Saturn's largest moon.

1807 The Slave Trade Act became law, ending the trade of enslaved people throughout the British Empire.

1436 Florence Cathedral

The Basilica di Santa Maria del Fiore in Florence, Italy, was consecrated (made holy) by Pope Eugenius IV. The huge brick dome of the cathedral was designed and built by Italian architect Filippo Brunelleschi and remains the largest ever built.

Born this day

1942 Aretha Franklin, Black American singer. Known as the Queen of Soul, this 18-time Grammy winner became the first woman to be honoured with a place in the Rock & Roll Hall of Fame.

1947 Elton John, British singer, songwriter, and performer. An LGBTQ+ icon, he is among the world's biggest pop stars and has sold more than 300 million records.

Selma march 1965

After police violence ended previous attempts, Black civil rights activist Martin Luther King, Jr marched 87 km (54 miles) from Selma to Montgomery in Alabama, USA, joined by nearly 25,000 supporters. They were protesting against restrictions for Black voters.

1169 Egyptian ruler

Islamic warrior Saladin became the first sultan, or ruler, of Egypt and Syria, establishing the Ayyubid Dynasty. His rule spread across parts of Arabia and Africa and he played an important role in wars in the Holy Land – sacred to Jews, Christians, and Muslims.

Also on this day

1859 French doctor Edmond Lescarbault believed he'd spotted a new planet and named it Vulcan. It's now thought he saw an asteroid.

1897 The first Māori lawyer Āpirana Turupa Ngata took his position at the Supreme Court in Auckland, New Zealand.

1979 A peace treaty between Egypt and Israel was finalized with a televised handshake between the leaders of the two countries in Washington, DC, USA.

Born this day

1931 Leonard Nimoy, US actor. He was best known for playing the sharp-eared Spock in the long-running science-fiction series *Star Trek*.

2012 Skateboarding stunt

A remarkable skateboarding feat, the 1080, was achieved for the first time by 12-year-old Tom Schaar in California, USA. The US skateboarder used a mega ramp to perform three full rotations in the air.

1927 Non-stop racing

The Italian car race Mille Miglia, meaning "Thousand Miles", was held for the first time. The competing drivers sped off in their sports cars from the city of Brescia at speeds of up to 77 kph (48 mph). The winner returned to Brescia in just over 21 hours.

March 27

47 BCE Queen Cleopatra

Cleopatra VII was reinstated as the joint ruler of Egypt, alongside her brother Ptolemy XIV. She was the last monarch of Egypt's Ptolemaic Dynasty.

1871 International rugby match

Around 4,000 fans watched Scotland beat England 1–0 in the world's first international rugby union match at Raeburn Place in Edinburgh, Scotland.

Born this day

1963 Xuxa, Brazilian presenter, actress, and singer. She has sold 50 million records, and won two Latin Grammy Awards for Best Children's Album.

1968 Surfing on the wind

The first US patent for the windsurfer sailboard – a surfboard attached to a mast and sail – was filed by Californian surfers Jim Drake and Hoyle Schweitzer.

2003 Prehistoric salamanders

The scientific journal *Nature* published a report on the earliest salamanders after thousands of fossils dating back 165 million years were found in volcanic ash in China and Mongolia.

Also on this day

1867 A group of Black Americans defied laws by sitting with white passengers in a streetcar in the first protest against segregation on public transport in the USA.

1981 In the biggest nationwide strike in Poland, 12 million people protested the violent methods used by security services against the workers' rights organization Solidarity.

Grand Canyon Skywalk

2007

Extending 21 m (70 ft) over the edge of the Grand Canyon in Arizona, USA, this skywalk first opened to visitors, offering stunning views. The glass walkway on this horseshoe-shaped structure creates the illusion of walking on air.

Born this day

1986 Lady Gaga, US pop star. Her powerful songwriting, distinctive voice, flamboyant style, and hit records have earned her 12 Grammy Awards as well as an Oscar.

Return of kabuki

2013

The Kabuki-za Theatre reopened in Tokyo, Japan, as the main stage for kabuki drama. This traditional form of Japanese dance-drama features performers in colourful costumes and elaborate masks or make-up.

Weightlifting championship

1891

The first World Weightlifting Championship was held in London, UK, with only seven athletes from six countries taking part. Britain's Edward Lawrence Levy took the first title as world champion. He went on to set 14 world records.

Also on this day

1939 The Spanish Civil War ended when nationalist troops entered Madrid, and General Francisco Franco took charge of the country.

1964 The second-biggest earthquake in recorded history hit Prince William Sound, Alaska, USA, producing a tsunami.

2011 Alain Robert, known as the French Spiderman, climbed the 830 m (2,723 ft) tall skyscraper Burj Khalifa in Dubai in six hours.

March 29

1958 Carbon curve

The first measurements of carbon dioxide levels in Earth's atmosphere were taken in the Mauna Loa Observatory in Hawaii, USA. The daily data is plotted on a graph called the Keeling Curve, which monitors the link between burning fossil fuels such as coal, oil, or petrol, and levels of carbon dioxide. This gas is the biggest cause of climate change.

1974 Terracotta Army

Farmers in Xian, China, found fragments of a clay figure in the soil, leading to the discovery of more than 8,000 life-size clay soldiers known as the Terracotta Army. These models were buried close to the tomb of the first Chinese emperor Qin Shi Huang to protect him in the afterlife.

Also on this day

1807 German astronomer Wilhelm Olbers spotted Vesta – the brightest asteroid in the sky.

1849 Maharaja of the Punjab, Duleep Singh, signed the Treaty of Lahore, giving the British East India Company land in India.

2017 British prime minister Theresa May triggered Article 50 of the Treaty on European Union to begin Brexit, the UK's departure from the EU.

Born this day

1905 Philip Ahn, Korean-American actor. He enjoyed a long career and is remembered with his own star on the Walk of Fame in California, USA.

1927 Speedy Slug

The Sunbeam 1000 HP Mystery broke the land speed record, travelling at more than 320 kph (200 mph) on Daytona Beach, USA. Nicknamed "The Slug", this specially built car was powered by two aircraft engines.

March 30

1842

First anaesthetic

US doctor Crawford Long gave ether to his patient James Venable while removing his neck tumour. This was the first-ever use of an anaesthetic for pain relief during an operation.

2017

Reusable rocket

The SpaceX booster launched from Cape Canaveral, USA, marking the first successful flight of a reused rocket. The same booster had flown into space the previous year.

Born this day

1908 Devika Rani, Indian film star. She played lead roles in films about women's issues and ran her own production company.

Also on this day

239 BCE Halley's Comet was observed for the first time by Chinese astronomers. The comet passes by Earth every 76 years or so.

1861 British chemist William Crookes announced his discovery of the element thallium.

1987 US actor Marlee Matlin became the first Deaf performer to win an Oscar for Best Actress, in *Children of a Lesser God.*

1923

World cruise

Ocean liner RMS *Laconia* sailed back into New York Harbor, USA, as the first passenger cruise ship to circle the world. With 400 passengers, RMS *Laconia* had visited 22 ports in 130 days.

March

31

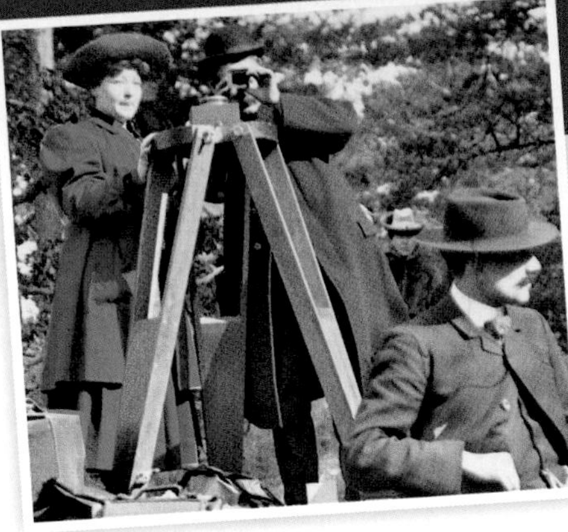

1896

Female director

Trailblazing French film director Alice Guy-Blaché released the short silent film *La Fée aux Choux* ("The Cabbage Fairy"), about a fairy who makes babies from cabbages. It was the first film ever directed by a woman.

2007

Earth Hour

More than 2 million homes and 2,000 businesses switched their lights off for an hour to help save energy during the first Earth Hour event, held in Sydney, Australia.

Born this day

1971 Ewan McGregor, Scottish actor. He has appeared in a diverse range of dramas and musicals, and has starred as the Jedi Knight Obi-Wan Kenobi in the *Star Wars* series.

1889

Eiffel Tower

The grand opening of the Eiffel Tower took place in Paris, France. Named after its designer Gustave Eiffel, the iron tower consists of 18,000 parts. Standing 324 m (1,063 ft) tall, it was the world's tallest building until 1930.

Also on this day

1854 Under threat of force, Japan opened its ports to US trade ships, ending centuries of isolation from the outside world.

1870 Thomas Mundy Peterson was the first Black American to vote in the US elections, after a new law allowed citizens of all races to vote.

1913 A musical recital in Vienna – later named the Skandalkonzert ("scandal concert") – was so unmelodic that the audience rioted to make it stop.

Nunavut

1999

In the Northwest Territories in northern Canada, a new homeland for an Indigenous people called the Inuit was created. In the Inuit language, Nunavut means "Our Land".

Also on this day

1976 Business partners Steve Jobs and Steve Wozniak launched the Apple Computer Company in California, USA.

2001 The Netherlands became the first country in the world to legalize marriage between two people of the same sex.

2013 In Saudi Arabia, construction began on the Jeddah Tower, planned to be the world's first 1 km (0.6 mile) high skyscraper.

1973

Project Tiger

With the Royal Bengal tiger, India's national animal, in danger of extinction from hunting and habitat destruction, the Indian government launched "Project Tiger". The organization works to safeguard tiger habitats and increase the numbers of these tigers living in the wild.

1983

Human chain protest

Seventy thousand women gathered to protest against nuclear weapons being installed. They made a 22 km (14 mile) human chain stretching from an US Air Force base in the UK to a nuclear weapons factory.

Born this day

1776 Sophie Germain, French scientist. She confounded 18th-century expectations of women by making great contributions to mathematics.

1940 Wangari Maathai, Kenyan environmental activist. She was the first African woman to be awarded the Nobel Peace Prize.

April

2

1930 African emperor

Haile Selassie became emperor of Ethiopia. A forward-thinking ruler, Selassie created modern Ethiopia, abolishing slavery and setting up the country's first written constitution.

Also on this day

1513 Spanish explorer Juan Ponce de León first saw land in what is now Florida, USA.

1851 Rama IV became the king of Siam (modern-day Thailand). He ruled until 1868.

1982 Argentina launched a military operation to capture the British-controlled Falkland Islands in the South Atlantic, triggering the Falklands War.

1877 Fired!

The first human cannonball act was performed by 14-year-old British acrobat Rossa Matilda Richter, known as Zazel, at the Royal Aquarium in London, UK.

Born this day

1805 Hans Christian Andersen, Danish author. He is best known for writing *The Little Mermaid*. His birthday is now celebrated as International Children's Book Day.

1939 Marvin Gaye, Black American singer and songwriter. The soul and R&B music he produced has influenced many other artists.

1931

Pitching a curve ball

One of the first women to play professional baseball, pitcher Jackie Mitchell shocked fans by striking out superstar hitters Babe Ruth and Lou Gehrig during a game in Tennessee, USA.

Also on this day

1864 The Northern army captured Richmond, Virginia – a stronghold of the Southern army – during the US Civil War.

1973 Martin Cooper of Motorola made the first public mobile phone call to Joel Engel, who headed a rival project at AT&T.

2009 The United Nations Declaration on the Rights of Indigenous Peoples (UNDRIP) was accepted by Australia.

Pony Express 1860

A mail delivery service powered by hardy riders on fast horses began between Missouri and California, USA. Messages could now be sent between the east and west coasts in just 10 days.

Osborne 1 1981

The first successful handheld computer was introduced at the West Coast Computer Faire in San Francisco, USA. It weighed 10 kg (22 lb), had a 12.7 cm (5 in) display screen, a 64K RAM, and a price tag of US $1,795.

Born this day

1934 Jane Goodall, British biologist and conservationist. She spent years studying wild chimpanzees at Gombe National Park, Tanzania.

1934 Pamela Allen, New Zealand children's author and illustrator. She has published more than 30 picture books since 1980.

Rise to power 1922

Joseph Stalin became Secretary General of the Communist Party of the Soviet Union. The role gave him power over the party, an important step on his path to taking full control of the Soviet Union.

Microsoft founded

1975

Childhood friends Paul Allen (left) and Bill Gates (right) set up Microsoft, a computer software company, at Albuquerque, USA. It eventually became one of the world's biggest technology companies.

Born this day

1928 Maya Angelou, Black American writer, poet, and civil rights activist. She rose to fame with *I Know Why the Caged Bird Sings* in 1970.

1873

The Kennel Club

Frustrated by the lack of rules for dog shows, a group of British dog lovers set up the world's first official club to register purebred dogs and record their activities.

Also on this day

1949 Twelve countries from across North America and Europe formed the North Atlantic Treaty Organization (NATO). This alliance was set up to protect against potential attacks by the Soviet Union.

1968 Black American civil rights leader Martin Luther King, Jr was assassinated at the Lorraine Motel in Memphis, Tennessee, USA.

2002 A peace agreement between the government of Angola and UNITA rebels ended 27 years of civil war in the country.

1932

A lemony cure

US scientist Charles Glen King identified vitamin C in lemon juice. He proved that this vitamin, found in many fruits and vegetables, could cure scurvy – a fatal disease caused by a lack of vitamin C.

April

5

1943

Surviving the sea

Brazilian fishermen rescued Chinese sailor Poon Lim, who had been adrift at sea for 133 days on a wooden raft after his ship sank in the Atlantic Ocean. He had survived on rainwater and fish.

1965 Lava lamp

An egg timer filled with strange bubbling liquids inspired British accountant Edward Craven Walker to design one of the most eye-catching light fixtures of the 1960s.

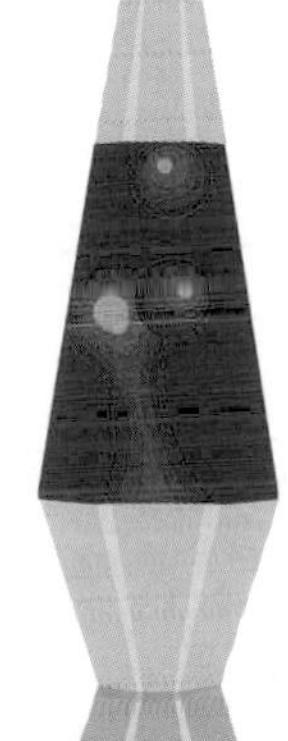

Also on this day

1722 Dutch seafarer Jacob Roggeveen became the first European to visit Easter Island (Rapa Nui) in the Pacific Ocean and meet its Indigenous people.

1818 Chile won its struggle for independence from Spain at the Battle of Maipú.

1998 The world's longest suspension bridge, the six-lane Akashi Kaikyo, opened in Japan. It crosses the Akashi Strait and connects the cities of Kobe and Iwaya.

Born this day

1973 Pharrell Williams, Black American musician and producer. Rising to fame as part of the music group N.E.R.D., he has scored major hits such as *Get Lucky* and *Happy*.

Robotic arm 2012

US whizz kid Easton LaChappelle took his design for a 3D-printed robotic arm to the Colorado State Science Fair. A meeting there with a girl with a US $80,000 prosthetic arm made him want to create affordable prosthetic alternatives. The next year Easton presented his ideas at a science fair at the White House.

April

6

1896

Modern Olympics

King George I of Greece and 60,000 spectators welcomed athletes from 13 countries as they prepared to compete in the first modern Olympics in Athens, 1,500 years after the Olympic Games were banned by Roman emperor Theodosius I.

Born this day

1483 Raphael, Italian painter and architect. Among his most important masterpieces are the paintings now hanging in the Raphael Rooms, a suite of apartments at the Vatican.

Axe the tax

1772

Catherine the Great of Russia abolished a hugely unpopular tax on beards that had been in place for more than 70 years. The day is now celebrated in Russia as Beard Day.

Winner takes it all

1974

Swedish pop group ABBA won the Eurovision Song Contest with their catchy song *Waterloo*, catapulting them to global stardom.

Also on this day

1909 US explorer Robert Peary claimed to have discovered the North Pole, but decades later an investigation cast doubts on this achievement.

1917 The USA entered World War I, declaring war against Germany after German attacks sank US merchant ships and claimed civilian lives.

1943 The classic children's tale *Le Petit Prince* (*The Little Prince*) by Antoine de Saint-Exupéry was first published in the USA.

April

7

1805 Musical masterpiece

German composer Ludwig van Beethoven's *Symphony No. 3* was performed for the public for the first time, in Vienna, Austria. Grander and more dramatic than other symphonies of the time, it marked the beginning of the Romantic era in music.

1795 Measuring in metric

France became the first country to officially adopt the metric system, which defined units of length, mass, and volume based on the dimensions of Earth.

1913 Keeping food cool

After making some improvements to the industrial refrigerator, US inventor Fred W Wolf filed a patent for his new design. He manufactured a simple, inexpensive fridge that could be plugged into the household electric supply.

Born this day

1954 Jackie Chan, Hong Kong-born Chinese film star. He is best known for mixing dangerous acrobatic stunts with comedy. He popularized kung fu in Hollywood and has starred in many movies.

Also on this day

1827 A year after inventing friction matches, British chemist John Walker started selling them in his shop.

1927 US Secretary of Commerce Herbert Hoover made the first public demonstration of a videophone, using it to call officials of the American Telephone & Telegraph company (AT&T), the creators of the device.

1987 The National Museum of Women in the Arts in Washington, DC, USA, opened to the public, displaying its vast collection of artworks by women.

April

8

1271

The fallen fortress

Considered impossible to capture, the Krak des Chevaliers fortress in Syria, built by European crusaders, was seized by Sultan Baibars, an important Islamic ruler.

1942

Unlikely soldier

A group of Polish soldiers adopted a brown bear cub in Iran and gave him the rank of Private. The bear became the most famous member of their regiment and was later promoted to Corporal.

2008

Turbine towers

The three power-generating wind turbines between the twin towers of the World Trade Centre in Bahrain were turned on together for the first time. No other skyscrapers had been designed with built-in wind turbines before.

Also on this day

1904 After nearly 1,000 years of recurring conflict, Britain and France signed the Entente Cordiale, finally making peace.

1974 Black American baseball star Hank Aaron hit his 715th home run to beat Babe Ruth's record, in front of more than 53,000 spectators.

1983 Live on television, US magician David Copperfield seemingly made the Statue of Liberty vanish for a few moments, shocking viewers with his astonishing trick.

Born this day

1941 Vivienne Westwood, self-taught British fashion designer. She became an icon of British fashion with her bold designs.

April

9

1865 Civil War ends

General Robert E Lee of the Southern Army surrendered to General Ulysses S Grant of the Northern Army at Appomattox Court House in Virginia, USA, effectively ending the US Civil War. The two sides had been fighting over the issue of slavery for four years.

1860 Oldest voice recording

French inventor Édouard-Léon Scott de Martinville recorded himself singing a French folk song on his phonautograph. Unheard for almost 150 years, his recording was brought to life by modern audio technology In 2008.

Also on this day

1867 The USA agreed to purchase Alaska from Russia for about two cents per acre.

1939 Barred from singing at Washington, DC's biggest concert hall, Black American musician Marian Anderson instead performed an open-air concert for 75,000 people at the Lincoln Memorial.

1947 An interracial group of Americans took a two-week ride on a bus through four southern states, challenging years of segregation on interstate buses.

Born this day

1822 Aron of Kangeq, Inuit hunter. He took up drawing and printmaking when bedridden with tuberculosis, and became one of the pioneers of modern Greenlandic art.

1288 Battle of Bach Dang

In a decisive naval battle, Vietnamese forces commanded by Tran Hung Dao (left) trapped and defeated Mongol invaders from China, on the Bach Dang River. After fierce fighting, they seized 400 enemy warships and captured the Mongol general Omar Khan.

April 10

1849

Accidental invention

US mechanic Walter Hunt received a patent for his invention, the safety pin. He'd had the idea for the useful item as he was twisting an ordinary piece of wire in his fingers.

Born this day

1993 Daisy Ridley, British actor. She rose to global fame after playing the lead role of Rey in the *Star Wars* films.

2017

Champion for education

At just 19 years old, Pakistani activist Malala Yousafzai became the United Nation's (UN's) youngest-ever Messenger of Peace. She is recognized internationally for drawing attention to the plight of 130 million girls around the world who do not have access to education.

1833

First global Black star

On his opening night, stage actor Ira Aldridge won over his audience as the first Black person to play Shakespeare's Othello at the famous Theatre Royal in London, UK. He went on to tour the world.

Also on this day

1815 Mount Tambora erupted in Indonesia. It was the most powerful eruption in recorded history – at least 10,000 people were killed.

1998 Signed on Good Friday, the Belfast Agreement ended 30 years of violent conflict over how Northern Ireland should be governed.

2019 The Event Horizon Telescope captured the first-ever photograph of a supermassive black hole.

April 11

1831 Lewis chess pieces

Found on the Isle of Lewis, Scotland, and dating back to the 12th century, these medieval artefacts were displayed to the public for the first time in Edinburgh, Scotland. The game pieces were carved from walrus tusk and sperm whale tooth.

Also on this day

1814 The Treaty of Fontainebleau was signed in France, ending Napoleon Bonaparte's rule as emperor and forcing him to leave the country.

1941 French officer Alain le Ray became the first soldier to escape from Germany's Colditz Castle, a maximum-security prison, during World War II.

Impressive skyscraper 1931

In the USA, the construction of New York City's Empire State Building was finished, following 7 million hours of work carried out by 3,400 workers over just 410 days. It was the world's tallest building until 1972.

2010 Balloon flight

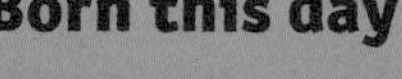

US pilot Jonathan Trappe spent 13 hours, 36 minutes, and 57 seconds flying over North Carolina, USA, using a cluster of 57 enormous helium balloons. During the overnight flight, he covered more than 175 km (109 miles) and reached a peak height of 2,278 m (7,474 ft).

Born this day

1991 Thiago Alcântara, Spanish footballer. He has played for many clubs, such as FC Barcelona, and also the Spanish national team.

April

12

1937 Whittle's jet engine

Overcoming doubts raised by scientists, British engineer Frank Whittle successfully tested his invention – the first jet engine designed to power an aircraft. The government helped finance his work during World War II.

Also on this day

1919 Architect Walter Gropius founded Bauhaus, an art and design school in Weimar, Germany. It gathered together Europe's most brilliant artists and designers.

1964 Black American civil rights activist Malcolm X gave his "Ballot or the Bullet" speech at the King Solomon Baptist Church in Detroit, USA.

1992 Europe's first Disneyland, originally called Euro Disneyland Park, opened near Paris.

Born this day

1913 Keiko Fukuda, Japanese-American martial artist. She was the highest-ranking female *judoka* in the sport's history.

1925 Evelyn Berezin, US computer designer. She developed one of the earliest computer systems for airline reservations.

Human in space 1961

Cosmonaut (Soviet astronaut) Yuri Gagarin spent 108 minutes orbiting Earth in his spacecraft *Vostok 1*, becoming the first person to travel into space. Gagarin's flight was remotely controlled from Earth by a computer program.

1861 Battle of Fort Sumter

The first major battle of the US Civil War took place, following decades of simmering tensions between the Northern and Southern states. Fort Sumter, controlled by the Northern Army, was bombarded by Southern forces.

April 13

2019 Stratolaunch

Originally designed as a flying launchpad for rockets, Stratolaunch – the world's largest aircraft by wingspan – flew for the first time, over the Mojave Desert in California, USA. The distance between its wingtips is longer than a football pitch.

1953 The name's Bond

British writer Ian Fleming's *Casino Royale* introduced the fictional British secret service agent James Bond. It was the first book in a series of 12 action-packed spy novels that were later turned into blockbuster movies.

2017

The ultimate challenge

Having already climbed the world's seven highest mountains and skied to the South Pole, 20-year-old Japanese adventurer Marin Minamiya became the youngest person to complete the Explorer's Grand Slam when she reached the North Pole.

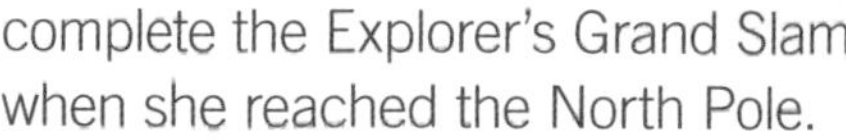

Born this day

1519 Catherine de' Medici, Italian noblewoman. She married King Henry II of France and had a powerful role in French politics as the mother of three future kings.

Also on this day

1204 Though tasked with recapturing Jerusalem, a western Christian army instead sacked the Byzantine city of Constantinople and stole its treasures.

1964 Bahamian-American actor Sidney Poitier became the first Black person to win the Best Actor Oscar, for the film *Lilies of the Field*.

1997 In a major golfing win, US golfer Tiger Woods became the youngest winner of the Masters Tournament at the age of 21.

April

14

1935

Dust storm

The day turned dark when an enormous cloud of sand and dust blew into the USA's drought-stricken Southern Plains, giving the area its famous name "The Dust Bowl".

Born this day

1932 Loretta Lynn, US country singer and songwriter. Throughout her 60-year career, she wrote songs that were inspired by her own life experiences.

Cloud of ash

2010

The explosive eruption of a volcano under the Icelandic ice cap of Eyjafjallajökull spewed huge quantities of ash into the atmosphere, causing air traffic chaos across large parts of Europe for a week afterwards.

Battle in space

1561

Residents of Nuremberg in Germany reported seeing hundreds of unidentified flying objects (UFOs) fighting with each other in the sky at sunrise. It's now thought they saw a sundog – a type of natural phenomenon similar to a rainbow.

Also on this day

1865 US president Abraham Lincoln was assassinated by John Wilkes Booth at Ford's Theatre in Washington, DC, USA.

1986 In Gopalganj, Bangladesh, 92 people were killed by the heaviest hailstones on record, with some ice chunks weighing up to 1 kg (2 lb).

1990 Georgians held the first-ever Day of the Georgian Language, celebrating their country's official language.

Blazing cathedral

2019

A massive fire, most likely caused by an electrical fault, engulfed the centuries-old Notre Dame Cathedral in Paris, France. The fire melted the building's lead roof, and toppled its 96 m (315 ft) high spire.

Born this day

1452 Leonardo da Vinci, Italian artist and engineer. He is best known for his painting the *Mona Lisa* and for designing various flying machines.

1469 Guru Nanak, religious leader. A Hindu by birth, he travelled widely in search of spiritual truth and founded the Sikh religion.

Also on this day

1868 Members of the Indigenous Māori tribe were elected to New Zealand's parliament for the first time following the Māori Representation Act.

1945 The Bergen-Belsen concentration camp in Germany was liberated by British forces, exposing the horrific extent of Nazi war crimes.

1955 US entrepreneur Ray Kroc opened his first McDonald's franchise in Illinois, USA, later turning the fast-food company into a global success.

1941

Vought-Sikorsky VS-300

Russian-American aircraft designer Igor Sikorsky's helicopter set a record in the USA by staying in the air for 1 hour, 5 minutes, and 14.5 seconds. Sikorsky's design became the model for future helicopters.

Atlantic tragedy

1912

On its first voyage, the HMS *Titanic* – the largest and most luxurious steamship of its time – hit an iceberg and sank in the freezing North Atlantic Ocean. More than 1,500 passengers and crew died.

April 16

1346

Dušan the Mighty

The powerful Serbian king Stephen Dušan crowned himself emperor of Serbia, Greece, and Bulgaria. During his reign, the Serbian Empire expanded to include most of southeast Europe.

Born this day

1755 Élisabeth Vigée-Le Brun, French painter. One of the most successful female artists of her time, she painted portraits of various famous women, including Queen Marie Antoinette.

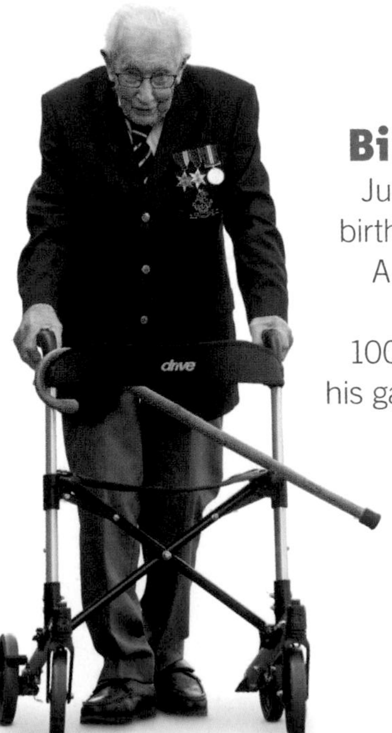

2020

Birthday walk

Just before his 100th birthday, former British Army officer Captain Tom Moore walked 100 sponsored laps of his garden, raising more than £30 million to support medical charities during the COVID-19 pandemic.

Also on this day

1746 The French-supported Jacobite army was defeated at the Battle of Culloden, ending their fight to seize the British throne.

1847 In New Zealand, a British officer shot a Māori chief by accident, causing conflict between Indigenous Māori and British settlers.

1853 A 21-gun salute was fired to celebrate India's first passenger train, which travelled from Mumbai (then called Bombay) to Thane, a distance of 34 km (21 miles).

Panda presents

1972

US president Richard Nixon and First Lady Pat Nixon welcomed two young giant pandas, Ling-Ling and Hsing-Hsing, to the Smithsonian's National Zoo at Washington, DC, USA. The popular pair had been sent as gifts by Chinese premier Zhou Enlai.

April 17

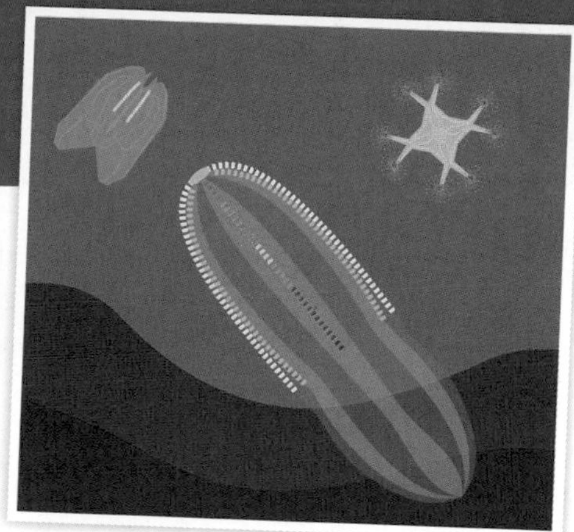

2017 Underwater wonders

Austrian underwater filmmaker Alexander Benedik filmed vibrant sea creatures living in the sub-zero waters below the ice caps at Tasiilaq, Greenland. He found colourful jellyfish and shrimps that glow in the dark.

Born this day

1974 Victoria Beckham, British style icon. She rose to international fame as a member of the Spice Girls, a bestselling 1990s pop group, before starting her own fashion label.

1964 Must-have motor

Customers rushed to buy the stylish and affordable Ford Mustang when it was unveiled at the World's Fair in New York City, USA. In just one day, almost 22,000 cars were sold in showrooms across the country.

Also on this day

1961 Cuban refugees, supported by the USA, began the Bay of Pigs invasion in an unsuccessful attempt to topple the communist government of Fidel Castro in Cuba.

1982 Canada gained full independence from the UK when British monarch Queen Elizabeth II signed Canada's new constitution into law.

2014 Aleksander Doba, a 67-year-old Polish kayaker, became the first person to paddle a canoe across the Atlantic Ocean from Europe to North America. He made the journey from Portugal to Florida in 196 days.

1964 Flying solo

US pilot Geraldine "Jerrie" Mock became the first woman to complete a solo flight around the world. It had taken her 29 days, 11 hours, and 59 minutes to circle the globe.

April

18

2019

Ancient carnivore

An ancient mammal species bigger than a polar bear was identified. The 22-million-year-old bones of *Simbakubwa kutokaafrika* had lain forgotten in a drawer at Nairobi National Museum, Kenya, for nearly 40 years.

Also on this day

1775 US patriot Paul Revere rode through the night to alert the US militia about an impending attack by British troops.

1906 A 7.9-magnitude earthquake struck San Francisco, USA, destroying much of the city and killing more than 3,000 people.

2018 Cinemas reopened in Saudi Arabia after a 35-year ban. Marvel's *Black Panther* was the first movie to be screened.

1938

Here comes Superman!

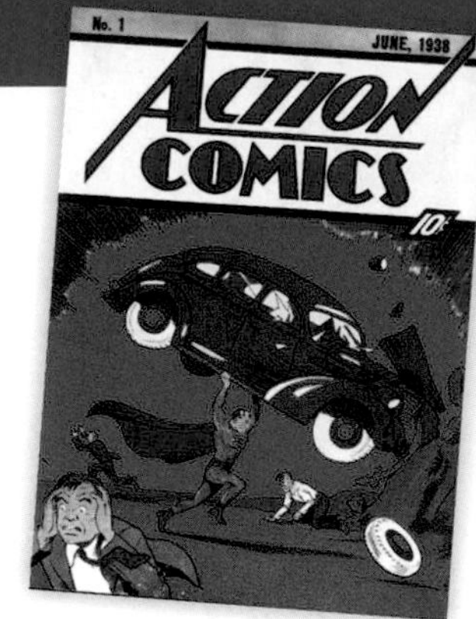

Comic book legend Superman appeared for the first time in *Action Comics #1*. Created by US writer and artist duo Jerry Siegel and Joe Shuster, Superman was the first comic book hero to have superpowers.

Born this day

1813 James McCune Smith, Black American physician. Born into slavery, he became the first Black person in the USA to earn a medical degree.

1506

St Peter's Basilica

In Rome, Italy, Pope Julius II laid the foundation stone of the new St Peter's Basilica. The enormous stone church was designed by architect Donato Bramante, whose work was continued after his death by other artists, including Michelangelo and Raphael. It took 150 years to build.

April 19

1971 First space home

The first-ever space station, *Salyut 1*, was launched into Earth's orbit as part of the Soviet Union's space programme. It stayed in space for 175 days and circled Earth nearly 3,000 times.

American Revolution 1775

The first battles of the US War of Independence between Britain and its colonies took place at Lexington and Concord in Massachusetts, in present-day USA.

Also on this day

1987 The USA's favourite cartoon family, the Simpsons first appeared in a series of short episodes on the *Tracey Ullman Show*.

1987 The UK's first medical unit for HIV and AIDS patients was opened by Diana, Princess of Wales, in London, UK.

2018 Swaziland's King Mswati III changed the country's name to eSwatini to celebrate 50 years of independence from British rule.

Born this day

1946 Duygu Asena, Turkish journalist and civil rights champion. She campaigned for equality and wrote about injustices towards women.

1968 Snowmobile trek

After journeying for 42 days on snowmobiles, US explorer Ralph Plaisted and his teammates Walter Pederson, Gerald Pitzl, and Jean-Luc Bombardier became the first people to reach the North Pole by travelling over the surface of the Arctic ice.

April

20

Born this day

1964 Andy Serkis, British film and voice actor, director, and motion capture artist. He is famous for portraying Gollum in *The Lord of the Rings*.

Triumph in Japan

2008

Claiming victory at Indy Japan 300, US racing driver Danica Patrick became the first woman to win an IndyCar Series race. She took the lead from the top contenders in the final few laps of the 200-lap race.

1961

Human rocket

In a pioneering 13-second flight, US engineer Harold Graham became the first person to be lifted off the ground by a jet propulsion device without being tethered. He rose 1.2 m (4 ft) into the air.

Also on this day

1611 English playwright William Shakespeare's tragedy *Macbeth* was performed for the first time at the Globe Theatre in London, England.

1862 French chemist Louis Pasteur and biologist Claude Bernard first tested their new method for preserving liquids such as milk.

2010

Disaster at sea

An explosion on *Deepwater Horizon*, an oil drilling rig off the coast of Louisiana, USA, caused an enormous fire and the death of 11 workers. Two days later, the rig sank, causing the world's worst-ever oil spill, which devastated many marine wildlife species.

April 21

1934 Monster mystery

A photograph was published appearing to show a monster swimming in the waters of Loch Ness, Scotland. It was later revealed to be a hoax.

Also on this day

753 BCE Legend has it that the city of Rome was founded on this day by twin brothers Remus and Romulus on the banks of the Tiber River.

1782 In present-day Thailand, Siamese king Rama I established his kingdom's capital, which became known as Bangkok.

1966 The last Ethiopian emperor, Haile Selassie I, visited Jamaica. His visit is celebrated as the annual Rastafari holiday, Grounation Day.

2015 High-speed train

The Central Japan Railway Company's experimental LO Series maglev train reached a top speed of 603 kph (375 mph) during a test run in Yamanashi, Japan.

Mughal victory 1526

The founder of the Mughal Empire, Babur, defeated the larger army of Ibrahim Lodi, the Sultan of Delhi, at the First Battle of Panipat in what is now northern India. Babur's victory marked the start of Mughal rule in the Indian subcontinent.

Born this day

1816 Charlotte Brontë, British author and poet. Her novels, such as *Jane Eyre*, are considered classics of English literature.

1926 Elizabeth II, Queen of the United Kingdom and 15 Commonwealth countries. She is the longest-reigning living monarch.

April 22

1823

Shoes on wheels

An early idea for in-line roller skates was patented by Robert John Tyers, a British fruit seller. Each skate was formed of a single row of five wheels attached to a wooden sole and a brake.

Born this day

1989 Aron Gunnarsson, Icelandic footballer. He has played more than 90 international matches and captained Iceland in the UEFA Euro 2016.

1970

First Earth Day

US politician Gaylord Nelson organized the first "Earth Day", a yearly event to raise awareness about the planet's environmental problems. Millions of Americans took part in protests and workshops.

Also on this day

1500 Portuguese explorer Pedro Álvares Cabral became the first European to arrive in South America, claiming the land that is now present-day Brazil for Portugal.

1993 China National Space Administration (CNSA), the national space agency of the People's Republic of China, was founded.

2016 The Paris Climate Agreement was signed by 195 countries in New York City, USA.

1915

Gas attack

In a surprise attack, the German army released 136 tonnes of poisonous chlorine gas on the battlefield at Ypres, Belgium, killing 1,100 Allied soldiers and injuring 7,000. It was the first time that a large-scale chemical attack had been carried out in a war.

April 23

2016 Chart topper

Music sensation Beyoncé became the first-ever artist to top the US Billboard 200 album chart with their first six albums, when her sixth studio album, *Lemonade*, went straight to number 1 on the US chart.

Born this day

1933 Annie Easley, Black American computer programmer. Employed by NASA, she developed software for the powerful Centaur rocket.

Also on this day

1920 Led by Mustafa Kemal Atatürk, the Grand National Assembly of Turkey rejected the rule of Sultan Mehmed VI, bringing an end to the 600-year-old Ottoman Empire.

2019 The government of Malawi and the World Health Organization (WHO) launched the first malaria vaccine.

2020 A 40-million-year-old fossil of a frog was found on Seymour Island, Antarctica, suggesting that amphibians may have lived on the icy continent in the past.

1867 Early animation

One of the first moving picture machines – the zoetrope – was patented by US inventor William E Lincoln. Viewers could make the animation spring to life by rotating the cylinder – which had images drawn on the inside surface – and looking through its viewing slits.

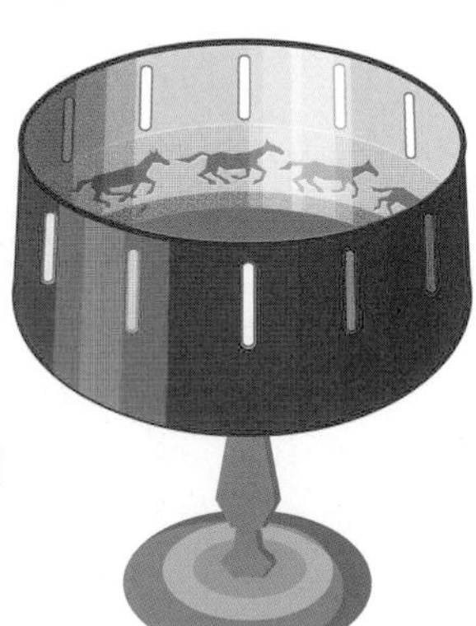

1616 Great playwright

Notable English playwright William Shakespeare died on this day. During his lifetime he wrote 39 plays and more than 154 sonnets (a type of love poem).

April

24

1888

Kodak moment

US inventor George Eastman started the Eastman Kodak Company, which mass-produced portable box cameras that could be used easily by anyone.

Also on this day

1184 BCE The legendary Trojan War ended on this day with the fall of the city of Troy to the Greeks, according to ancient historians.

1990 Gruinard Island, Scotland, was declared safe after being out-of-bounds for 48 years. The uninhabited island had been a testing site for biological weapons during World War II.

2020 In Egypt, archaeologists announced they had discovered the 3,500-year-old mummy of an unknown teenage girl.

2018

Streaming music

For the first time in music history, the money made from listeners paying to stream music on services such as Spotify and Apple Music was greater than that from the sales of music CDs.

1918

Tank combat

Three German A7V tanks faced off against three British Mark IV tanks at the Battle of Villers-Bretonneux in France, during World War I. It was the first time in military history that tanks had fought against each other.

Born this day

1982 Kelly Clarkson, US singer. She won a record deal on the first season of the TV series *American Idol*, and went on to have several hit singles and albums.

April 25

1719 Robinson Crusoe

British writer Daniel Defoe's novel, about a sailor shipwrecked on an island for 28 years, was published in London, UK. The story has since been translated into more than 100 languages.

1960 Operation Sandblast

The nuclear-powered submarine USS *Triton* finished circumnavigating (travelling around) the globe underwater. It had travelled 66,672 km (36,000 nautical miles) in 85 days.

Born this day

1917 Ella Fitzgerald, Black American jazz singer. Known as the Queen of Jazz, she became famous for her vocal range. During her 60-year career, she won 14 Grammys and was awarded the Presidential Medal of Freedom.

Also on this day

1792 French highwayman Nicolas Jacques Pelletier became the first person to be executed for his crimes by guillotine.

1944 The Sikorsky YR-4B became the first helicopter to be used in combat, when it was brought in to rescue four US and British soldiers in Burma (now Myanmar) during World War II.

1946 Nazi occupation and Benito Mussolini's dictatorship ended in Italy. Italians now celebrate this date yearly as Liberation Day.

Gallipoli campaign

1915

Allied troops began an attack on Turkey after it sided with Germany during World War I. The eight-month campaign failed and hundreds of thousands were killed or wounded. The campaign is remembered in Australia and New Zealand each year on ANZAC Day.

April

26

1986

Chernobyl nuclear disaster

During an accident at the Chernobyl nuclear power station in Ukraine, large amounts of radioactive material were spewed out into the atmosphere. The material spread and exposed millions of people to harmful nuclear radiation.

Born this day

1888 Anita Loos, US writer. A successful author, she was also the first female scriptwriter in Hollywood.

1918 Fanny Blankers-Koen, Dutch athlete. She won four golds at the 1948 Summer Olympics at the age of 30 while pregnant with her third child.

Democracy at last

1994

After years of being governed by a regime that denied Black citizens even basic rights, South Africans of all races voted for a new government. Nelson Mandela was elected the first Black president.

Also on this day

1803 More than 3,000 meteors rained down on the city of L'Aigle in France, finally convincing scientists that meteors came from space.

1989 One of the deadliest tornadoes in history struck the Manikganj district of Bangladesh, killing around 1,300 people and injuring 12,000.

2019 The Waorani people of Ecuador won a historic court case against the government to save their land from oil drilling.

April 27

Airbus A380 — 2005

The world's largest passenger plane – the Airbus A380 – took to the skies for the first time, with a crew of six. Taking off from Toulouse-Blagnac airport in France, it flew for 3 hours and 54 minutes before landing.

2011 Tornado tragedy

More than 300 lives were lost when a record-breaking 216 tornadoes hit the USA on the same day. Alabama was the worst-hit state, with 238 deaths.

Born this day

1927 Coretta Scott King, Black American civil rights leader. Wife of Martin Luther King, Jr, she spent her life promoting his philosophy of non-violence, social justice, and human rights.

Also on this day

1943 Three years after getting himself arrested to collect inside information on the Auschwitz concentration camp, Polish officer Witold Pilecki finally escaped.

1956 World heavyweight champion Rocky Marciano retired from boxing, remaining undefeated in his 49 professional matches.

2018 North Korean leader Kim Jong-un and South Korean leader Moon Jae-in met in a summit to establish peace between their two countries.

2006 Freedom Tower

Construction of the Freedom Tower began in New York City, USA. It is the tallest building in the country and shares its name with the North Tower of the original World Trade Center, destroyed by terrorists on 9/11 in 2001.

April

28

224 CE Battle of Hormozdgān

Sasanian king Ardashīr I defeated the Parthian king Artabanus V and set up the Sasanian Empire in ancient Persia. He went on to become one of Persia's greatest rulers, and his empire lasted more than 400 years.

2001 Space tourist

US millionaire Dennis Tito travelled to the International Space Station (ISS) on board a Russian *Soyuz* spacecraft. He funded the trip himself at a cost of US $20 million, becoming the first space tourist.

Born this day

1974 Penelope Cruz, Spanish actor. She became an international star after her leading roles in many Spanish-language films.

Also on this day

1869 Chinese and Irish workers set a record by laying more than 16 km (10 miles) of the Pacific Railroad in the USA in one day.

1952 The US occupation of Japan after World War II ended when the San Francisco Peace Treaty came into effect.

2019 On reaching the bottom of the Mariana Trench (the deepest part of the Pacific Ocean) in a submersible, US diver Victor Vescovo found plastic waste.

1947 Kon-Tiki expedition

Norwegian scientist Thor Heyerdahl and his crew of five set sail from Peru for Polynesia on the Kon-Tiki – a raft made of locally available balsa wood. They wanted to prove that ancient South Americans could have travelled the 6,900 km (4,300 miles) to the Polynesian islands.

April

29

Also on this day

1770 Explorer James Cook and his crew landed at Botany Bay in Australia, beginning British interest in colonizing the continent.

1961 The World Wildlife Fund (WWF) was set up to raise money to protect animals and habitats that are threatened by humans.

2011 Millions of TV viewers watched as Prince William, Duke of Cambridge, married Catherine Middleton in a lavish ceremony at London's Westminster Abbey.

Most wanted

1944

Nancy Wake, one of Britain's leading special agents in World War II, parachuted into France. There, she assembled a resistance group to attack German forces. She eventually reached the top of the Nazis' most-wanted list.

1429

Maid of Orléans

During the Hundred Years' War between France and England, 17-year-old Joan of Arc led the French army to free the city of Orléans, which had been besieged by the English. She became a legendary figure and was made a patron saint of France in 1920.

Born this day

1863 William Randolph Hearst, Sr, US newspaper publisher and entrepreneur. He was the founder of Hearst Corporation, one of the USA's largest media companies.

1899 Edward Kennedy "Duke" Ellington, Black American musician. Often called America's greatest jazz composer, he wrote more than 2,000 songs.

April 30

2005 Tower of buns

Revived after a 26-year pause, the Bun Festival was hosted on Cheung Chau island in Hong Kong. People raced up tall towers covered with buns, which they collected for good fortune.

Founding Father 1789

George Washington took his oath as the first president of the newly formed United States of America. During the American Revolution, he had led the Thirteen Colonies to independence from British rule.

Born this day

1985 Gal Gadot-Varsano, Israeli actor. She rose to fame playing the superhero Wonder Woman in a series of Hollywood films based on the DC Comics character.

1993 World Wide Web

British scientist Tim Berners-Lee made the software for his invention, the World Wide Web, free for public use. Anyone could now use it to share information between computer systems on the internet.

Also on this day

1006 Astronomers around the world watched as the night sky was lit up by the brightest supernova (exploding star) in recorded history.

1888 In the deadliest hailstorm on record, hailstones as large as goose eggs killed 246 people in Moradabad, India.

2013 Queen Beatrix gave up her throne for her son Willem-Alexander, who became king of the Netherlands.

May 1

2005

Glorious goal

At 17, Argentinian footballer Lionel Messi played as a substitute and scored his first goal for FC Barcelona. He went on to become a football legend, having scored more than 700 goals by 2021.

1840

Penny Black

The first prepaid sticky postage stamp was issued in the UK. Called the Penny Black, it showed a portrait of Queen Victoria. Before stamps, people who received letters had to pay the cost of postage.

Born this day

1852 Calamity Jane, hero of the American Wild West. She was known for her bravery and shooting skills, as well as her charitable nature.

Also on this day

1707 The Acts of Union joined the nations of England and Scotland together to create the United Kingdom of Great Britain.

1999 The US animated show *SpongeBob SquarePants* first aired on Nickelodeon. It is the longest-running series on this TV channel.

1890

Workers' Day

Many countries recognized International Workers' Day as a public holiday. It was held on this day in remembrance of the 1886 Haymarket Affair in the USA, in which a peaceful protest of Chicago workers turned into a deadly fight with the police.

May 2

1945 Battle for Berlin

In the final European battle of World War II, the Soviet Red Army seized the German capital of Berlin. This event led to the downfall of Adolf Hitler's Nazi regime.

Rainbow Warrior 1978

The Greenpeace ship *Rainbow Warrior* set sail on a global campaign against harmful ocean activities, including dumping nuclear waste and whale and seal hunting.

Born this day

1972 Dwayne Johnson, American-Canadian wrestler. Better known as The Rock, he went on to take centre stage as an action film star.

1975 David Beckham, British footballer. He played with Manchester United and won multiple league titles and cup victories.

Also on this day

1611 The King James Bible was published. It went on to sell more than a billion copies as the most popular English translation of the Bible.

1670 England's King Charles II gave control of a vast area of what would later become Canada to the Hudson Bay Company.

1922 Constellation convention

The modern list of 88 constellations was agreed at the first meeting of the International Astronomical Union in Rome, Italy. More than half of these groups of stars are based on ancient Greek constellations.

2000 Geocaching games begin

US computer whizz Dave Ulmer hid a small container called a geocache in the woods by Beavercreek, Oregon, USA, kickstarting the pastime of geocaching. Players use satellite navigation and codes from the internet to locate hidden items.

Also on this day

1803 The USA nearly doubled in size with the Louisiana Purchase. French leader Napoleon Bonaparte sold the land to raise war funds.

1947 Japan's Constitution came into effect after World War II. It limited the emperor's power and banned the government from starting wars.

1978 The first spam email, which featured a computer advert, was sent to 400 users in the USA.

1979 Iron Lady

Margaret Thatcher was elected Britain's prime minister, making her the first woman to take the top job. The Iron Lady was the only 20th-century prime minister to win three consecutive terms in office.

1960 Musical sensation

A musical comedy about love and life, *The Fantasticks* opened in New York City, USA. With 17,162 performances in the following 42 years, this show would become the longest-running musical of all time.

Born this day

1933 James Brown, Black American singer and songwriter. Originally a gospel singer, he became a soul and funk star.

Battle of the Coral Sea

1942

The first sea battle between aircraft carriers began as the Japanese navy fought the combined American and Australian forces during World War II. The Allies won, gaining control of the Coral Sea.

1912

Teenage campaigner

In one of her many campaigns to promote equality for women, Chinese-American teenager Mabel Ping Hua-Lee arrived on horseback to lead almost 10,000 people in a parade for suffrage (the right to vote for all) in New York City, USA.

Also on this day

1919 Mass protests by students in Beijing, China, resulted in the May Fourth Movement, which encouraged equality and education for women.

2013 The Walt Disney Company began an annual celebration of *Star Wars*, with special events held at its theme parks.

2019 Kenyan runner Biegon Andrew Kiplangat took a wrong turn during a marathon in Qingdao, China. He had to be helped back on track, before winning the race.

Born this day

1929 Audrey Hepburn, British actor. She is famous for her iconic role in *Breakfast at Tiffany's*.

1607

English settlers

A party of 104 English pioneers established a settlement on the shores of Virginia in North America. Eventually known as Jamestown, it became the first successful English colony on the continent.

May 5

Cinco de Mayo 1862

Following the French invasion of Mexico, Mexican troops defeated a far larger battalion of French soldiers at the Battle of Puebla. This triumph is still celebrated every fifth of May (*cinco de mayo*).

Born this day

1892 Dorothy Garrod, British archaeologist and professor. In 1939, she became the first woman to be made a professor at Cambridge University, UK.

1988 Adele, British singer and songwriter. She became a global superstar after record-breaking sales of her first album, which showcased her remarkable voice.

1921 Perfume of choice

French fashion designer Coco Chanel released her bestselling Chanel No. 5 fragrance. This luxury scent combined 80 ingredients in a rectangular bottle.

1860 One Italy

Italian general Giuseppe Garibaldi set off on the Expedition of the Thousand. He sailed from Genoa and overthrew the Kingdom of the Two Sicilies in a key development that led towards the unification of Italy.

Also on this day

1260 Kublai Khan became ruler of the vast Mongol Empire in East Asia. He would eventually become emperor of China.

1958 The Children's Peace Monument was unveiled in Japan on the annual Children's Day to honour the many thousands of children who died in the Hiroshima tragedy of 1945.

1984 Itaipu Dam in South America began generating electricity. It was the world's largest hydroelectric dam until 2012.

May 6

Launch of iMac 1998

Apple launched its first all-in-one desktop computer, the iMac. It featured a colourful, translucent case with matching keyboard and mouse, a CD drive, built-in speakers, and very easy setup. It was Apple's most successful product in years.

Royal home 1782

Building work started on the Grand Palace, the royal residence of the king of Siam (Thailand), after the capital city was moved to Bangkok from Thonburi. The royal family lived there until 1925, and now the palace is a museum.

The end of airships 1937

A fire on board the German passenger airship *Hindenburg* resulted in a crash in New Jersey, USA, killing 35 passengers. The public lost confidence in this mode of travel and the era of airships ended.

Born this day

1856 Sigmund Freud, Austrian neurologist. He developed a method to help patients with mental health problems by exploring their past.

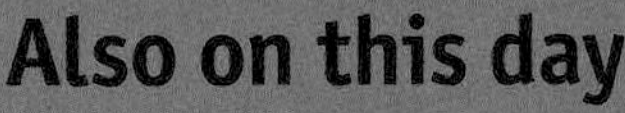

Also on this day

1954 British athlete Roger Bannister became the world's first person to run a mile in less than four minutes.

1994 The Channel Tunnel opened, joining Britain and France with a 50 km (31 mile) railway under the English Channel.

2002 South African innovator Elon Musk founded the space travel company SpaceX, with the ultimate goal of colonizing Mars.

May 7

Pirate treasure 2015

Underwater explorers found a 55 kg (121 lb) silver bar off the coast of Saint Marie Island in Madagascar. It was believed to be a piece from the legendary loot of Scottish pirate Captain William Kidd.

1867 Dynamite in demand

Swedish chemist Alfred Nobel patented dynamite, a new explosive that could be shaped and sold in the form of sticks. Unlike earlier explosives, it didn't explode spontaneously, which made it safer to handle. The invention helped make Nobel a millionaire.

1953 Colossal catch

After a two-hour battle, fisherman Louis Marron landed the heaviest fish ever caught using a rod and reel – a 536 kg (1,180 lb) swordfish caught off the coast of Chile.

Also on this day

1945 Germany surrendered unconditionally to the Allied forces during World War II, in the city of Reims in France.

1946 Masaru Ibuka and Akio Morita founded the Tokyo Telecommunications Engineering Corporation, which went on to become the Japanese technology giant Sony.

1986 Canadian mountaineer Patrick Morrow completed his quest to climb the highest peak on each of the world's seven continents, becoming the first person to do so.

Born this day

1748 Olympe de Gouges, French playwright and women's rights activist. She challenged gender inequality through her work.

Victory in Europe Day

1945

Cities across western Europe and North America celebrated the defeat of Nazi Germany in World War II. The hard-fought victory had come at the cost of millions of lives and widespread destruction.

2014

A rare find

Diver David Mearns found the oldest known astrolabe – an astronomical device used by sailors for navigation. It was found in the wreckage of the Portuguese ship *Esmeralda*, which sank in 1503.

Born this day

1926 David Attenborough, British broadcaster and naturalist. He is famous for his spectacular TV documentaries about natural history.

1975 Enrique Iglesias, Spanish-American singer. He is known as the King of Latin Pop.

Also on this day

1834 The first part of Hans Christian Andersen's *Fairy Tales* was published in Copenhagen, Denmark. It included the story of "The Princess and the Pea".

1902 Nearly 30,000 people died when Mount Pelée volcano erupted over the town of St Pierre, Martinique.

1996 The new constitution of South Africa was the first in the world to protect the rights of LGBTQ+ people.

1984

Thames barrier

Thousands watched as the UK's Queen Elizabeth II opened a set of 20 m (66 ft) tall steel gates built across the River Thames to prevent it from flooding central London.

May 9

1950

Smokey Bear

During a forest fire in New Mexico, USA, firefighters rescued a bear cub with burnt legs and paws clinging to a tree. Nicknamed Smokey Bear, the cub went on to become a famous icon for forest fire prevention.

Also on this day

1901 The first Parliament of the Commonwealth of Australia was opened at a grand ceremony in Melbourne by the UK's Prince George, who later became King George V.

1950 French foreign minister Robert Schuman suggested European powers produce coal and steel jointly so that they would be less likely to go to war again. This was the first step towards the creation of the European Union (EU) many years later.

2017

Dinosaur eggs

Scientists studying a nest of 90-million-year-old fossilized dinosaur eggs found in China in 1993 named the species *Beibeilong sinensis*, meaning "baby dragon from China". It was a giant feathered dinosaur.

1941

Enigma machine

The British Royal Navy captured a German submarine, from which it recovered one of the Enigma machines used by the Nazis to turn secret German messages to unreadable codes during World War II. British code breakers would eventually learn how to read the codes.

Born this day

1921 Sophie Scholl, German student activist. She was a member of White Rose, a non-violent, anti-Nazi resistance group. Scholl was executed in 1943 at the age of 21.

1979 Rosario Dawson, US actor. She co-founded Voto Latino, an organization that encourages young Hispanic people to vote.

May 10

1752

Sparks in the sky

French scientist Thomas François Dalibard drew sparks from a thunderstorm with a 15 m (50 ft) iron rod raised towards the clouds near Paris, France. The experiment demonstrated that lightning is a form of electricity.

War leader

1940

Winston Churchill replaced Neville Chamberlain as the United Kingdom's prime minister. Churchill led the country through World War II and played a major role in the Allied victory.

Born this day

1960 Merlene Ottey, Jamaican-Slovenian athlete. A track and field sprinter, she competed in every Summer Olympics from 1980 to 2004.

1869

The golden spike

A spike made of 18 carat gold was driven into a railway track in Utah, USA, to mark the completion of the USA's first transcontinental railroad. The track connected Sacramento in the west with Omaha in the east.

Also on this day

1857 Indian troops began an unsuccessful revolt against the British in the First War of Independence.

1933 Student groups supporting the Nazi regime burned books by Jewish and liberal writers, claiming the books were "un-German".

1994 Following a historic election victory, Nelson Mandela became South Africa's first Black president.

May 11

Setting a record

1893

Amateur French cyclist Henri Desgrange covered 35.325 km (21.950 miles) in one hour at the Vélodrome Buffalo cycling track in Paris, France, setting the first hour record in cycling.

Born this day

1904 Salvador Dalí, Spanish artist. He was known for his surrealist style, which made use of unusual, dreamlike imagery.

1906 Jacqueline Cochran, US racing pilot. She was the first woman to fly faster than the speed of sound.

330 CE

Founding Constantinople

A new capital for the Roman Empire was established by Emperor Constantine at the city of Byzantium. It was renamed Constantinople after its founder. Today it is the city of Istanbul in Turkey.

Also on this day

1846 Following a border dispute between the USA and Mexico, US president James K Polk asked Congress to declare war on Mexico.

2000 According to official records, the population of India reached 1 billion people.

2019 Scientists at Mauna Loa Observatory in Hawaii announced that the carbon dioxide level in Earth's atmosphere had reached levels not seen for 300 million years.

868

Diamond Sutra

The oldest printed book in existence was created in ancient China. The sacred Buddhist text was discovered in a hidden cave near Dunhuang, China, in 1900.

May 12

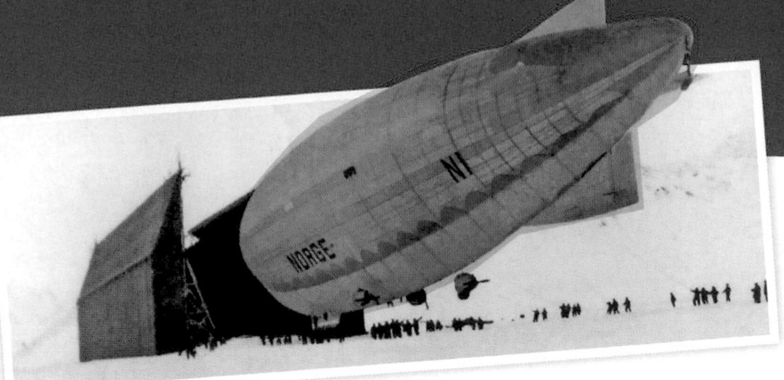

Also on this day

1941 German inventor Konrad Zuse presented the Z3, the first fully automatic computer, at the German Laboratory for Aviation in Berlin.

2002 Former US president Jimmy Carter became the first US leader to visit Cuba since Fidel Castro rose to power during a violent revolution in 1959.

2017 A malicious software called WannaCry infected more than 400,000 computers across the world. It locked users' computer files, then demanded a ransom to release them.

1743 Queen of Bohemia

Maria Theresa, the daughter of Emperor Charles VI, was crowned on this day, becoming the first female monarch of Bohemia (in modern-day Czechia). Her reign lasted for 40 years.

1926 Polar record

Norwegian explorer Roald Amundsen, US pilot Lincoln Ellsworth, and Italian engineer Umberto Nobile, along with 13 other crew members, made the first-ever flight over the North Pole, in an enormous airship called *Norge*.

Born this day

1820 Florence Nightingale, British nurse. She treated wounded soldiers in the Crimean War and pioneered nursing as a respectable career for women.

1968 Tony Hawk, US skateboarder. Nicknamed Birdman, he popularized skateboarding with his gravity-defying moves.

1881 Tram travel

Lichterfelde in Berlin, Germany, welcomed the world's first electric tram. In the first three months after it opened, the tram carried a total of about 12,000 passengers along its 2.5 km (1.5 mile) long route.

Also on this day

1861 Farmer John Tebbutt spotted Comet C/1861 J1 – one of the brightest comets seen in the 19th century – as it passed over Windsor, Australia.

1943 The Axis forces finally surrendered to the Allies in Tunisia, following intense battles in the deserts of northern Africa in World War II.

1968 Around 800,000 protesters marched in Paris, France, demanding the resignation of President Charles de Gaulle for incidents of police brutality.

1958

Ten-year journey

Australian adventurer Ben Carlin became the first person to circle the globe in an amphibious vehicle (one that can move on land and on water), called *Half-Safe*, when he returned to Canada after 10 years of travel.

1909

Giro d'Italia

In Italy, a little before 3 am, 127 cyclists set off from Milan on the world's first multi-stage bicycle race. Over the next two weeks, they cycled nearly 2,500 km (1,553 miles) across the country before returning to Milan on 30 May.

1995

Everest pioneer

When British climber Alison Hargreaves reached the summit of Mount Everest without a companion or any bottled oxygen, she became the first woman in the world to accomplish such a feat.

Born this day

1986 Robert Pattinson, British actor. Rising to fame for his role as a vampire in the popular *Twilight* movies, he is now a leading actor in Hollywood.

1796

First vaccine

British doctor Edward Jenner injected eight-year-old James Phipps with pus taken from the blisters of a milkmaid infected with cowpox. The vaccine gave the child immunity (resistance) against a similar but much more deadly disease called smallpox.

Born this day

1984 Mark Zuckerberg, US tech innovator and entrepreneur. He co-founded the social media site Facebook while still a student at Harvard University, USA.

Fantastic flip

2016

Brazilian surfer Gabriel Medina stunned spectators and surfing fans around the world by landing the first-ever backflip in a competition, earning a perfect score of 10 from the judges.

Also on this day

1918 The practice of observing a two-minute silence originated on this day, when people in Cape Town, South Africa, stood still to remember those killed in World War I.

1948 A new and independent Jewish state called Israel was established, after the United Nations (UN) divided Palestine between Jews and Arabs.

1955 The Soviet Union and countries in Eastern Europe signed the Warsaw Pact, a military alliance against external attacks.

Bear in danger

2008

Following a legal campaign by environmentalists, the polar bear was finally listed as "threatened" in the USA, signalling that action was needed to protect the Arctic species. Polar bears are at risk because climate change is melting their sea-ice habitat.

May

15

Also on this day

1897 In Berlin, German physicist Magnus Hirschfeld founded the Scientific-Humanitarian Committee – the first organization in history to fight for LGBTQ+ rights.

1926 Mickey Mouse appeared on screen for the first time – in Walt Disney's silent short film *Plane Crazy*.

1972 The Ryukyu Islands were finally returned to Japan and renamed Okinawa, after 26 years of US military control.

221 CE

Three Kingdoms

After the fall of the Han Dynasty in China, General Liu Bei set up the state of Shu-Han. This was one of three states that were collectively known as the Three Kingdoms.

2007

Scratch is released

The computer programming language Scratch, developed in the USA, was made freely available to the public, allowing users to easily create their own games and animations.

1869

Votes for women

In New York City, USA, Elizabeth Cady Stanton and Susan B Anthony founded the National Woman Suffrage Association, an organization that campaigned for women to be given the right to vote.

Born this day

1857 Williamina Fleming, Scottish astronomer. She worked at the Harvard College Observatory in Boston, USA, where she discovered the Horsehead Nebula in 1888.

1987 Andy Murray, Scottish tennis player. He was the world's number one male tennis player in 2016, and has won three Grand Slam singles titles.

May

16

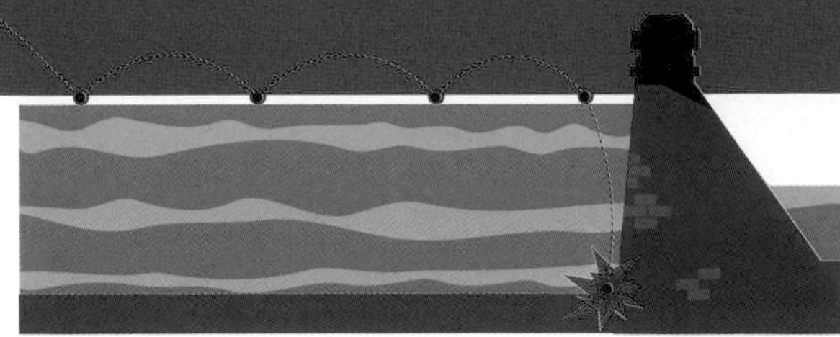

1888

Electric talk

In a lecture to engineers in New York City, USA, Serbian-American inventor Nikola Tesla demonstrated his new alternating-current power system, which is still in use today.

Dambuster raid

1943

During World War II, British planes unleashed a new weapon – "bouncing bombs" that skimmed across water. The bombs destroyed a series of dams in Germany's Ruhr region, flooding the area and killing 1,300 people.

Born this day

1966 Janet Jackson, Black American singer and actor. This successful pop and R&B star has sold more than 100 million records.

Also on this day

1832 Chilean miner Juan Godoy discovered large amounts of silver in the ground near Copiapó, Chile, sparking the Chilean Silver Rush.

1929 The Academy of Motion Picture Arts and Sciences gave out its first annual awards – nicknamed the Oscars – in California, USA.

1985 British scientists working in Antarctica announced that they had found an 18.9 million sq km (7.3 million sq mile) hole in the ozone layer over the South Pole.

Kick volleyball

1945

Teams from Penang, Malaysia, played in the first official competition of Sepak Takraw – a fast-paced game of foot volleyball popular in Southeast Asia, in which players use their feet, knees, or heads to get a ball over a high net and score.

May 17

1859 Aussie rules

The rules for Australia's version of football were established by members of the Melbourne Cricket Club. It's thought the sport was invented to keep cricketers fit during their off-season.

Born this day

1971 Queen Máxima, Queen Consort of the Netherlands. She works to help immigrants, especially women, settle into Dutch society.

1900 Wonderful Wizard of Oz

US author Lyman Frank Baum gave the first printed copy of his novel to his sister Mary. The story, about a young girl's adventures in the magical land of Oz with her friends the lion, the tin man, and the scarecrow, was later made into a much-loved film.

1970 Papyrus boat voyage

Norwegian scientist Thor Heyerdahl set sail from Morocco in an attempt to cross the Atlantic Ocean. Heyerdahl and his crew travelled in a papyrus boat, crafted by the Aymara people of Bolivia. They arrived in Barbados 57 days later.

Also on this day

1861 Scottish scientist James Clerk Maxwell showed the first colour photograph – a picture of a tartan ribbon – at King's College London, UK.

1902 The Antikythera Mechanism – the world's first-known mechanical computer – was identified among the artefacts recovered from an ancient Greek shipwreck.

1954 The US Supreme Court ruled that having separate schools for white and Black students was illegal.

May

18

1804

Emperor Napoleon

After conquering much of Europe, French military leader Napoleon Bonaparte became the self-appointed emperor of France. He introduced government reforms, but constant battles overseas led to his downfall.

Also on this day

1291 The city of Acre, the last stronghold of Christian Crusaders in the Holy Land, was captured by Muslim forces.

1893 Meri Te Tai Mangakāhia became the first woman to speak to the all-male Māori Parliament in New Zealand.

1991 The first British astronaut – 27-year-old Helen Sharman – travelled to the *Mir* space station on a Soyuz spacecraft.

Lawnmower deal

1830

Trimming lawns became easier after inventor Edwin Budding and manufacturer John Ferrabee struck a deal to start making the world's first lawnmowers in Gloucestershire, UK.

Born this day

1955 Chow Yun-fat, Chinese actor and screenwriter. He starred in the Oscar-winning movie *Crouching Tiger, Hidden Dragon.*

1970 Tina Fey, US actor, comedian, and writer. She found fame as a presenter and performer on US TV show *Saturday Night Live.*

1927

Hollywood cinema

Thousands lined Hollywood Boulevard in Los Angeles, USA, for the opening of Grauman's Chinese Theatre. The famous cinema has hosted many movie premieres, including *Star Wars* in 1977.

Royal wedding

2018

Hundreds of millions of people watched on TV as the UK's Prince Harry wed US actor Meghan Markle at St George's Chapel in Windsor, UK.

Born this day

1948 Grace Jones, Jamaican-American singer, songwriter, model, and actor. She is known for her unique style and creative flair.

2003 JoJo Siwa, US entertainer and YouTube star. In 2020, *Time* magazine included her in its list of the world's 100 most influential people.

Dark Day

1780

A mysterious darkness spread across New England, USA, and parts of Canada, causing people to light candles at midday. The cause was never found.

Also on this day

1845 Explorer Sir John Franklin set sail from Britain with a crew of 128 to find the Northwest Passage in the Arctic. They later perished at sea.

1910 Earth passed through the tail of Halley's Comet during a spectacular close approach and the comet was photographed for the first time.

2020 Global greenhouse gas emissions fell by 17 per cent due to lockdowns to fight the spread of COVID-19.

1906

Through the Alps

The 20 km (12 mile) Simplon Tunnel through the Alps mountains opened, linking Italy and Switzerland. It was the world's longest railway tunnel until 1982.

May 20

1498 Passage to India

Portuguese explorer Vasco da Gama arrived at Calicut in India, ensuring his place in history by becoming the first European to reach India by sea. The breakthrough route enabled Portuguese colonists to begin trading with Asia.

Monkey business 2005

Scientists announced their discovery of a new species of monkey. The kipunji lives in the highland forests of Tanzania, Africa, and has a population of just over 1,000.

Born this day

1908 James Stewart, US actor. He starred in the Christmas classic *It's A Wonderful Life*.

1946 Cher, US singer and songwriter. Known for her eclectic style, she has enjoyed a career in music and film spanning six decades.

1999 Grand Canyon jump

Daredevil US motorcyclist Robbie Knievel jumped 69 m (228 ft) across the Grand Canyon in Arizona, USA, to a backdrop of fireworks as viewers watched on live TV. He lost control of his vehicle on landing and broke his leg.

Also on this day

1570 The first modern atlas, called *Theatrum Orbis Terrarum* (Theatre of the World), was released by Flemish cartographer Abraham Ortelius.

1927 US aviator Charles Lindbergh flew from New York City, USA, to Paris, France, in the first solo transatlantic flight.

1990 NASA's Hubble Space Telescope took its first photograph – a spectacular starry image of the Pincushion Cluster in the Carina constellation.

May 21

1871 Up the mountain

Europe's first mountain railway opened in Switzerland. The Vitznau–Rigi Railway climbs Mount Rigi from Vitznau on the shore of Lake Lucerne. It was the brainchild of Swiss engineer Niklaus Riggenbach, who wanted passengers to enjoy the breathtaking alpine views.

Also on this day

1792 The eruption of Mount Unzen in Japan triggered an earthquake, a landslide, and a 100 m (330 ft) tall tsunami.

1904 The Fédération Internationale de Football Association (FIFA), the highest governing body for the sport of football, was founded in Paris, France, by seven European nations.

2010 The first spacecraft powered by solar radiation, IKAROS was launched by Japanese space agency JAXA.

Console unwrapped 2013

US software corporation Microsoft unveiled its Xbox One console, which could be used to play games or watch TV shows and films. More than 48 million consoles were sold in the seven years following its launch.

Born this day

1994 Tom Daley, British diver. He has won 10 gold medals at Commonwealth, European, and World championships.

1932 Earhart's flight

The first woman and second person to fly solo across the Atlantic Ocean, US aviator Amelia Earhart took off from Newfoundland, Canada, and landed 15 hours later in Londonderry, Northern Ireland.

1980

Hunger game

The first Pac-Man machine was installed at an amusement arcade in Tokyo, Japan. Created by video-game designer Toru Iwatani, this classic game about a hungry character in a maze became the most successful arcade game ever.

Born this day

1987 Novak Djokovic, Serbian tennis player. He is one of the world's most successful players, with 18 Grand Slams to his name.

1762

Fountain of love

The Trevi Fountain was opened in Rome, Italy. Carved from marble, this spectacular fountain is visited by around 1,000 tourists every hour who toss coins in the water to bring good luck in love.

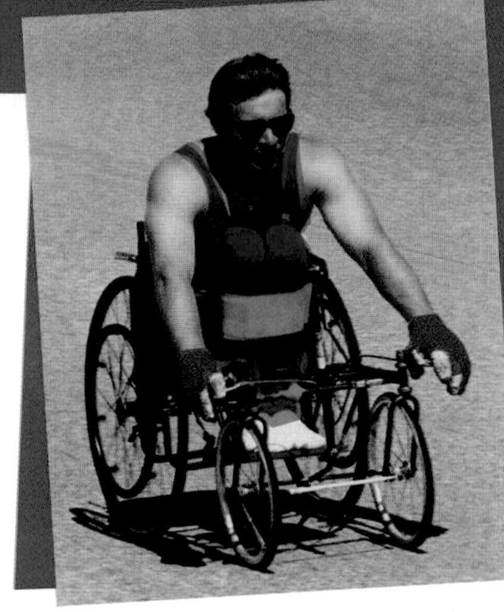

1987

Man in Motion

After two years travelling by wheelchair on the Man in Motion World Tour, Canadian athlete Rick Hansen returned to Vancouver, Canada. He had wheeled more than 40,000 km (24,800 miles) to highlight the potential of disabled people.

Also on this day

1900 Swiss sailor Hélène de Pourtalès became the first woman to compete, and to win gold, at the Olympics.

1918 Spanish newspaper *ABC* reported the outbreak of a deadly flu epidemic, known as the Spanish Flu. Many historians now think the outbreak began in France.

1960 The biggest earthquake in recorded history, at 9.5 on the Richter scale, devastated Valdivia in Chile.

May

23

1934

Partners in crime

US outlaws Bonnie Parker and Clyde Champion Barrow were ambushed, shot, and killed by police officers in Louisiana, USA. Their crime spree of murder and robbery had finally caught up with them after two years on the run.

Born this day

1848 Otto Lilienthal, German aviator. He was known as the "Flying Man", and his multiple successful flights were covered in newspapers published at the time.

1908 Hélène Boucher, French pilot. She set impressive world records for flight altitudes and speeds.

1618

Lucky escape

Angered by their Catholic king's decision to stop the building of a Protestant church, a mob in Bohemia, in present-day Czech Republic, threw the king's representatives out of the windows of Prague Castle. Luckily, the men survived.

Astronomer's island

1576

Danish astronomer Tycho Brahe was gifted Hven Island by King Frederick II, where he set up the Uraniborg Observatory. While working there, Brahe made important discoveries, such as the exact length of a year.

Also on this day

1915 During World War I, Italy declared war on Austria-Hungary and sided with the Allies.

1962 US surgeon Ronald Malt reattached a young boy's severed arm – it was the first time this type of operation had been successful.

2015 Ireland became the first country to legalize same-sex marriage as a result of a public vote.

May

24

2018 Cat-free zone

The world's longest cat-proof fence was completed at Newhaven Wildlife Sanctuary, Australia. Measuring 44 km (27 miles) long, it protects native birds and marsupials, such as the rufous hare-wallaby, from wild cats.

Born this day

1686 Daniel Gabriel Fahrenheit, Polish-born physicist. He invented the first widely used thermometer and devised the Fahrenheit temperature scale used in the USA today.

Also on this day

1798 Inspired by similar uprisings in France and the USA, an Irish rebellion was a major landmark in the country's long struggle for independence from British rule.

1822 The Battle of Pichincha took place on the slopes of the Pichincha volcano in present-day Ecuador, bringing victory for South American rebels and ending Spanish rule.

1956 The first Eurovision Song Contest was staged in Lugano, Switzerland, with seven countries taking part.

1844 Morse code

US inventor Samuel Morse and machinist Alfred Vail sent the first message by telegraph, from Washington, DC, to Baltimore, USA. The message "What hath God wrought?" was coded with dots and dashes.

1883 Mega bridge

The opening of the Brooklyn Bridge in New York City, USA, was celebrated with fireworks and a musical performance. The world's longest suspension bridge at the time, it connected the boroughs of Manhattan and Brooklyn.

May

25

Also on this day

1521 Holy Roman Emperor Charles V declared Protestant priest Martin Luther a heretic (unbeliever), worsening divisions in the Christian Church.

1810 Argentina became the first South American nation to declare independence from Spain.

1861 During the US Civil War, Canadian-born soldier Sarah Edmonds joined the Northern Army, disguised as a man named Franklin Thompson.

Born this day

1939 Ian McKellen, British actor. During his 60-year career, he has been cast in a variety of roles, both on stage and on screen.

1970 Octavia Spencer, Black American actor. She is the first Black female actor to be nominated for an Oscar two years in a row, winning one for her role in *The Help*.

2001

Peak of success

US adventurer Erik Weihenmayer became the first blind person to climb to the summit of Mount Everest. He was featured on the cover of *Time* magazine in celebration of his achievements.

Black Lives Matter

2020

In the USA, a Black man named George Floyd was killed by a police officer, triggering protests around the world and bringing global attention to the #BlackLivesMatter (BLM) movement, which stands against police brutality towards Black people.

1940

Miracle of Dunkirk

The evacuation of 338,226 Allied troops began on the beach of Dunkirk in France during World War II. More than 800 boats came to rescue the soldiers, who had become trapped between invading German forces and the North Sea.

1923 Le Mans race

The first 24 Hours of Le Mans – one of the world's most famous car races – began near Le Mans, France. In this annual competition, drivers compete to cover the furthest distance in 24 hours.

1897

Gothic thriller

Dracula, a horror novel about the bloodsucking vampire Count Dracula by Bram Stoker, was published. London bookshops were the first to stock this terrifying Gothic classic, which was later translated into many languages and adapted for film and TV.

Born this day

1966 Helena Bonham Carter, British actor. She is best known for playing quirky characters in period dramas and Bellatrix Lestrange in the *Harry Potter* series of films.

Also on this day

1954 A wooden funeral ship, built to take the soul of Egyptian pharaoh Khufu to heaven, was discovered buried next to the Great Pyramid at Giza, Egypt.

1998 Australia's first National Sorry Day was held. The annual event commemorates the mistreatment of First Australians by European settlers.

2019 Alan "Nasty" Nash won the World Toe Wrestling title for a record-breaking 16th time.

May

27

1931

High-flier

Swiss physicist Auguste Piccard and assistant Paul Kipfer set a record for the highest flight and became the first humans to enter Earth's stratosphere. Travelling in an aluminium capsule attached to a hydrogen balloon, they reached a dizzying 15,781 m (51,775 ft) over Augsberg, Germany.

Born this day

1837 Wild Bill Hickok, legendary gunfighter and folk hero in America's Wild West. He built his reputation by telling false or exaggerated tales about his exploits.

Battle of Tsushima

1905

In this epic naval battle, fought in the waters off Japan during the Russo–Japanese War, Japanese forces almost wiped out the Russian fleet.

1937

Golden Gate Bridge

After four years of construction, the Golden Gate Bridge – the world's longest suspension bridge at the time – opened in San Francisco, USA, with a special pedestrian day. About 200,000 people joined the celebrations on the bridge before vehicles began crossing the next day.

Also on this day

1941 An attack by British battleships sank the gigantic German vessel *Bismarck* in the Atlantic Ocean off France.

1963 Jomo Kenyatta was announced as the first prime minister of Kenya. Thousands took to the streets of Kenya's capital Nairobi to celebrate.

1997 The first entirely female polar expedition arrived at the North Pole, having travelled from Ward Hunt Island in Canada by skis and sledges.

585 BCE

Predicting an eclipse

Greek philosopher Thales correctly foretold a solar eclipse in Asia Minor, as recorded in *The Histories* by Herodotus. The darkening skies brought a sudden end to the Battle of Halys.

Born this day

1968 Kylie Minogue, Australian actor and singer. Known as the Princess of Pop, she has sold more than 70 million records worldwide.

2018

Cheese champion

After winning his 21st race, British soldier Chris Anderson was hailed as the greatest Double Gloucester Cheese Rolling champion ever. At this annual event in Brockworth, UK, participants run down a hill to catch a rolling round of cheese.

1907

Racing motorcycles

The Isle of Man TT race started with 25 competitors riding their motorcycles for 254 km (158 miles). The prize for the winner was a silver statue and £25. This annual race is a deadly test of speed and skill on mountainous roads with 264 corners.

Also on this day

1830 US president Andrew Jackson signed the Indian Removal Act, which took away the land rights of Indigenous American peoples.

1932 The Afsluitdijk Dam was completed in the Netherlands, with an incredible 32 km (20 miles) of flood defences against the North Sea.

1936 British mathematician Alan Turing submitted his article *On Computable Numbers*, which described a universal computing machine.

Truth talk 1851

Former enslaved person and women's rights activist Sojourner Truth addressed the Women's Conference in Ohio, USA. Her powerful speech, known as "Ain't I a woman?", was published in US newspapers, helping to spread the message of gender and racial equality.

1453 Fall of Constantinople

Ottoman ruler Sultan Mehmed II seized the city of Constantinople (modern-day Istanbul), following a siege lasting 53 days. This marked the end of the once-powerful Byzantine Empire.

Born this day

1975 Mel B, British pop singer. She found fame as Scary Spice in the girl group Spice Girls. She is also an actor and a talent show judge.

On top of the world 1953

New Zealand explorer Edmund Hillary and Sherpa mountaineer Tenzing Norgay became the first people to set foot on the summit of Mount Everest – the highest peak on Earth.

Also on this day

1766 The discovery of a gas, now known as hydrogen, was revealed by British chemist Henry Cavendish at the Royal Society in London, UK.

1935 The German Messerschmitt Bf 109 fighter plane flew for the first time, serving later in World War II.

2019 The YouTube channel T-series, which plays Bollywood film trailers and music videos, became the first to have 100 million subscribers.

May

30

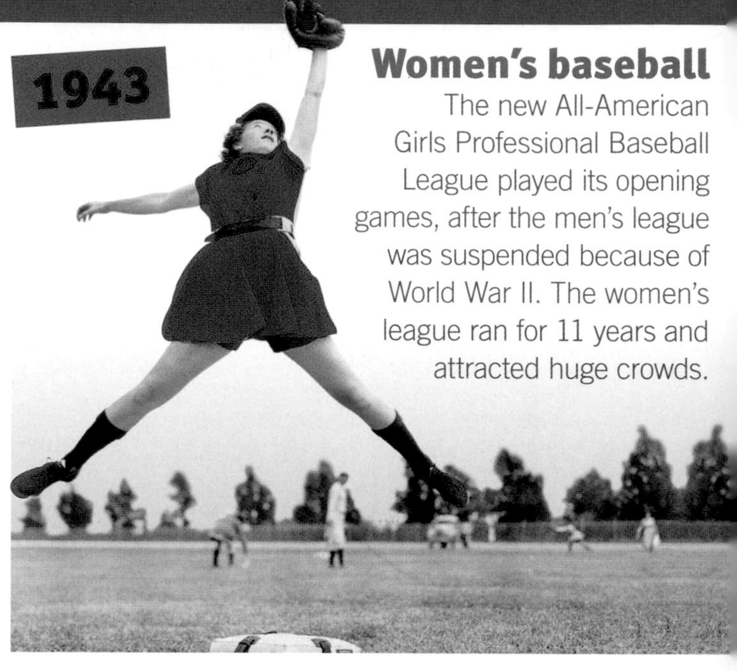

1943 Women's baseball

The new All-American Girls Professional Baseball League played its opening games, after the men's league was suspended because of World War II. The women's league ran for 11 years and attracted huge crowds.

1848 Keep it cool!

US entrepreneur William Young filed a patent for his ice cream freezer, after adapting inventor Nancy Johnson's original design. People could now make their own ice cream at home.

Born this day

1975 Marissa Ann Mayer, US entrepreneur and software engineer. She helped to develop the Google search engine before becoming president of Yahoo!.

Also on this day

1431 Accused of witchcraft and heresy, Joan of Arc was burned at the stake in Rouen, France.

1868 To mark the first Decoration Day (now called Memorial Day) in the USA, flowers were placed on the 20,000 graves of those who died in the US Civil War.

1975 The European Space Agency (ESA) was established, with 10 countries signing up to show their commitment to space exploration.

1899 Bandit Queen

Canadian-born outlaw Pearl Hart robbed a stagecoach at gunpoint in Arizona, USA – one of the last robberies of its kind. The so-called Bandit Queen became famous as one of the few female criminals in the Wild West.

2016

Viral video

Catchy K-Pop hit *Gangnam Style* by South Korean rapper Psy became the first video to get 2 billion views on YouTube and was the site's most-watched video for nearly five years. Psy's routine sparked a global dance craze.

1740

Frederick the Great

Frederick II took over the throne of Prussia, a European kingdom that included northern Germany and Poland. He won many battles and turned Prussia into a powerful nation.

Also on this day

1879 The first electric railway, built by German engineer Werner von Siemens, was shown at the Berlin Trade Exhibition in Germany.

1910 Four provinces joined to form the Union of South Africa under a single government.

1970 The Huascarán debris avalanche, set off by the Ancash earthquake, devastated Yungay, Peru. It was the worst avalanche in history.

Born this day

1921 Chien-Shiung Wu, Chinese American scientist. She researched nuclear weapons for the Manhattan Project.

1930 Clint Eastwood, US actor and director. The star of the *Dirty Harry* film series, he has had a 60-year-long career.

1895

Breakfast cereal

A patent for "flaked cereal" was filed by US doctor John Harvey Kellogg. While researching healthy foods for his patients, he had flaked a dough mixture, which he then served with milk – cornflakes.

1279 BCE

Powerful pharaoh

Ramesses II became pharaoh of the New Kingdom of ancient Egypt, beginning a 66-year-long reign in which he expanded the empire and built impressive monuments.

June 1

1809 Winning walk

Scottish walker Captain Robert Barclay Allardice set out to walk 1,000 miles in 1,000 hours to win a bet of 1,000 guineas. He completed this task on 12 July, and his feat helped to popularize competitive walking in the 19th century.

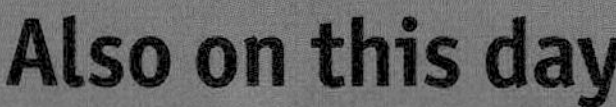

Also on this day

1773 Dairy farmer Wolraad Woltemade rescued 14 sailors by riding his horse into the sea near the Cape of Good Hope, South Africa.

1831 The north magnetic pole was discovered by British explorer James Clark Ross and his team.

1868 The Treaty of Bosque Redondo was signed by Navajo leaders and the US government, ending their long-running conflict.

1930 Fast train

The *Deccan Queen*, a daily passenger train, made its first journey from Bombay (now Mumbai) to Pune, India. It was the country's first superfast train.

Born this day

1985 Tirunesh Dibaba, Ethiopian long-distance track athlete. She won two Olympic gold medals in the 5,000 m and 10,000 m events in 2008, and another in 2012.

1996 Tom Holland, British actor. Starting his career with the musical *Billy Elliot*, he rose to fame with his role as Spider-Man in the Marvel Cinematic Universe films.

Limiting light 2002

The first and only country to outlaw light pollution, Czechia introduced shields for all outdoor lights so that they only illuminated the areas they needed to.

June 2

1692 Witch trials

In Salem, USA, people (mostly women) accused of practising witchcraft began to be convicted. They were sentenced to death by hanging, not burned at the stake as popularly believed.

Also on this day

1924 US president Calvin Coolidge signed the Indian Citizenship Act, granting citizenship to all US-born Indigenous people.

1946 In a public vote in Italy, a majority of the citizens voted in favour of changing the country from a monarchy to a republic.

2003 The European Space Agency (ESA) launched its *Mars Express* probe from the Baïkonur Cosmodrome in Kazakhstan.

Born this day

1977 Zachary Quinto, US actor and producer. He starred as the villain Sylar in the TV series *Heroes* and as Spock in some of the *Star Trek* films.

1953 Coronation on TV

Watched on TV by millions of people worldwide, Elizabeth II was crowned Queen of the United Kingdom, Canada, Australia, New Zealand, and other Commonwealth territories in a ceremony at Westminster Abbey in London, UK.

Combahee River Raid 1863

US anti-slavery activist Harriet Tubman led a group of 150 Black soldiers along South Carolina's Combahee River during the US Civil War, freeing more than 700 enslaved people. She was the first woman to direct a major US military operation.

June

3

Also on this day

1969 ***The Very Hungry Caterpillar***, a bestselling children's book by US writer Eric Carle, was published.

1992 **The Earth Summit**, a UN conference on environmental issues, began in Rio de Janeiro, Brazil.

1992 **The High Court of Australia** ruled that First Australian communities had the legal right to own their ancestral lands.

2017

Climbing El Capitan

US climber Alex Honnold became the first person to scale the massive El Capitan rock formation in Yosemite National Park, California, USA, without any ropes or safety equipment.

2010

Preparing for Mars

A group of six volunteers went into isolation to experience the conditions of a mission to Mars. As part of an experiment called MARS-500, they were locked away in a chamber in Russia for 520 days – the duration of a real Mars mission – with little contact with the outside world. Scientists studied the effects on their health to help prepare for a future crewed flight to the Red Planet.

Born this day

1986 **Rafael Nadal**, Spanish tennis player. He has won 20 Grand Slam singles tournaments, including a record 13 French Open titles. Between 2005 and 2007, he won 81 consecutive matches on clay courts – a record – and is widely agreed to be the greatest clay court player of all time.

June 4

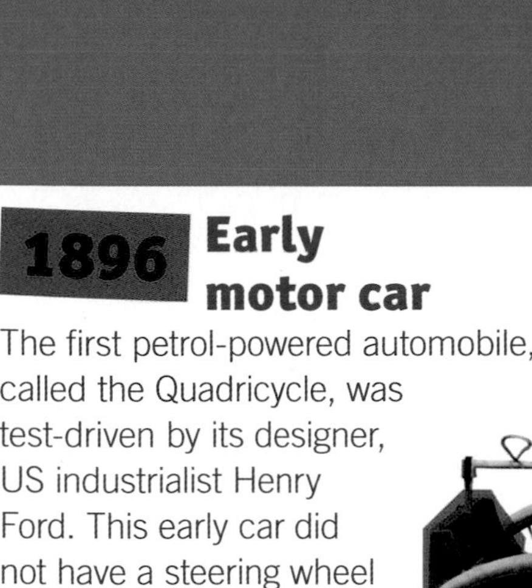

1896 Early motor car

The first petrol-powered automobile, called the Quadricycle, was test-driven by its designer, US industrialist Henry Ford. This early car did not have a steering wheel or brakes, and was built using everyday items such as bicycle wheels and a doorbell button for the horn.

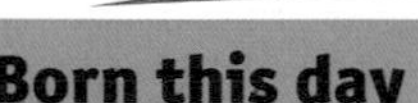

Born this day

1975 Angelina Jolie, US actor, filmmaker, and activist. She has starred in movies such as *Girl, Interrupted* and *Maleficent*, and campaigns in support of children's education and the rights of women.

Trolleys R Us 1937

Humpty Dumpty, a supermarket chain in Oklahoma, USA, introduced the world's first shopping trolleys. The cart was invented by the chain's owner, Sylvan Goldman.

Also on this day

1783 The hot-air balloon, invented by the Montgolfier brothers, first took to the sky above Annonay, France.

1887 French microbiologist Louis Pasteur founded the Pasteur Institute in Paris, France. This centre of research into infectious diseases went on to make many medical breakthroughs.

1920 The Treaty of Trianon was signed by the Allied powers and the Kingdom of Hungary after the end of World War I. Hungary lost two-thirds of its territory.

A cheesy decision

1411

King Charles VI of France decreed that only the people of Roquefort-sur-Soulzon could produce Roquefort, a pungent cheese that gets its flavour from a fungus, *Penicillium roqueforti*, found in local caves.

June

5

1851

Changing times

US author Harriet Beecher Stowe's novel *Uncle Tom's Cabin* was published in the newspaper *Washington National Era*. The story, about the sufferings of enslaved people in the USA, laid the groundwork for the movement to end slavery.

Born this day

1971 Mark Wahlberg, US actor and film producer. He found fame in the hip-hop group Marky Mark and the Funky Bunch, and has appeared in many acclaimed Hollywood films, including *The Departed*.

1988

Circling the globe

Kay Cottee returned to Sydney Harbour on her yacht *Blackmores First Lady* after completing a non-stop, 189-day journey around the world on her own. The Australian sailor was the first woman to achieve this feat.

Also on this day

1848 The lowest temperature possible, known as absolute zero, was defined by British-Irish scientist William Thomson as equivalent to –273.15°C (–459.67°F).

1883 The long-distance European passenger train *Express d'Orient*, later called the *Orient Express*, began its first journey from Paris, France, to Vienna, Austria.

1972 The UN Conference on the Environment, held in Stockholm, Sweden, was the first international meeting to focus on protecting the environment at a global level.

1956

Elvis the Pelvis

After his first hit single, *Heartbreak Hotel*, US singer Elvis Presley confirmed his status as the King of Rock 'n' Roll on *The Milton Berle Show*.

June 6

Drive-in cinema

1933

US entrepreneur Richard Hollingshead, Jr opened the world's first drive-in cinema in New Jersey, USA. He used a 1928 Kodak projector and a white screen hung between two trees so that people could enjoy watching films in their cars.

Also on this day

1896 Norwegians George Harbo and Frank Samuelson became the first people to row across the Atlantic Ocean, covering 5,262 km (3,270 miles) in 55 days.

1912 A volcanic eruption in the Katmai National Park and Preserve in Alaska, USA, led to the formation of the Novarupta volcano. It was the largest eruption of the 20th century.

2017

Island iguanas

A new species of iguana called *Brachylophus gau*, found only on Gau island in the Fijian archipelago, was discovered by researchers.

1523

Rebel leader becomes king

Swedish nobleman Gustav Vasa, who had led rebel forces in the Swedish War of Liberation, was elected king of Sweden. Swedes celebrate this day as their National Day.

Born this day

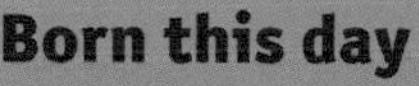

1875 Thomas Mann, German writer. Known for novels such as *Doctor Faustus*, he received the Nobel Prize in Literature in 1929.

1956 Björn Borg, Swedish tennis player. He was the first male player to win five consecutive Wimbledon titles.

Allies to the rescue

1944

In an operation code-named "Operation Overlord", 150,000 Allied soldiers stormed the beaches of Normandy, France, to liberate the country from German occupation during World War II. This day is known as D-Day.

June

7

1654

Teen power

Louis XIV, also known as the Sun King, was crowned king of France at the age of 15. During his 72-year reign, France grew to become the most powerful nation in Europe.

Also on this day

1099 The city of Jerusalem was captured by Christian crusaders during the First Crusade, the first of a series of religious wars waged in the Holy Land.

1494 Spain and Portugal signed the Treaty of Tordesillas, agreeing to divide their claims to territories in South America.

1893 Protesting against racial segregation, Indian lawyer Mohandas Karamchand Gandhi, later known as Mahatma Gandhi, refused to leave the first-class compartment of a train in South Africa.

Born this day

1981 Anna Kournikova, Russian tennis player. She was one of the best women's doubles players in the world.

1968

Wonder park

LEGOLAND® Billund Resort, the first LEGOLAND® theme park, opened in Denmark. The park features scale models of cities and famous landmarks, built with more than 20 million LEGO® bricks.

June 8

793

Victorious Vikings

Seafaring warriors and raiders from Scandinavia, known as Vikings, attacked the monastery on the island of Lindisfarne, off the coast of England. They killed the monks and looted valuables in what was the first of many raids throughout the British Isles.

Born this day

1823 Robert Morris, Black American lawyer. One of the first Black lawyers in the USA, he challenged racial segregation in schools by filing a lawsuit against the state of Boston.

1938

Bony remains

The remains of a skull and jawbone of an early human ancestor were found by schoolboy Gert Terblanche in a cave in South Africa. This species was named *Paranthropus robustus*.

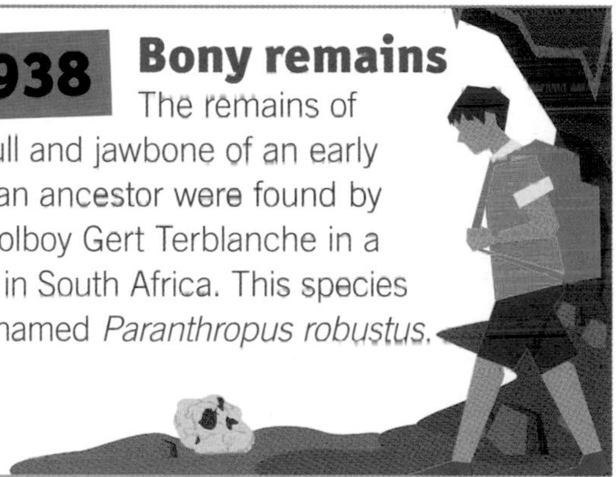

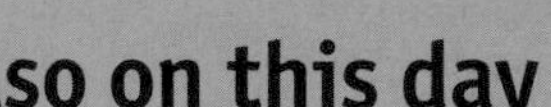

1869

Vacuum-cleaning

Ives W McGaffey of Chicago, USA, patented one of the world's first vacuum cleaners. His machine had to be cranked by hand to generate a suction force while the device was pushed across the floor.

Also on this day

1783 The Laki volcanic fissure in Iceland erupted, spewing dangerous gases into the atmosphere. This poisonous haze spread across Europe, causing crop failure and famine.

1896 A Peugeot Victoria Type 8 was stolen in France in the first known instance of car theft.

1992 World Ocean Day was first celebrated during the Rio de Janeiro Earth Summit to raise awareness about protecting Earth's oceans.

June 9

Balancing act 1815

The Congress of Vienna, a conference to discuss how to ensure lasting peace in Europe after the defeat of French emperor Napoleon Bonaparte, came to a close. Ambassadors agreed to reorganize some national borders in the hope of keeping power balanced between nations.

Also on this day

1898 China was forced to lease Hong Kong's New Territories rent-free to the UK for a period of 99 years.

1909 The first woman to drive across the USA from coast to coast, Alice Huyler Ramsey set off in her car from New York City.

1934 Disney's Donald Duck made his first appearance in the animated short film *The Wise Little Hen.*

1946 Beloved ruler

Bhumibol Adulyadej was crowned king of Thailand. Much loved by his people, Bhumibol reigned for more than 70 years, until his death in 2016, making him one of the longest-serving monarchs in history.

Born this day

1981 Natalie Portman, Israeli-born US actor and filmmaker. A star of many blockbuster movies, she won the Best Actress Oscar for her performance in *Black Swan*.

1534 A passage to Asia

On a voyage to the northern lands of North America in search of gold, spices, and a new route from Europe to Asia, French navigator Jacques Cartier reached the Saint Lawrence River. He became the first European explorer to map the region.

2015 A quiet place

Tests carried out in a specially built chamber at the headquarters of technology company Microsoft in Redmond, Washington, USA, revealed that it was the quietest place in the world. The chamber's walls absorb all echoes, preventing any sound.

Racing to Paris 1907

Starting from the French embassy in Beijing, China, five teams set off on a gruelling 16,000 km (10,000 mile) automobile race to Paris, France.

671 Clock Day

A type of water clock called a *rokoku* was introduced in Japan for the first time during the reign of Emperor Tenji. This device kept time by measuring the flow of water from one vessel to another. Japanese citizens still celebrate this date as Clock Day.

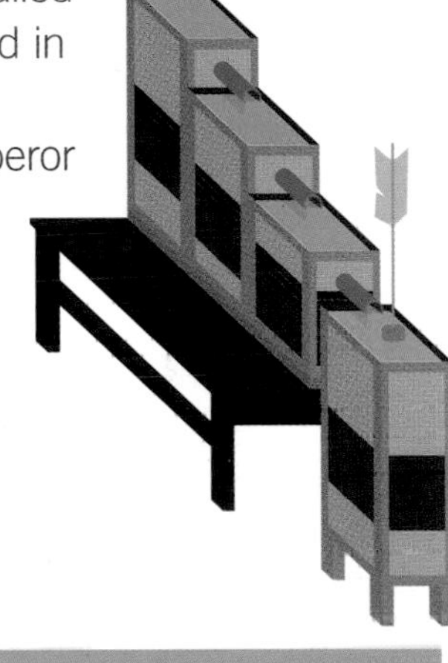

Born this day

1922 Judy Garland, US actor, singer, and dancer. She became an international star playing Dorothy in the 1939 film *The Wizard of Oz*.

Also on this day

1829 In Britain, the first annual Boat Race between Oxford and Cambridge universities, held on the River Thames in London, took place. Oxford won.

1940 Italian dictator Benito Mussolini declared war on Britain and France, bringing Italy into World War II.

2016 Scientists in Iceland announced that injecting carbon dioxide into volcanic rocks can turn it into stone. This locks up the gas underground, preventing it from reaching the atmosphere.

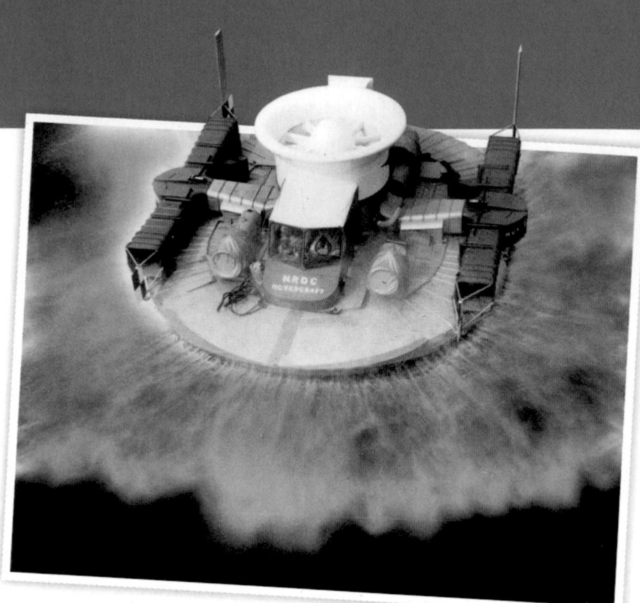

1959

Historic hover

The first public display of a hovercraft off the coast of the Isle of Wight, UK, achieved a top speed of 126 kph (78 mph).

Also on this day

980 Vladimir the Great was crowned ruler of Kievan Rus', a kingdom in eastern Europe.

1754 Scottish chemist Jacob Black discovered that heating calcium carbonate produced a gas that could extinguish a flame. This gas is now known as carbon dioxide.

1895 In France, competitors in the first-ever motorcar race set off on a 1,178 km (732 mile) route from Paris to Bordeaux, and back.

Born this day

1910 Jacques Cousteau, French ocean explorer, conservationist, and documentary maker. He popularized the sport of scuba diving, which uses equipment he helped develop.

1971

First senator

Neville Bonner became the first person from the First Australian communities to take on a role as a representative in the Australian Parliament.

1993

Jurassic success

The movie *Jurassic Park*, which brought dinosaurs to life, was released in US cinemas. It went on to become the world's highest-grossing film until the release of *Titanic* four years later.

June

12

Also on this day

1550 The city of Helsingfors (present-day Helsinki) was founded by King Gustav I of Sweden. It is now the capital of Finland.

1991 Russian politician Boris Yeltsin won the country's first democratic presidential election to become the first president of Russia.

2018 North Korean leader Kim Jong-un met President Donald Trump of the USA in Singapore to explore ways of improving relations between their two countries.

1817 Early bicycle

German inventor Karl von Drais demonstrated his *Laufmaschine* ("running machine") for the first time. This early bicycle had no pedals, so riders had to push along the ground with their feet.

Born this day

1979 Robyn, Swedish singer, DJ, and record producer. She found international fame with hit singles such as *Show Me Love*, and has had a big influence on electronic music.

1942 Dutch diary

For her 13th birthday Jewish teenager Anne Frank was given an autograph book, which she decided to use as a diary. Over the next two years, she documented her life in hiding during the Nazi occupation of the Netherlands in World War II. Her memoirs were published after her death as *Diary of a Young Girl*.

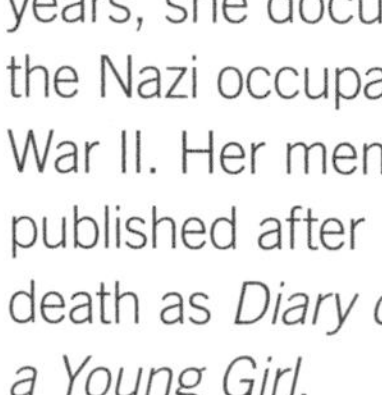

A great escape 1962

Guards at Alcatraz, a formidable prison on an island in San Francisco Bay, USA, discovered that three inmates had escaped overnight. The prisoners had left dummy heads made out of plaster to fool the prison guards.

June

13

1944

London bombed

The Luftwaffe (German Air Force) fired 11 long-range V-1 flying bombs – known as "doodlebugs" – at London during the Blitz. Of these, four hit the city.

2000

Landmark meeting

In the first-ever summit since Korea was divided, President Kim Dae-jung (left) of South Korea and Kim Jong-il (right), the North Korean leader, met in the North Korean capital, Pyongyang.

Born this day

1873 Alice Stebbins Wells, first US female police officer. She worked at the Los Angeles Police Department.

1879 Lois Weber, US silent film actor. She also wrote 114 films, directed 135 films, and ran her own film studio.

Also on this day

1611 German astronomer Johannes Fabricius was the first to write about sunspots – temporary dark spots on the surface of the Sun.

1983 The *Pioneer 10* space probe became the first human-made object to cross Neptune's orbit.

2013 The AeroVelo Atlas helicopter flew for 64.1 seconds to become the only winner of a 33-year-old contest for human-powered helicopters.

2010

Oracle Paul

An octopus called Paul selected the German flag, correctly predicting the winner of Germany's first match in the 2010 FIFA World Cup. Paul went on to predict the outcomes of all seven of Germany's matches, as well as the final game between Spain and the Netherlands.

June

14

Extinct mammal

2016

The Australian government announced the extinction of the small rodent species Bramble Cay melomys. This was the first mammal to die out as a result of climate change caused by human actions.

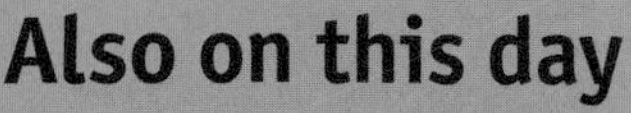

Also on this day

1800 Napoleon Bonaparte led the French army to victory over Austria in the Battle of Marengo, increasing his military reputation and influence.

1940 In World War II, German forces invaded Paris, the French capital city. The rest of the country surrendered shortly afterwards.

1982 Argentina surrendered to the UK in the Falklands War after two months of conflict over ownership of the Falkland Islands in the South Atlantic Ocean.

Born this day

1923 Judith Kerr, German-British children's author. She is known for *The Tiger Who Came to Tea* and the *Mog* series, as well as for her Holocaust education work.

1998

Basketball best

US basketball legend Michael Jordan won a record-breaking sixth championship after scoring in the last seconds for the Chicago Bulls, beating rivals Utah Jazz 87–86 in a nail-biting match in Salt Lake City, USA.

Death camp

1940

The first prisoners arrived at Auschwitz, a concentration camp built by the Nazis during World War II in occupied Polish territory. This group consisted of 728 Polish political activists.

June 15

2006

Marine sanctuary

The waters of the USA's Northwestern Hawaiian Islands became the Papahānaumokuākea Marine National Monument. The sanctuary was later expanded to cover 1,510,000 sq km (583,000 sq miles), making it one of the world's largest protected areas.

Born this day

1950 Michel Lotito, French entertainer. Known as Mr Eat-All, he chomped through objects including bicycles, TVs, and a whole aeroplane.

1878

Horse in motion

British photographer Eadweard Muybridge took a series of photographs of a galloping horse. They formed an image sequence, called *The Horse in Motion*, which marked a milestone in making moving pictures.

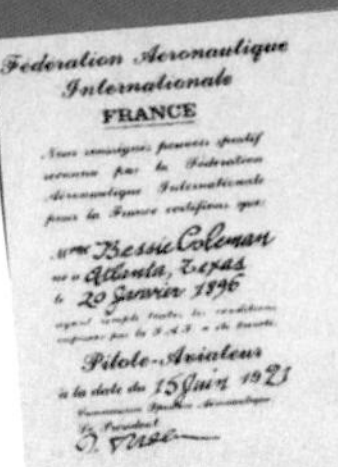

1921

Soaring high

After being refused flight training in the USA, aviator Bessie Coleman earned her flying licence in France, becoming the first Black woman to qualify as a pilot. She became a professional stunt pilot, performing aerial acrobatics.

Also on this day

1215 English nobles forced King John I of England to sign the Magna Carta, a document that stated that rulers were not above the law.

1960 A freak heat burst, known as "Satan's Storm", hit the town of Kopperl, Texas, USA, with temperatures suddenly rising to 60°C (140°F).

1991 Mount Pinatubo in the Philippines exploded, sending an ash cloud 40 km (28 miles) into the air, in the 20th century's second-largest volcanic eruption.

1950 Record final

A record-breaking crowd of at least 173,850 fans gathered at Rio de Janeiro's Maracanã Stadium in Brazil, to watch Uruguay beat hosts Brazil 2–1 in the FIFA World Cup Final. This remains the largest football crowd ever.

Born this day

1829 Geronimo, Apache leader. He defended his homeland by fighting against US troops and settlers.

1972 John Cho, Korean-born American actor. He starred as Hikaru Sulu in the later *Star Trek* films.

1963 Space trip

Cosmonaut (Russian astronaut) Valentina Tereshkova became the first woman to travel into space, aboard the spacecraft *Vostok 6*. She spent almost three days in orbit before reentering the atmosphere and safely parachuting to Earth.

Also on this day

1373 The Anglo-Portuguese Treaty was signed by the rulers of England and Portugal, and remains the world's oldest active treaty.

1911 Technology company IBM was founded as the Computing-Tabulating-Recording Company in Endicott, New York, USA.

2016 Shanghai Disneyland in China opened to the public. The theme park attracted more than 5 million visitors in its first six months.

1961 Defection drama

At a Paris airport, Russian ballet star Rudolf Nureyev escaped the clutches of the Soviet secret police, and asked the French authorities for asylum (refuge).

June 17

1885
Green goddess

A ship carrying the Statue of Liberty, transported as 350 individual pieces, sailed into New York Harbor, USA. This gift from France celebrated the friendship between the two nations and is an enduring symbol of democracy.

Born this day

1980 Venus Williams, Black American tennis player. One of the sport's greatest players, she has won four Olympic golds and seven Grand Slam singles titles.

1947
Global flight

The US airline Pan Am launched the world's first round-the-world flight service. The plane set off from LaGuardia airport in New York City, USA, and stopped in 17 cities before returning on 30 June.

Also on this day

1775 US troops killed many British soldiers in the Battle of Bunker Hill during the American Revolutionary War.

1843 The first violent clash over land ownership between British settlers and the Māori people broke out in the Wairau Valley, New Zealand.

1922 Portuguese pilots Gago Coutinho and Sacadura Cabral completed the first flight across the South Atlantic Ocean.

1631
Monument of love

Mumtaz Mahal, the beloved wife of Mughal emperor Shah Jahan, died in childbirth. In her memory, the heartbroken monarch ordered the construction of the Taj Mahal, a magnificent, ivory-white marble tomb in Agra, a city in present-day India.

June 18

Also on this day

1429 Under Joan of Arc's inspirational leadership, French forces defeated the English army in the Battle of Patay, during the Hundred Years' War.

1940 French army officer Charles de Gaulle gave a rousing speech urging the people of France to resist the Nazi occupation of their country.

1980 Shakuntala Devi, an Indian mathematician known as the "human computer", mentally multiplied two random 13-digit numbers in just 28 seconds.

618

Tang emperor

After the fall of the Sui Dynasty in China, official Li Yuan seized power and founded the Tang Dynasty, ruling as Emperor Gaozu. The dynasty he established lasted three centuries.

2000

Greatest golfer

US golfer Tiger Woods won the 100th US Open Championship at Pebble Beach, California, USA, by a record-breaking 15 strokes.

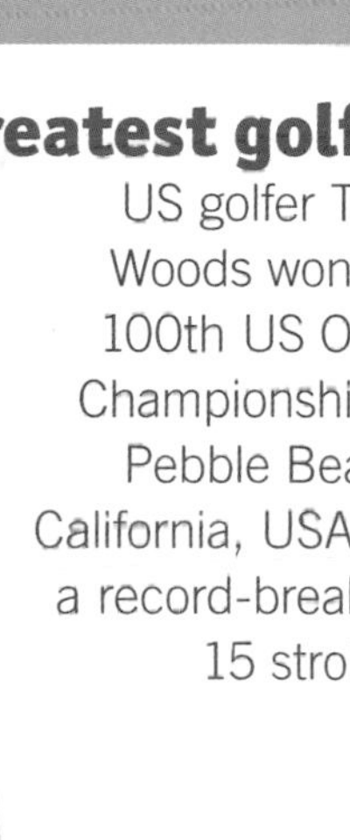

Born this day

1942 Paul McCartney, British singer and musician. One of the two principal songwriters in the legendary band The Beatles, he went on to have a successful solo career. He has won 18 Grammy Awards and more than 30 of his songs have topped the US Billboard Hot 100 chart.

1815

Battle of Waterloo

After a string of conquests in Europe, French emperor Napoleon Bonaparte was finally defeated in a battle near Waterloo, in present-day Belgium, by a combined force of British, Dutch, and German soldiers. Both sides made heavy use of cannon fire.

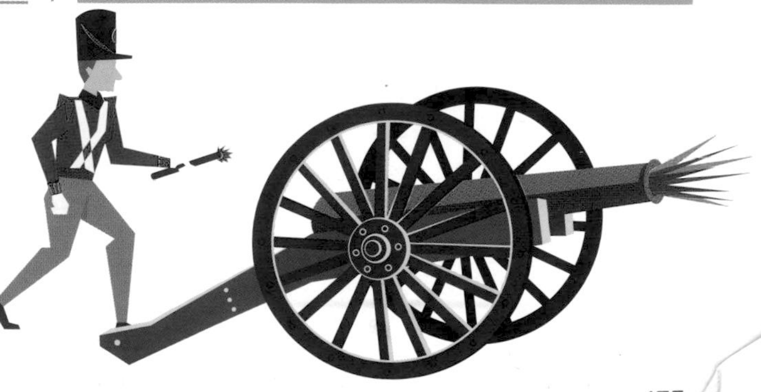

June 19

2017 Studying cats

Researchers studying the remains of ancient felines revealed that cats have changed little since they were first domesticated by humans about 10,000 years ago.

Born this day

1978 Dirk Werner Nowitzki, German basketball player. He is considered one of the greatest European players.

1978 Zoe Saldana, US actor. She has played memorable characters in blockbusters such as *Avatar* and several of the Marvel Cinematic Universe films.

1905 The first cinema

In their shop in Pittsburgh, USA, John P Harris and Harry Davis set up the first nickelodeon – a cinema where people could watch "moving pictures" for five cents (a nickel).

Also on this day

1865 At the end of the US Civil War, Texas was one of the last states to announce that all enslaved people were now free. The day is now celebrated nationwide as Juneteenth.

1910 In Germany, the airship *Deutschland*, the world's first commercial passenger aircraft, took to the skies on its first flight.

1913 The white minority government in South Africa passed the Natives Land Act, restricting the land rights of the majority Black population.

1846 Baseball first

In the first officially recorded game of modern baseball, a team called the New York Nine smashed the Knickerbockers 23–1 in Hoboken, New Jersey, USA.

June

20

1975 Shark scare

US director Steven Spielberg's terrifying movie *Jaws*, about a great white shark with a taste for human flesh, was released in US cinemas. The film kept many Americans away from beaches throughout the summer of 1975.

Born this day

1949 Lionel Richie, Black American singer. He started out as the lead vocalist of the funk and soul band Commodores before becoming a successful solo artist in the 1980s.

1967 Nicole Kidman, Australian actor. She has starred in films such as *Lion*, *Paddington*, and *The Golden Compass*.

2005 Ape artist

Three paintings by the chimpanzee Congo sold for £14,000 at an auction in London, UK. He had learned how to draw aged two after being offered a pencil.

1944 First rocket

A German A-4 rocket became the first human-made object to enter space when it was blasted 176 km (109 miles) above Earth's surface.

Also on this day

1790 During the French Revolution, King Louis XVI attempted to escape the angry citizens of Paris, France, but was arrested the following day.

1895 The Kiel Canal opened in northern Germany. It is now the busiest human-made waterway in the world.

1903 On a track at the Indiana State Fairgrounds, USA, racer Barney Oldfield became the first person to drive a mile in one minute.

June

21

1970

Trophy winners

A sparkling performance by the legendary Pelé helped Brazil to win the FIFA World Cup for the third time – a feat that earned them the right to keep the original World Cup trophy.

1976

Four colours

Using a supercomputer, US-based mathematicians Kenneth Appel and Wolfgang Haken solved an age-old maths problem. They proved that to colour a map so that no two neighbouring countries shared the same colour, only four colours were needed.

Born this day

1982 Prince William, member of the British Royal Family. The son of Prince Charles and Princess Diana, he is the second-in-line to the British throne.

1985 Lana Del Rey, US singer. She shot to fame with her first single, *Video Games*, in 2011.

Also on this day

2004 ***SpaceShipOne*** became the first privately funded crewed craft to reach outer space.

2009 A new law gave the people of Greenland more say in how their land was governed, though the island remained part of the Kingdom of Denmark.

1893

First Ferris wheel

The original Ferris wheel took its first spin at the World's Columbian Exposition in Chicago, USA. Fairgoers paid US 50 cents for the 20-minute ride.

1869 Wacky wheel

US inventor Georg Bergner beat his rivals to file the first patent for a vehicle called a monowheel – a large, pedal-powered wheel inside which the rider would sit. It failed to catch on.

1986 Greatest goal

At a FIFA World Cup game in Mexico, Argentinian footballer Diego Maradona weaved past three English players to score one of the greatest goals in football history. Argentina won the match 2–1 and went on to win the World Cup.

Born this day

1949 Meryl Streep, US actor. She has been nominated for more than 20 Oscars – far more than any other actor – and has won three times, for her roles in *Kramer vs Kramer*, *Sophie's Choice*, and *The Iron Lady*.

1960 Erin Brockovich, US environmental activist. Her successful case against Pacific Gas & Electric company for polluting groundwater inspired a Hollywood film.

1948 Windrush generation

Hundreds of passengers from the Caribbean on the ship *Empire Windrush* set foot on British soil. The contribution these migrants made to the UK is now celebrated on this date as Windrush Day.

Also on this day

1940 France surrendered to Germany in World War II, and signed an agreement that brought much of the country under Nazi rule.

1941 Nazi Germany launched Operation Barbarossa, a surprise invasion of the Soviet Union. In time, the Soviet army pushed the Germans back.

1978 Charon, the largest of Pluto's five moons, was discovered by US astronomers James Christy and Robert Harrington.

1281 Divine wind

Mongol forces arrived in Hakata Bay off Kyūshū island in an attempt to invade Japan. But the Mongol armada was nearly destroyed by a typhoon, forcing them to retreat. This was the second Mongol invasion of Japan to be foiled by bad weather, leading the Japanese to believe they had been saved by divine winds, or *kamikaze*.

Also on this day

1757 The British East India Company defeated the Nawab of Bengal at the Battle of Plassey, gaining control over the region.

1894 The International Olympic Committee was founded in France, with members from 13 countries. It organized the first modern Olympic Games in 1896, and continues to arrange the Olympics every four years.

2016 In a historic public vote, 52 per cent of the UK's population chose to leave the European Union.

1961 Protecting Antarctica

Twelve countries came together to enforce the Antarctic Treaty, which banned military activity on the continent and encouraged peaceful cooperation between the nations in scientific research carried out in Antarctica.

Born this day

1912 Alan Turing, British mathematician. Among the greatest scientific minds of the 20th century, he is best known for breaking encrypted German codes during World War II, and for his work in developing computer science.

June 24

1374
Dance mania

Thousands of people in Aachen, Germany, started dancing uncontrollably in a bout of dancing mania. The reasons for this phenomenon are not known, though illness, religious devotion, and poisonous fungi have all been suggested.

Born this day

1987 Lionel Messi, Argentinian football player. He joined Barcelona FC as a teenager, and eventually became their top player. A famous dribbler of the ball, he scored more than 1,200 goals in his career, and won the prestigious *Ballon d'Or* award six times.

2010
An epic match

The longest tennis match on record began at Wimbledon, UK, between the USA's John Isner (below left) and Nicolas Mahut (below centre) from France. After an exhausting 11 hours and 5 minutes of play over three days, Isner finally won the fifth set and the match.

1896
Honorary degree

Educator Booker T Washington became the first Black American to receive an honorary degree from Harvard University in the USA. Washington founded what is now Tuskegee University in Alabama, USA, and started an organization to support Black American businesses.

Also on this day

2012 The last Pinta Island giant tortoise, named Lonesome George, died aged 102. His species, which lived on the Galápagos Islands of Ecuador, died out because of hunting.

2017 Female footballers from many countries played a match in a crater on Mount Kilimanjaro, Tanzania, at an altitude of 5,714 m (18,746 ft). It is the highest-altitude football match on record.

June

25

1867

Keep out!

US inventor Lucien B Smith patented barbed wire. A cheaper alternative to wooden fencing, it was designed to keep free-roaming animals out of farmers' fields.

Rainbow flag

1978

Designed by US drag performer Gilbert Baker, an eight-coloured flag was first flown at the annual Pride Parade in San Francisco, USA. Today, most common versions of the flag have at least six colours and represent the unity and diversity of the global LGBTQ+ community.

Also on this day

1876 Indigenous American warriors successfully defended their land by defeating the US Army at the Battle of Little Bighorn.

1950 North Korea invaded South Korea, starting the Korean War.

1951 US network CBS made the world's first colour TV broadcast – though very few people saw it as hardly anyone had a colour TV set.

Born this day

1852 Antoni Gaudí, Catalan architect. His distinctive modern buildings in Barcelona, Spain, have become the city's biggest tourist sights.

1963 George Michael, British singer. He was part of the music duo Wham! before finding further pop success as a solo singer.

Wheelie wonder

1999

US cyclist Kurt Osburn completed the longest bicycle wheelie journey when he arrived at Orlando, Florida, USA. He had travelled 4,569 km (2,840 miles) from Hollywood, California, in 74 days.

June

26

1948 Berlin airlift

The Allies made the first airdrop of essential supplies into West Berlin, Germany. All other routes to this part of the city had been blocked by Soviet troops in an effort to squeeze out Allied forces.

Born this day

1911 Babe Didrikson Zaharias, US athlete. She won gold medals for hurdling and javelin at the 1932 Olympics, and also excelled at golf, baseball, and basketball.

1993 Ariana Grande, US singer and actor. After rising to fame in the hit TV series *Victorious*, she became a chart-topping musical sensation known for her powerful voice.

The spell is cast 1997

The world's most famous boy wizard was introduced to British readers when *Harry Potter and the Philosopher's Stone* – the first book in J K Rowling's *Harry Potter* series – was published in the UK.

First barcode 1974

Sharon Buchanan, a cashier at the Marsh Supermarket in Troy, Ohio, USA, scanned the first item to be sold using a barcode – a pack of chewing gum.

Also on this day

1498 The bristle toothbrush was invented in China, made out of a bamboo stick and wild pig's hair.

1794 At the Battle of Fleurus, French forces used a hot-air balloon to spy on the enemy – the first-ever military use of an aircraft.

1976 Tall tower

In Toronto, Canada, the 553 m (1,815 ft) CN Tower opened its doors to the public for the first time. It was the world's tallest freestanding structure until 2007.

Also on this day

1898 Canada-born US adventurer Joshua Slocum became the first person to sail around the world alone, in a fishing boat called *Spray*.

1905 The crew on the Russian battleship *Potemkin* revolted against their officers – the first step towards the 1917 Russian Revolution.

Fancy flip

2014

French motocross rider Tom Pagès stunned fans in Madrid, Spain, when he pulled off a gravity-defying bike flip – the world's first in a competition – to win the Red Bull X-Fighters freestyle motocross event.

1871

One currency

In order to simplify Japan's money system, the Meiji government signed an act to introduce the yen as its national currency, replacing the old system in which powerful land owners issued their own money.

Born this day

1966 Jeffrey Jacob (J J) Abrams, US filmmaker. Having found fame with the hit spy TV series *Alias*, Abrams went on to direct movies, including *Star Trek* and *Star Wars: The Force Awakens*.

A worm welcome

2009

Using only a garden fork, 10-year-old Sophie Smith established a world record by "charming" 567 worms up to the surface of a small patch of land in 30 minutes, at the World Worm Charming Championship in Cheshire, UK.

1838

Victoria crowned

The coronation of Queen Victoria was held at Westminster Abbey in London, UK. She had begun her 64-year reign at the age of 18.

Also on this day

1914 Archduke Franz Ferdinand of Austria-Hungary was assassinated in Sarajevo, in what is now Bosnia and Herzegovina, triggering a series of events that led to World War I.

1919 The Treaty of Versailles was signed in Paris, France, formally ending World War I.

2007 The bald eagle was removed from the endangered species list after a rise in numbers.

2009

Party planning

British physicist Stephen Hawking threw a party for time travellers – he sent out invitations the following day in the hope that future partygoers might arrive by time machine.

Born this day

1906 Maria Goeppert Mayer, German-born US physicist. She made important discoveries about the structure of atoms.

1971 Elon Musk, South African-born US entrepreneur. He is the owner of tech companies SpaceX, Tesla, and Neuralink.

1969

Stonewall riots

A police raid on the Stonewall Inn, a gay club in New York City, USA, turned violent when members of the LGBTQ+ community fought back. The resulting riots boosted the cause of LGBTQ+ rights in the USA, and the first gay pride marches were held exactly a year later.

1994 Mammoth discovery

A near complete skeleton of a pygmy mammoth was found on Santa Rosa Island, USA. Palaeontologists later discovered that the skeleton was 13,000 years old.

Cruise launch 1900

The first ship built as a cruise liner, the German *Prinzessin Victoria Luise,* was launched. All its 120 luxury cabins were first class, and it featured a gymnasium and library.

Born this day

1941 Stokely Carmichael, Black civil rights activist. Born in Trinidad, he moved to the USA aged 11 and went on to be an influential leader of the Black Power movement for racial equality.

1978 Nicole Scherzinger, US singer. She found fame in the girl band The Pussycat Dolls before moving on to solo success.

Also on this day

1995 US Space Shuttle *Atlantis* became the first Shuttle to dock with the Russian space station Mir.

2007 The first Apple iPhone hit US stores to huge demand from customers.

2014 The Islamic State of Iraq and the Levant declared itself a caliphate, a Muslim state modelled on the early Islamic empire in Iraq and Syria.

Theatre blaze 1613

The original Globe Theatre in London, England, burned down during a performance of William Shakespeare's *Henry VIII*. Sparks from a cannon in the attic set the thatched roof ablaze but thankfully, no one was hurt.

June 30

A balancing act

1859

French daredevil Charles Blondin became the first person to cross Niagara Falls, on the US/Canada border, on a tightrope. He used no safety nets or harnesses.

First Black astronaut

1967

After passing his flight training, Black American pilot Robert Henry Lawrence, Jr was selected to join the US Air Force's Manned Orbiting Laboratory, a secret espionage programme. This made him the first Black astronaut.

Also on this day

1908 A massive explosion over a remote area of Siberia, Russia, flattened an estimated 80 million trees. It was probably caused by an asteroid breaking up above Earth's surface.

1960 The present-day Democratic Republic of the Congo gained independence from Belgium.

2016 The United Nations agreed to take action to protect people from discrimination and violence based on their sexual or gender identities.

London landmark

1894

Tower Bridge, in London, UK, was officially declared open after eight years of construction. The bridge remains one of the city's most famous landmarks.

Born this day

1985 Michael Phelps, US swimmer. Nicknamed the Flying Fish, he is the most successful Olympic athlete of all time, with a record 23 gold medals.

July 1

Born this day

1961 Diana Spencer, Princess of Wales, a member of the British royal family. Known as the "people's princess", she supported many charitable causes.

1971 Missy Elliott, Black American rapper. One of the most successful female rappers, she is best known for hit singles such as *Get Ur Freak On* and *Work It.*

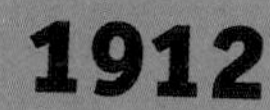

1912 Gender bender

Popular actor and male impersonator Vesta Tilley appeared on stage dressed as a man during a royal performance at the Palace Theatre in London, UK. The watching Queen Mary was so shocked to see a woman's legs that she covered her face.

Tour de France 1903

The first stage of this long-distance bicycle race began in Paris, France. The Tour de France became an annual event, and the most famous cycling race in the world.

1867 Canada united

The Constitution Act united the British colonies of Canada, Nova Scotia, and New Brunswick into the self-governing Dominion of Canada. The day is now celebrated as Canada Day to commemorate this step towards full independence.

Also on this day

1908 The Morse code SOS officially became a global distress signal and began to be used by ships in danger.

1968 The Treaty on the Non-Proliferation of Nuclear Weapons was signed by 62 countries to stop the spread of nuclear weapons.

1997 After more than a century of British rule, Hong Kong was returned to China.

July 2

Also on this day

1823 Residents of Brazil's Bahia province celebrated independence from Portuguese colonizers.

1937 US aviator Amelia Earhart went missing while flying over the Pacific Ocean in her attempt to become the first woman to fly around the globe.

1964 Following decades of mass protests, US president Lyndon B Johnson signed the Civil Rights Act, outlawing racial discrimination.

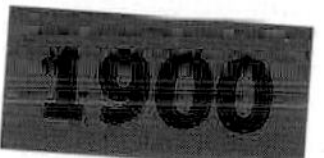

1900

First Zeppelin flight

German inventor Ferdinand von Zeppelin flew his airship Zeppelin LZ 1 over Lake Constance, Germany. It was the first flight of a rigid airship and covered more than 5 km (3 miles) in about 18 minutes.

2005

Live 8

A series of concerts, called Live 8, was broadcast on 182 television networks and 2,000 radio stations, with about 1,000 musicians performing live in cities across the world. They performed in support of campaigns to increase government aid from rich nations to poor nations.

The Amistad revolt

1839

Led by Sengbe Pieh (also called Joseph Cinqué), a group of 53 enslaved Africans killed their Spanish captors on the ship *Amistad*. They were captured and tried by the USA, but later allowed to return to their homeland.

Born this day

1929 Imelda Marcos, wife of president Ferdinand Marcos of the Philippines. She was notorious for her lavish spending, even as most of the country struggled with poverty.

July

3

1987

Across the ocean

British billionaire Richard Branson and Swedish pilot Per Lindstrand set a world record when they became the first people to cross the Atlantic Ocean in a hot-air balloon. They landed in Limavady, Northern Ireland, having flown 4,947 km (3,074 miles) from Maine, USA.

Born this day

1962 Tom Cruise, US actor. One of the most successful film stars of all time, he has played the lead role in more than 40 films, including blockbuster action movies such as *Top Gun* and the *Mission Impossible* series.

Fastest steam engine

1938

The British steam engine *Mallard* reached a speed of 203 kph (126 mph) near Grantham, UK, setting a world speed record for steam locomotives that remains unbroken.

Also on this day

1863 The Northern Army achieved its first major victory over Southern forces at the Battle of Gettysburg, turning the tide in the US Civil War.

1886 Engineer Karl Benz drove his three-wheeled Motorwagen – the world's first automobile – through the streets of Mannheim in Germany.

1928 Shades of red, blue, and green came alive on screen when Scottish inventor John Logie Baird demonstrated the first colour TV.

Magic trick

2004

Led by US magician Monty Witt, 129 magicians formed the world's longest linking ring chain. They joined together 534 steel rings at a convention of the International Brotherhood of Magicians in Cleveland, USA.

July 4

1054

Dazzling explosion

Astronomers in China observed an exploding star, or supernova, that remained visible for two years in the constellation Taurus. It left behind a cloud of debris now called the Crab Nebula.

Also on this day

1187 Muslim forces regained control of Jerusalem by defeating the Christian Crusader army at the Battle of Hattin in the Middle East.

1959 Ecuador made the Galápagos Islands its first national park 100 years after the publication of Charles Darwin's book *On the Origin of Species*, which was partly inspired by his visit to the islands.

1997 The *Sojourner* rover landed on Mars and spent 83 days exploring the Red Planet.

1956

Record rainfall

The world record for the largest amount of rain to fall in a single minute was recorded in Unionville, Maryland, USA. During a storm that flooded homes, flattened crops, and disrupted telephone lines, 31.2 mm (1.23 in) of rain fell in the space of 60 seconds.

Born this day

1868 Henrietta Swan Leavitt, US astronomer. She discovered a way to measure the distance between Earth and various galaxies.

1776

Independence Day

After years of revolutionary war, 13 British colonies in North America adopted the Declaration of Independence, a document that announced their separation from Great Britain and named them the United States of America.

1687 Laws of motion

English scientist Isaac Newton's *Mathematical Principles of Natural Philosophy* was published in Latin. Legend has it that a falling apple inspired the scientist to study how things move and the forces affecting them.

Born this day

1968 Susan Wojcicki, CEO of YouTube. One of the most powerful women in the technology industry, she was part of Google's founding team.

1996 Dolly the sheep, the world's first cloned mammal. She was born at an institute in Scotland and was named after US singer Dolly Parton.

Clash of tanks 1943

Nearly 8,000 tanks were used by German and Soviet forces at the Battle of Kursk in western Soviet Union. Despite heavy losses, the Soviets crushed their opponents.

2009 Treasure trove

The largest-ever hoard of Anglo-Saxon treasure was discovered in a field in Staffordshire, UK, by metal detector enthusiast Terry Herbert. The find included more than 5 kg (11 lb) of gold and thousands of jewels.

Also on this day

1948 The UK government launched the National Health Service (NHS) to offer free health care to its population.

1950 Israel passed the Law of Return, allowing every Jewish person to settle in the country and become a citizen.

1994 Amazon was founded by Jeff Bezos out of his garage in Bellevue, USA. It is now one of the world's largest companies.

July

6

2019 Ancient tombs of Japan

The Kofun tombs of Japan were declared a World Heritage Site by the United Nations. These large burial mounds were built more than 1,300 years ago and take various forms, including keyhole shapes, squares, and circles.

Born this day

1907 Frida Kahlo, Mexican painter. She is best known for the colourful self-portraits that she painted after getting injured in a bus accident.

2016

Gotta catch 'em all!

The launch of Pokémon GO, a real-world mobile game, had people across the world hunting fictional Pokémon creatures using their mobile phones.

Lawrence of Arabia 1917

When the Arabs revolted against Turkish rulers in the Middle East, British intelligence officer T E Lawrence became their close ally and helped them capture the port of Aqaba, from where they received British aid.

Also on this day

640 The Battle of Heliopolis in Egypt ended Roman rule and marked the beginning of Muslim rule.

1942 To escape the Nazis, Jewish diarist Anne Frank and her family went into hiding in Amsterdam in the Netherlands.

1964 The film *A Hard Day's Night* was released. It was the first film starring British rock band The Beatles.

Also on this day

1911 The first international treaty for wildlife conservation – the North Pacific Fur Seal Convention – was signed. It aimed to stop open-water seal hunting.

1950 The implementation of the Population Registration Act, which classified people according to race, set off racial tensions in South Africa.

2005 Terrorists detonated explosives on public transport in London, UK, during the morning rush hour, killing 52 people.

1881

Pinocchio

Italian author Carlo Collodi's classic about a naughty wooden puppet first appeared as a series of stories in the Italian magazine *Giornale per i bambini*. The stories were later collected and published as *The Adventures of Pinocchio* in 1883.

1978 

Tennis legend

Czech-American tennis player Martina Navratilova won the first of her nine Wimbledon singles titles, a record that still stands. She reached the finals 12 times and achieved six consecutive wins from 1982 to 1987.

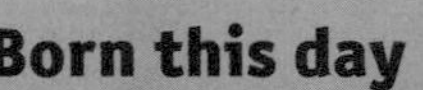

Born this day

1980 Michelle Kwan, US figure skater. She has won two Olympic medals, five World Figure Skating Championships, and nine US Figure Skating Championships.

1981 Mahendra Singh Dhoni, Indian cricketer. A great batsman and wicketkeeper, he captained India to victory in the 2011 One-day World Cup.

First sliced bread

1928

Customers were surprised when a bakery in Chillicothe, Missouri, USA, began selling the world's first pre-sliced bread. It was marketed as "the greatest forward step in the baking industry since bread was wrapped".

July

8

1817 Roller-coaster

The world's first roller-coaster opened in an amusement park in Paris, France. The *Promenades Aériennes* featured wheeled carts that hurtled down curving tracks at up to 64 kph (40 mph).

Born this day

1593 Artemisia Gentileschi, Italian painter. Among the most successful women painters of the 17th century, she became famous for her bold, colourful, and realistic paintings of women from the Bible.

1853

Mission to Japan

With a fleet of four ships, US Navy officer Matthew Perry sailed into the harbour of Uraga, Japan, hoping to force the nation to open to US trade after more than 200 years of isolation.

Also on this day

1497 Portuguese explorer Vasco da Gama set sail with a fleet of four ships on the world's first sea voyage from Europe to India.

1775 British colonies in North America signed the Olive Branch Petition in an attempt to avoid war with Great Britain. The petition was rejected by the British king and war followed.

1947 The US military reported the discovery of a mysterious "flying disc" near Roswell, New Mexico, sparking decades of conspiracy theories about alien spacecraft.

Girl power

1996

The Spice Girls, an all-female British pop group, released their smash-hit single *Wannabe*. The song won over young fans across the world with its emphasis on strong friendships between women.

July 9

1877

First Wimbledon

The world's first official lawn tennis tournament began in Wimbledon, UK. British sportsperson Spencer Gore beat 21 other amateur players to win the first Gentlemen's Singles title 10 days later.

1958

Megatsunami

A 7.8 magnitude earthquake caused a massive rockslide in Lituya Bay in Alaska, USA. The displaced seawater formed into a series of giant waves – some as tall as 524 m (1,720 ft) – that struck land.

1922

Swimming champion

Before finding fame playing the character of Tarzan in Hollywood films, US swimming champion Johnny Weissmuller made history by finishing a 100 m freestyle race in less than a minute in California, USA.

Also on this day

1981 The famous video-game character Mario first appeared in the Japanese video game *Donkey Kong*.

1982 Michael Fagan successfully dodged the high-security measures in place at London's Buckingham Palace and broke in. He found his way to the Queen's bedroom, before being discovered and arrested shortly afterwards.

Born this day

1935 Haydée Mercedes Sosa, Argentinian folk singer. She sang songs in support of oppressed people.

1956 Tom Hanks, US actor and director. He has starred in more than 90 films, and gave voice to the character of Woody in the *Toy Story* films.

2018 First giant dinosaur

Two hundred million year old fossils of *Ingentia prima*, the earliest known giant dinosaur, were found in Argentina. At 10 m (33 ft) long and weighing 9 tonnes, this species was about three times larger than other dinosaurs alive at that time.

Born this day

1891 Edith Quimby, US medical researcher and physicist. She helped develop radioactive techniques to detect and treat cancer, and found ways to limit patients' side effects.

1995 Ada Hegerberg, Norwegian footballer. She won the UEFA Best Women's Player in Europe Award in 2016.

Battle of Britain begins 1940

One of the most famous air battles of World War II began when the Luftwaffe (German air force) invaded the skies over Britain. They were defeated by the British Royal Air Force (RAF).

Heroic hound 1943

When his platoon came under fire in Sicily, Italy, during World War II, US army dog Chips charged towards and attacked the Italian soldiers firing machine guns, forcing them to surrender. Chips was awarded many medals for the defence of his platoon.

Also on this day

1913 In the Mojave Desert's Death Valley in California, USA, the hottest-ever temperature of 56.7°C (134°F) was recorded.

1962 The world's first communications satellite, Telstar, was launched into space by NASA.

1962 In the USA, a patent was filed for a plastic bag with handles – the invention soon replaced paper bags worldwide.

1405 Treasure voyage

Chinese admiral Zheng He, with his fleet of 317 ships, received the command to set sail on his first voyage of exploration to Southeast Asia and India in search of treasure.

1897 Arctic tragedy

Swedish explorer S A Andrée and two companions set off from Norway in a disastrous attempt to reach the North Pole by hot-air balloon. They disappeared and the balloon was not found until 33 years later.

Born this day

1923 Tun Tun, Indian comedian and singer. The first female comedian in Bollywood, she appeared in more than 100 films.

1957 Michael Rose, Jamaican musician. He was lead singer of the reggae group Black Uhuru, who in 1985 won the first-ever Grammy Award for Best Reggae Album.

Also on this day

1801 French astronomer Jean-Louis Pons found the first of the 37 comets discovered by him.

1914 US baseball legend Babe Ruth made his debut in the Major League as a pitcher.

2018 Scientists reported finding 2.1-million-year-old stone tools in China, suggesting that humans left Africa much earlier than assumed.

1899 Founding FIAT

A group of investors, including Italian entrepreneur Giovanni Agnelli, founded FIAT (Fabbrica Italiana Automobili Torino) in Turin, Italy. Under Agnelli's leadership, FIAT became the largest manufacturer of cars in the country.

July

12

1770 Spinning jenny

James Hargreaves of Lancashire, UK, patented the spinning jenny, a machine that turns raw cotton fibre into thread for weaving. The invention helped trigger Britain's Industrial Revolution.

Born this day

1997 Malala Yousafzai, Pakistani activist. She survived an assassination attempt after campaigning for girls' rights to education. She is the youngest recipient of the Nobel Peace Prize.

Also on this day

1576 The Mughal Empire seized control of Bengal in the Indian subcontinent after defeating Sultan Daud Khan Karrani at the Battle of Rajmahal.

1776 British explorer James Cook set sail on an attempt to find the Northwest Passage – a sea route through the Arctic Ocean. He was killed while visiting Hawaii.

1863 The British colonial army invaded Indigenous Māori land at Waikato, New Zealand.

1971 The tricoloured Australian Aboriginal Flag was flown for the first time in Adelaide, Australia, on National Aborigines Day.

1493 Nuremberg Chronicle

The *Nuremberg Chronicle* by German historian Hartmann Schedel was published. One of the most richly illustrated books of the 15th century, it chronicled the history of the Christian world.

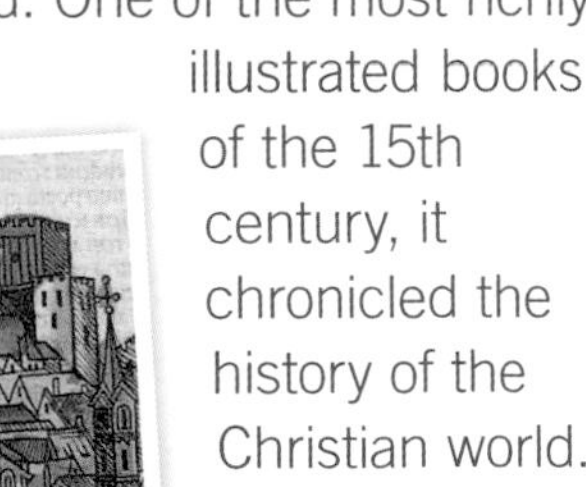

1985 Live Aid concert

A 16-hour charity concert was held in Wembley Stadium in London, UK. Broadcast globally, it raised an estimated £150 million for famine relief in Ethiopia.

Born this day

1942 Harrison Ford, US actor. He is best known for playing Han Solo in *Star Wars* and Indiana Jones in *Raiders of the Lost Ark*.

1944 Ernő Rubik, Hungarian inventor. Obsessed with puzzles since childhood, he created the Rubik's Cube in 1974.

2013 Black Lives Matter

Outraged by the release of George Zimmerman, who had killed unarmed Black teenager Trayvon Martin, US activist Alicia Garza posted a message on Facebook with the hashtag #BlackLivesMatter. It became a rallying cry for racial justice.

Also on this day

1772 British explorer James Cook set sail on a fruitless attempt to discover a vast continent thought to cover much of Earth's southern hemisphere.

1930 The first FIFA World Cup competition began in Montevideo, Uruguay.

1977 New York City, USA, suffered one of its worst blackouts after lightning struck its power grid. In the darkness, looters ransacked stores.

First cat show

About 170 cats, including Siamese, African, and French breeds, were exhibited at the Crystal Palace in London, UK. The world's first cat show was a thundering success, with more than 20,000 visitors.

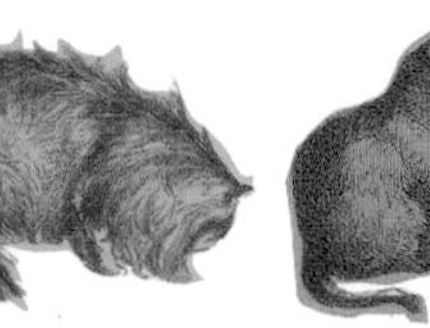

July 14

1712 Steam engine

The Newcomen engine – one of the first commercially successful steam engines – was put to work pumping water out of mines in Tipton, UK. It helped pave the way for Britain's Industrial Revolution.

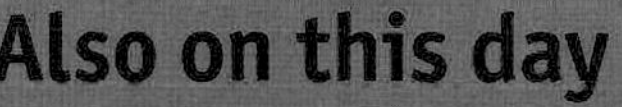

Also on this day

1957 After winning the 1957 election in her constituency, Rawya Ateya joined Egypt's National Assembly to become the first female member of parliament in the Arab world.

2011 Five days after becoming an independent country, South Sudan became the 193rd member of the United Nations.

2012 The first International Non-Binary People's Day was celebrated for individuals who do not identify as either male or female.

Billy the Kid 1881

Notorious American Wild West gunfighter Billy the Kid (Henry McCarty) was shot and killed at the age of 21 by law officer Patrick Floyd Garrett. The outlaw had committed at least nine murders.

Born this day

1917 Ben Enwonwu, Nigerian painter and sculptor. Known for his modernist style, Enwonwu became one of the most influential African artists of the 20th century.

1941 Maulana Karenga, Black American activist. He created the week-long celebration *Kwanzaa* to honour African heritage in the USA.

1789 Storming of the Bastille

Hundreds of angry French citizens attacked the Bastille, a prison and fortress in Paris. The battle kickstarted the French Revolution and its anniversary is now celebrated as Bastille Day.

July 15

Also on this day

1099/1244 Christian forces captured the city of Jerusalem in the Holy Land in 1099, bringing the First Crusade to an end. Exactly 145 years later to the day, the Crusaders lost Jerusalem to a Muslim army in 1244.

1965 The *Mariner 4* spacecraft flew as close as 9,846 km (6,118 miles) to Mars. Its photos of the Red Planet were the first taken from space of a planet other than Earth.

2010 Argentina became the first South American country to legalize same-sex marriages.

1890

Table tennis

David Foster, a British inventor, filed a patent for the game of table tennis. His version featured a rubber ball, rackets with strings, and a small wooden perimeter fence.

1799

Code breaker

The Rosetta Stone, a rock carved with the same inscription in three different ancient languages, was discovered near Rashid, Egypt. It helped scholars decipher the hieroglyphic writing used in ancient Egypt.

Born this day

1606 Rembrandt, Dutch painter. He was a master of different styles and subjects, such as portraits (including his own) and landscapes.

1914 Prince Birabongse Bhanudej, Thai prince, sailor, pilot, and racing driver. He was the first Southeast Asian driver to compete in Formula 1 racing.

The Great Stink

1858

A bill was passed to clean out the waste dumped in the River Thames in London, UK, to rid the city of the "Great Stink" it caused. This led to an improved sewer system.

July

16

1935 Pay for parking

Invented by US publisher Carl C Magee, the world's first parking meter – called "Park-O-Meter No. 1" – was installed in Oklahoma City, USA. More than 140,000 meters were set up in the USA by the 1940s.

1945 Nuclear test

The world's first nuclear bomb was detonated in the desert in New Mexico, USA. Code-named "Trinity", this test marked the beginning of the Atomic Age.

Also on this day

622 The start date of the Islamic calendar. It marks the first new moon after Prophet Muhammad moved to Medina.

1809 Led by Pedro Murillo, the citizens of La Paz, Bolivia, revolted against their Spanish rulers.

1911 Italian-Argentine women's rights activist Julieta Lanteri used a legal technicality to become the first woman in South America to vote.

Born this day

1911 Ginger Rogers, US actor, dancer, and singer. She starred in more than 70 Hollywood films, winning an Oscar for Best Actress for *Kitty Foyle*.

2017 All-time great

Swiss tennis player Roger Federer defeated Croatian Marin Čilić in three straight sets to claim his eighth Wimbledon men's singles title, setting a new record.

Disneyland opens

Built under the supervision of Walt Disney, the Disneyland theme park in California, USA, opened for the first time. The park now welcomes millions of visitors every year.

Also on this day

709 BCE The first confirmed total solar eclipse to be recorded in history was seen by Chinese astronomers, according to the ancient text *Lüshi Chunqiu*.

1936 An uprising by nationalist rebels opposed to Spain's left-wing government triggered the start of the Spanish Civil War, which would last until 1939.

Born this day

1954 Angela Merkel, German politician. She became Germany's first female chancellor (head of government) in 2005 and was re-elected in 2009, 2013, and 2018.

1717

Floating orchestra

The *Water Music* by German-born composer George Frideric Handel was performed for the first time at a concert that took place on a barge on the River Thames in Britain. King George I, who watched from another boat, asked for the music to be replayed multiple times.

Great Fire of Rome

64 CE

A fire broke out in a shop near Rome's Circus Maximus, a huge chariot-racing stadium. Fanned by strong winds, the blaze spread quickly and destroyed nearly two-thirds of the city within nine days.

Born this day

1918 Nelson Mandela, South African freedom fighter and political leader. A member of the African National Congress, he fought against racial segregation. He served as the country's first Black president from 1994 to 1999.

1863

Civil War hero

Black American soldier William Harvey Carney took part in the Battle of Fort Wagner in the US Civil War. He would later receive the Medal of Honor, the USA's most prestigious military award, for his bravery.

Also on this day

1892 Ukrainian-French microbiologist Waldemar Haffkine injected himself with the first effective human cholera vaccine, which he had developed at the Pasteur Institute in Paris, France.

2005 Brazilian windsurfers Flavio Jardim and Diogo Guerreiro completed their 8,120 km (5,045 mile) journey along the coast of Brazil, setting a world record for the longest windsurfing journey.

1976

Perfect 10

Romanian gymnast Nadia Comăneci scored the first perfect 10 in Olympic gymnastics after a flawless routine on the uneven bars at the Montreal Olympics. Unable to display a 10, the scoreboard showed "1.00" instead.

July 19

1903

Cycling champ

With a lead of three hours, French cyclist Maurice Garin beat 60 competitors to win the first Tour de France. Only 21 riders managed to complete the 19-day race across France.

Paris Métro

1900

The first line of the Paris Métro subway system was opened to the public during the Summer Olympics in Paris, France. The line linked Porte Maillot in the west of the city with Porte de Vincennes in the east.

Also on this day

1848 The first women's rights convention was held at Seneca Falls, New York, USA.

1912 After a 200 kg (441 lb) meteorite exploded in the sky above Holbrook in Arizona, USA, nearly 16,000 fragments rained down on the city.

2019 Kenya unveiled Africa's largest wind power plant on the shores of Lake Turkana.

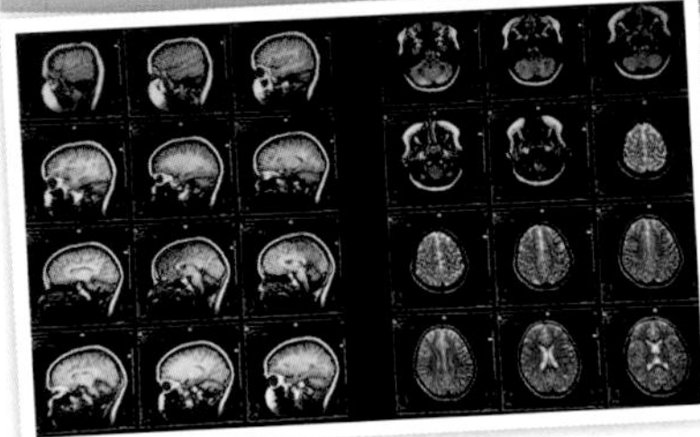

1983

Brain in 3D

US doctor Michael W Vannier and his team published a series of scans created using computed tomography (CT). These scans were put together to create the first three-dimensional picture of inside a person's head.

Born this day

1965 Evelyn Glennie, Scottish percussionist. Almost completely deaf, she has trained herself to feel music with other parts of her body.

1969

Moon landing

US astronaut Neil Armstrong became the first human to walk on the Moon, while half a billion people back on Earth watched him live on television. He was soon joined by fellow US astronaut Buzz Aldrin (left).

Born this day

1822 Gregor Mendel, Austrian scientist. He studied how physical traits are passed on from parents to children, by carrying out experiments using pea plants.

1919 Edmund Hillary, New Zealand mountaineer. He was the first person to reach the top of Mount Everest and both the North and South poles.

Also on this day

1960 Sri Lankan politician Sirimavo Bandaranaike became the world's first female prime minister.

1968 About 1,000 disabled athletes participated in the first Special Olympics in Chicago, USA.

1976 A broken knee couldn't stop Japanese gymnast Fujimoto Shun from winning a gold medal at the Montreal Olympics.

Long-lost treasure

1985

After searching for 15 years, US explorer Mel Fisher located the 17th-century Spanish ship *Nuestra Señora de Atocha* off the coast of Florida, USA. On board were tons of precious gold, silver, and emeralds.

Stunts on wheels

2018

US athlete Aaron Fotheringham set three huge wheelchair stunt world records for the longest ramp jump, the tallest quarter-pipe drop-in, and the highest hand plant, at the Woodward West summer camp in California, USA.

Also on this day

1865 "Wild Bill" Hickok shot down Davis Tutt in a gunfight in Springfield, Missouri, USA, that came to be known as the first "Wild West" showdown.

1919 Azerbaijan became the first Muslim country to grant women aged 20 and above the right to vote.

1983 Soviet research station Vostok in Antarctica noted a ground temperature of –89.2°C (–128.6°F), the lowest ever recorded on Earth.

Sumo champ 2017

Hakuhō Shō beat Takayasu Akira in Nagoya, Japan, winning his 1,048th sumo match and setting the record for most career wins in the sport.

1904 World's longest railway

The Trans-Siberian Railway was completed after more than 10 years of construction. It runs for 9,289 km (5,772 miles) between the Russian cities of Moscow in the west and Vladivostok in the east.

Born this day

1972 Catherine Nyambura Ndereba, Kenyan athlete. A legendary long-distance runner, she has won the Boston Marathon four times and the Chicago and World Championship marathons twice.

Muscle power 2012

US adventurer Erden Eruç returned to Bodega Bay, USA, after completing the first solo trip around the globe to be achieved by using only human muscle power. Over five years of travel, he had covered 66,299 km (41,196 miles) by cycling, walking, canoeing, kayaking, and rowing.

1802

Unifying Vietnam

Emperor Gia Long captured the northern city of Hanoi in Vietnam, bringing the entire country under his rule. He established the Nguyen Dynasty, the last in Vietnamese history.

2009

Long eclipse

The longest solar eclipse to be seen in the first two decades of the 21st century lasted for 6 minutes and 39 seconds. It was visible to millions of people across Asia.

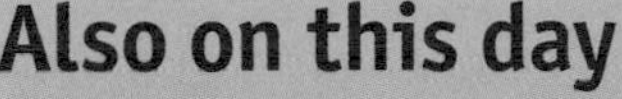

Also on this day

1342 Continuous rain caused the banks of several European rivers, including the Danube and Rhine, to burst. The St Mary Magdalene's flood, as it came to be known, was the worst ever recorded in central Europe.

1997 The first issue of Japanese manga (comic) *One Piece* was published. The series went on to sell more than 450 million copies.

2015 The oldest pieces of a copy of the Qur'an, the religious book of Islam, were dated by radiocarbon testing as about 1,370 years old.

Born this day

1992 Selena Gomez, US singer and actor. She appeared in Disney TV programmes as a child star before developing her film career. She has also enjoyed chart success with her band, and as a solo artist.

1933

Global flight

The first solo flight around the world was completed when US aviator Wiley Post landed in New York City, USA, after flying for seven days, 18 hours, and 49 minutes. His journey had taken him over 25,099 km (15,596 miles).

2010 One Direction

After five teenagers appeared separately on UK talent show *The X Factor*, they were brought together as boy band One Direction by judge Simon Cowell. They quickly became one of the world's most popular pop groups.

Also on this day

1952 The almost 150-year reign of the Muhammad Ali Dynasty in Egypt ended when the army overthrew King Farouk and established a republic.

1980 Vietnamese astronaut Pham Tuân became the first non-Soviet Asian to go into space, on board Soviet spacecraft *Soyuz 37*.

2015 NASA scientists announced the discovery of Kepler-452b, an Earthlike planet in the habitable zone of a Sunlike star.

Full speed ahead 1966

US former military pilot Don Wetzel tested the rocket-powered *Black Beetle* train. Speeding along a flat, straight track, it reached a top speed of 296 kph (183 mph) – an unbeaten US railway record.

Born this day

1931 Te Atairangikaahu, Māori queen. Her 40-year rule made her the longest-reigning Māori monarch.

1989 Daniel Radcliffe, British actor. He starred as Harry Potter in the film adaptations of J K Rowling's novels.

2012 Cycling record

The first woman to set a record for cycling around the globe, British-German endurance athlete Juliana Buhring began her journey in Naples, Italy. She finished 152 days later, after travelling more than 29,000 km (18,000 miles) on a bicycle.

2019 Global warming

Scientific studies revealed that although temperatures on Earth had risen and fallen over the past 2,000 years, the average global temperatures peaked in the 20th century due to human activities.

Born this day

1966 Aminatou Ali Ahmed Haidar, Moroccan human rights activist. She advocates for the independence of Western Sahara from Morocco.

1969 Jennifer Lopez, US singer and actor. She is a bestselling pop artist and one of the highest-earning entertainers in the USA.

Also on this day

1847 Led by Brigham Young, a group of 148 Mormons arrived in the Great Salt Lake Valley in Utah, USA. There, they founded Salt Lake City.

1943 More than 700 British RAF bombers began eight days of air raids on Hamburg, Germany, during World War II.

1944 About 300 Mexican soldiers formed a US military squadron called the Aztec Eagles. They went on to fight against Japan on the Pacific front in World War II.

1911 Inca city

In the Andes mountains of Peru, US archaeologist Hiram Bingham was led to Machu Picchu, becoming the first Westerner to see the ruins of this 15th-century Inca city.

July 25

1909

Winning flight

In an achievement that won him £1,000, French aviator Louis Blériot became the first person to fly across the English Channel. He rose to fame as one of leading pilots of the era.

Born this day

1920 Rosalind Franklin, British scientist. She made huge contributions to the discovery of the double-helix structure of DNA.

1967 Matt LeBlanc, US actor. He is best known for playing Joey Tribbiani in the popular TV show *Friends*.

2006 Toumani Diabaté

The renowned Malian musician Toumani Diabaté released his famous album *Boulevard de l'Indépendance*. He was one of the first artists to record music with a *kora* (a West African stringed instrument resembling a lute).

Also on this day

1814 At the Battle of Niagara Falls (in modern-day Ontario, Canada), Canadian and British troops defended their territory against US forces.

1984 Cosmonaut (Soviet astronaut) Svetlana Savitskaya became the first woman to perform a spacewalk, while working on the Soviet Union's *Salyut 7* space station.

1984 IVF baby

Louise Brown was born in the UK. She was the world's first baby conceived by in vitro fertilization (IVF), a type of fertilization that takes place outside a woman's body.

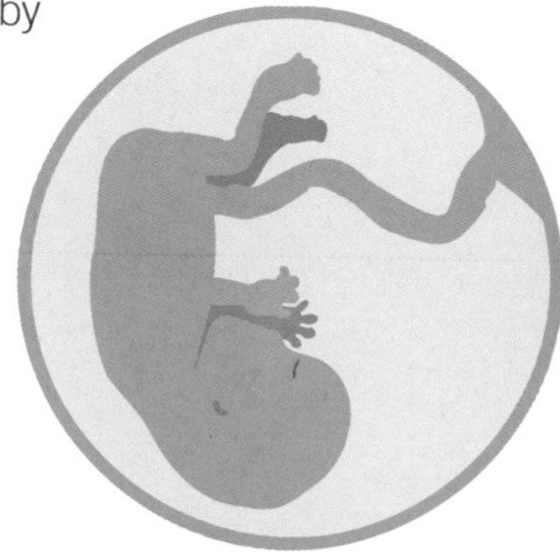

2016 Presidential candidate

At the Democratic National Convention in Philadelphia, USA, Hillary Clinton became the first-ever female US presidential nominee from a major political party.

Born this day

1964 Sandra Bullock, US actor. She has starred in many popular Hollywood films, such as *Speed*, *The Blind Side*, and *Gravity*.

The Congo Basin 2012

As part of a UN-led project, 10 countries across Central Africa agreed to monitor the rainforests of the Congo Basin in order to reduce illegal logging, mining, and construction in the region.

1509 Rise of Vijayanagara

Krishnadevaraya (on the left) became the ruler of the Vijayanagara Empire in what is now southern India. He expanded his empire through conquest and also promoted the arts.

Also on this day

1920 At 72, Swedish shooter Oscar Swahn won silver at the Antwerp Olympics in Belgium, becoming the oldest Olympic medallist in history.

1943 Dense smog covered Los Angeles, USA. Some feared a chemical attack by Japan, but the main cause was identified as traffic fumes.

July

27

1896 Wireless messaging

Italian inventor Guglielmo Marconi demonstrated his wireless telegraph in London, UK, sending a Morse code signal from one post office to another located 300 m (980 ft) away.

Born this day

1923 Masutatsu Ōyama, Korean-Japanese martial artist. He fought hundreds of contests, and some barehanded battles with bulls, before founding the *Kyokushin* karate style.

Also on this day

1377 Following a plague outbreak, the city of Ragusa (present-day Dubrovnik, Croatia) introduced the first compulsory quarantine, making people entering the city isolate themselves for 30 days.

1921 Canadian scientists Frederick Banting and Charles Best discovered insulin, the hormone that controls the level of sugar in the blood. It would eventually be used to treat diabetes.

1953 North Korea and South Korea signed an armistice agreement that ended the fighting in the Korean War.

Bugs Bunny 1940

The beloved cartoon rabbit first appeared on screen in the animated short film *A Wild Hare*. Bugs Bunny went on to star in many more cartoons.

1996 Beach volleyball

In the women's final of the first Olympic beach volleyball event, held in Atlanta, USA, Jackie Silva (left) and Sandra Pires beat fellow Brazilians Mônica Rodrigues and Adriana Samuel (right).

The Spanish Armada

1588

The English navy set eight of their ships on fire at night and sent them towards the Spanish Armada, a fleet of ships anchored at the harbour in Calais, France. The Spanish panicked and their ships scattered, leading to an easy victory for the English the following day.

Born this day

1866 Beatrix Potter, British author and illustrator. She created more than 20 children's books featuring animal characters such as Peter Rabbit.

1923 Xia Peisu, Chinese computer scientist. She researched and designed Model 107, the first computer to be built in China.

Silent protest

1917

Ten thousand people marched silently down New York City's Fifth Avenue in protest against the race-based killings of Black Americans in the USA.

1939

Anglo-Saxon helmet

Archaeologists unearthed the remains of an elaborately decorated helmet from a burial site at Sutton Hoo in Suffolk, UK. This rare Anglo-Saxon object is made of iron, and has a cap, a neck guard, a face mask, and cheek shields, which protected the warrior from every angle.

Also on this day

1821 Led by Argentinian general José de San Martín, the people of Peru defeated Spanish colonial forces to gain independence.

1914 Austria-Hungary declared war on Serbia, triggering World War I, after a Serbian man killed Austria's Archduke Franz Ferdinand.

1976 A devastating 7.6 magnitude earthquake struck Tangshan, China, destroying most buildings in the city and damaging roads and bridges.

1981 Fairytale wedding

Surrounded by a massive global media hype, Prince Charles, heir to the British throne, married Diana Spencer, the youngest daughter of a British nobleman, at St Paul's Cathedral in London, UK.

Also on this day

1030 King Olaf II Haraldsson of ancient Norway died at the Battle of Stiklestad. He was later declared a saint by the church, and his popularity helped the spread of Christianity in the country.

1921 Politician Adolf Hitler became the leader of the extremist Nazi Party in Germany. The Nazis would eventually take charge of the country in 1933.

Born this day

1959 Sanjay Dutt, Indian actor. He overcame a number of personal challenges to become a famous Bollywood movie star.

1981 Fernando Alonso, Spanish driver. He was one of the youngest winners of the Formula 1 World Drivers' Championship, and has competed in other motorsports, such as rally racing and the Indianapolis 500, as well.

Arc de Triomphe 1836

French king Louis-Philippe unveiled the Arc de Triomphe, a monument dedicated to the memory of soldiers who had died fighting for France in war. Located in Paris, it is one of the country's most famous landmarks.

July 30

2016

Leap of faith

US daredevil Luke Aikins jumped out of an aircraft at an altitude of 7,620 m (25,000 ft) without a parachute over Simi Valley in California, USA. He landed safely in a giant net and walked away with no injuries.

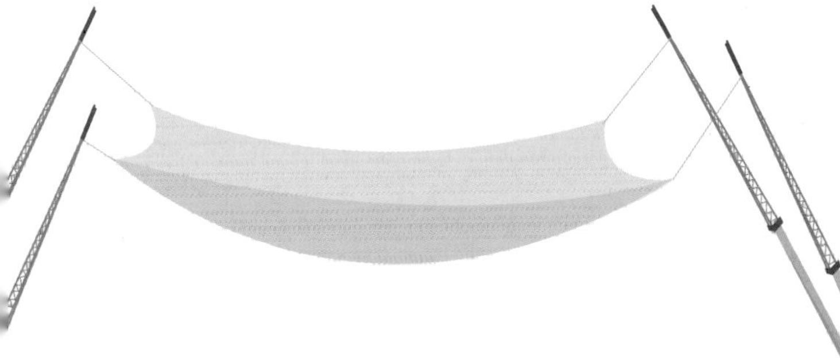

The joy of friendship

2011

The United Nations (UN) observed the first International Day of Friendship. It celebrated the importance of close bonds between people, communities, and countries, and raised awareness of how these relationships can help us during hard times.

Also on this day

762 Abbasid ruler Al-Mansur founded Baghdad, in modern-day Iraq. The "Round City" became the thriving capital of his empire.

2009 Japanese astronaut Koichi Wakata returned to Earth in a fresh pair of underpants after wearing his previous pair for a month while on board the International Space Station (ISS). He was testing to see whether the specially designed garment would eventually start to smell.

Born this day

1947 Arnold Schwarzenegger, Austrian-American bodybuilder, actor, and politician. In his varied career, he has won the Mr Universe title, starred in Hollywood films, and served as governor of California, USA.

Oldest working zoo

1752

Holy Roman Emperor Franz I founded the Vienna Zoo in the grounds of Austria's famous Schönbrunn Palace. It was opened to the public in 1778.

Born this day

1973 Andy Macdonald, US skateboarder. He has won the World Cup Skateboarding Series nine times.

Daredevil flight

2003

Austrian skydiver Felix Baumgartner became the first person to fly across the English Channel using a carbon wing. He jumped from a plane above Dover, UK, and soared 35 km (22 miles), before landing safely near Calais, France.

Also on this day

1581 Johann von Schönenberg became the Archbishop of Trier, Germany. He went on to lead one of Europe's biggest witch trials.

1658 Aurangzeb took the throne as the sixth Mughal emperor. During his reign, the Mughal Empire reached its largest size.

2013 The US White House honoured Black American Kimberly Bryant as a "Champion of Change". She founded Black Girls Code, an organization that teaches computer skills to young girls.

First Moon drive

1971

US astronauts David Scott and James Irwin from NASA's *Apollo 15* mission became the first people to drive a vehicle on the Moon when they set off to explore in the four-wheel, electric Lunar Roving Vehicle (LRV).

August 1

Scouts' honour

1907

The first Scout camp started on Brownsea Island, UK, organized by British Army officer Robert Baden-Powell. During the camp, children learned skills such as cooking outdoors and reading maps. This day is now celebrated as World Scouts' Day.

Born this day

1901 Francisco Guilledo, Filipino boxer, also known as Pancho Villa. He became the first Asian to win the World Flyweight Championship, in 1923.

1979 Jason Momoa, US actor. He has appeared in the television series *Stargate Atlantis* and *Game of Thrones*, and the movie *Aquaman*.

First music channel

1981

MTV (Music Television) was launched in the USA. The first music video played on the channel was *Video Killed the Radio Star* by the British band The Buggles.

Also on this day

1834 The Slavery Abolition Act (1833) came into force, ending slavery in the British Empire, except in Saint Helena and the Indian subcontinent.

1944 During World War II, the Warsaw Uprising began, when resistance fighters in Warsaw, Poland, attempted to end German rule.

1984 The Lindow Man, a 2,000-year-old bog body (a body preserved by natural processes in a peat bog) was found by a farmer in the UK.

Robot globetrotter

2015

After safe trips through the Netherlands, Germany, and Canada, Canadian hitchhiking robot hitchBOT ended its US journey early in Philadelphia, when it was destroyed.

August 2

Underwater crossing 1870

The Tower Subway, a tunnel dug underneath the River Thames in London, UK, opened to the public. Inside the tunnel, wooden railway carriages carried passengers from one side of the river to the other. The tunnel later became a walkway.

Also on this day

1776 In North America, 13 British colonies signed the US Declaration of Independence, pronouncing the end of British rule.

1944 Thousands of Romani people were killed by the Nazis at Auschwitz concentration camp in Poland. This day is now remembered as Roma Holocaust Memorial Day.

1990 Led by dictator Saddam Hussein, Iraqi troops invaded neighbouring Kuwait, leading to the start of the first Gulf War.

1971

Memorial on the Moon

The crew of the US mission *Apollo 15* placed a small sculpture named Fallen Astronaut on the Moon, together with a plaque showing the names of 14 US and Russian astronauts who lost their lives while working to advance space exploration.

Born this day

1979 Reuben Kosgei, Kenyan athlete. Aged 21, he became the youngest-ever winner of Olympic gold in the 3,000 m steeplechase.

Winning general

Roman military general Julius Caesar won a major victory against the Kingdom of Pontus at the Battle of Zela in modern-day Turkey. Caesar celebrated his win by declaring, *"Veni, vidi, vici"* ("I came, I saw, I conquered").

August 3

1862 Respected nurse

US nurse Clara Barton was allowed to take medical supplies to soldiers on the battlefields of the US Civil War. Her dedication to caring for the wounded and sick later led her to establish the American Red Cross.

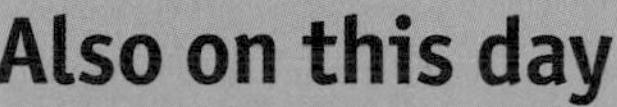

Also on this day

1492 Italian explorer Christopher Columbus set sail from Spain to find a westward route to India, but he instead arrived in the Americas.

1914 At the beginning of World War I, Germany declared war on France.

1946 Santa Claus Land, the world's first themed amusement park, opened in Indiana, USA.

1958 Nuclear submarine

The USS *Nautilus*, the world's first nuclear-powered submarine, reached the North Pole after travelling underneath the Arctic ice cap for nearly 1,600 km (1,000 miles).

2017 Super striker

French football club Paris Saint-Germain announced that they had signed popular Brazilian goal scorer Neymar for a whopping sum of €222 million.

Born this day

1904 Dolores del Río, Mexican actor. She was one of the first female actors in Latin America – her successful career in cinema lasted for more than 50 years.

1964 Lucky Dube, South African reggae musician. One of the country's biggest-selling reggae artists, he recorded songs in Zulu, English, and Afrikaans.

August 4

2006 X-treme stunt

US motocross racer Travis Pastrana performed the first-ever double backflip on a motorcycle at the 12th X Games in Los Angeles, USA. He earned the top score of 98.6 and finished the games with three gold medals.

2011 First electric helicopter

French engineer Pascal Chrétien, who built the electric-powered Solution F/Chretien helicopter, flew it for the first time on this day. Tethered to the ground, the aircraft hovered 50 cm (19 in) off the ground for just over two minutes.

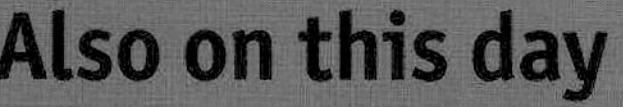

Also on this day

1944 After more than two years in hiding, Jewish teenager Anne Frank and her family were found and arrested by Nazi officials in Amsterdam, Netherlands.

1945 One of the world's first electronic bugs (listening devices) was hidden in the study of the US ambassador in Moscow. For the next seven years, Soviet agents used it to spy on the USA, before it was discovered.

2020 A massive explosion in a warehouse at the Port of Beirut, Lebanon, severely injured 6,500 people and killed more than 200.

Born this day

1901 Louis Armstrong, Black American trumpet player and singer. He transformed jazz music with his performances and unique singing style.

1929 Kishore Kumar, Indian singer and actor. He sang more than 2,000 songs in different Indian languages.

Siege of Odawara 1590

The Hōjō clan surrendered to the army of samurai lord Toyotomi Hideyoshi, ending the three-month-long siege of Odawara Castle. This event marked a step towards Hideyoshi's unification of Japan.

August 5

2020 Pacific plants

An international group of scientists revealed that New Guinea island in the Pacific Ocean has the greatest plant diversity of anywhere worldwide. It's home to 13,634 plant species – a fifth of which are orchids.

2013 Happy birthday!

To celebrate a year since *Curiosity*'s successful landing on Mars, scientists at NASA programmed the rover to play the song "Happy Birthday". It was the first time a tune had been played on a planet other than Earth.

Also on this day

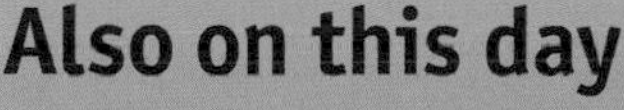

1963 The UK, the USA, and the Soviet Union signed an international treaty restricting the testing of nuclear weapons to underground sites.

1993 Magic: The Gathering, the first-ever trading card game, was launched.

Born this day

1962 Patrick Ewing, Jamaican-American basketball player and coach. He played for the New York Knicks for 15 years, and won two Olympic gold medals in 1984 and 1992.

1888 Motoring history

German entrepreneur Bertha Benz completed the first long-distance journey in an automobile when she drove 104 km (65 miles) from Mannheim to Pforzheim in Germany to test the Benz Patent-Motorwagen – the world's first factory-built motor vehicle.

August 6

1926

Speedy swimmer

US athlete Gertrude Ederle became the first woman to swim the English Channel, beating the men's record by two hours. During her swim, she faced huge waves, freezing temperatures, and jellyfish.

Born this day

1955 Lucille Ball, US actor. A well-known entertainer, she starred in popular sitcoms and was the first woman to lead a major Hollywood studio.

1945 Attack on Hiroshima

During World War II, the USA dropped an atomic bomb – the first one used in war – on Hiroshima, Japan. Almost 80,000 people died immediately. Thousands more later died from radiation exposure.

1960

Do the Twist

After Black American singer Chubby Checker performed "The Twist" on *The Dick Clark Show*, a new dance trend, involving a twisting movement of the hips, spread across the USA.

Also on this day

1965 US president Lyndon Johnson signed the Voting Rights Act, making it illegal for election officials to discriminate against Black voters.

1991 The world's first website went live – it was created by British computer scientist Tim Berners-Lee.

2015 Scientists in Hong Kong revealed the first interactive ant map, which tracked the whereabouts of ants all around the world.

August 7

High wire walk

1974

To the astonishment of people watching 400 m (1,312 ft) below, French tightrope artist Philippe Petit walked on a wire strung between the tops of the towers of the World Trade Center in New York City, USA.

1942

Talking in code

During World War II, a US marine unit with 15 Navajo code talkers landed on the Pacific island of Guadalcanal to help fight against Japan. The code talkers used the Navajo language to encode US military messages, as Japanese forces could not understand it.

Born this day

1975 Charlize Theron, South African-American actor and producer. She won an Academy Award for Best Actress for her work.

Also on this day

1819 Venezuelan general Simón Bolívar defeated Spanish forces at the Battle of Boyacá, which helped free Venezuela and Colombia from Spanish rule.

1987 US swimmer Lynne Cox became the first person to swim between the USA and the Soviet Union.

1996 After studying a Martian meteorite that landed in Antarctica, scientists announced they had found strong evidence that simple life forms may have existed on Mars more than 3.6 billion years ago.

1948

Historic jump

US athlete Alice Coachman became the first Black woman to win an Olympic gold medal with her victory in the high jump event at the London Olympic Games. Her 1.68 m (5.6 ft) leap set a world record at the time.

August 8

1876 Electric pen

US inventor Thomas Edison patented an electric pen that made stencils of documents, which could then be used to make copies. It was one of the first copying machines.

1709 Flying balloon

Brazilian priest Bartolomeu de Gusmão demonstrated the first flight of a model hot-air balloon, which rose about 4 m (13 ft) into the air.

Born this day

1879 Emiliano Zapata, Mexican revolutionary. During the Mexican Revolution, he fought for the right of peasants to own land.

1969 Faye Wong, Chinese singer and actor. Also called the "Diva of Asia", she has written and sung many songs in Cantonese and Mandarin.

Also on this day

1963 A British gang stole more than £2 million from a train on its way to London in what is now called the Great Train Robbery.

1967 The Association of Southeast Asian Nations (ASEAN) was founded to promote development in the region.

1988 Protesters seeking democracy took to the streets in the People Power Uprising in Burma (Myanmar), demanding an end to military rule.

1992 Dream team

A star-studded US basketball team won gold at the Olympic Games in Barcelona, Spain. Considered to be one of the best basketball squads ever put together, the group featured top players of the time, including Michael Jordan and Magic Johnson.

August 9

2019 Ace acrobat

At the US National Gymnastics Championships in Kansas City, USA, gymnast Simone Biles stunned the judges and the audience by pulling off a "double-double" dismount on the balance beam – a feat that had never been performed in a competition before.

Born this day

1914 Tove Jansson, Finnish author and cartoonist. She wrote a series of books and comic strips featuring a family of hippo-like characters called the Moomins.

1993 Dipa Karmakar, Indian gymnast. She was the first female Indian gymnast to compete at the Olympics.

Blue jeans 1872

US entrepreneur Levi Strauss and tailor Jacob Davis filed a patent for a pair of durable trousers made out of a thick cotton fabric called denim for the workers in California's gold mines. Denim jeans have since become an everyday item of clothing.

Also on this day

1942 Indian leader Mahatma Gandhi launched the Quit India Movement, demanding an end to British rule in India.

1945 US forces dropped a second atomic bomb – code-named "Fat Man" – over Nagasaki, Japan, during World War II.

2007 The bald eagle was removed from the US list of Threatened and Endangered Species after successful efforts to protect its habitat.

Super sprinter 1936

Black American sprinter Jesse Owens won his fourth gold medal in the 4x100 m relay race at the Berlin Olympics, after winning the 100 m, 200 m, and long jump events. His victories challenged German leader Adolf Hitler's views on white supremacy.

August 10

1937

Rock on!

The first electric guitar, known as the Rickenbacker Frying Pan, was patented by US inventor G D Beauchamp. A versatile instrument, the electric guitar revolutionized 20th-century music.

1993

Champion of justice

US lawyer Ruth Bader Ginsburg was sworn in as an Associate Justice of the US Supreme Court. She championed women's rights and dedicated her career to tackling gender inequality.

Sinking shocker

1628

Crowds watched in horror as the Swedish warship *Vasa* sank within 20 minutes of setting sail for the first time. According to modern archaeologists, its bronze cannons and ornamentation made it too heavy.

Also on this day

1792 Protesters stormed the king's residence at the Tuileries Palace in Paris, France, during the French Revolution.

1924 The Summer Deaflympics was held in Paris, France. Nine countries took part in the first games for Deaf athletes.

2017 A 100-year-old fruit cake, left by British explorers, was discovered preserved in Antarctica by scientists from New Zealand.

Born this day

1962 Suzanne Collins, US writer. She began her career writing for children's television shows and is best known for *The Hunger Games* series of books.

August 11

Also on this day

1858 The Eiger in the Swiss Alps was conquered by mountaineers. Irishman Charles Barrington and Swiss mountain guides Christian Almer and Peter Bohren became the first people to scale the 3,967 m (13,015 ft) tall mountain.

1919 Germany's first president, Friedrich Ebert, signed the Weimar Constitution into law, which gave all adult citizens the right to vote in elections.

1934 The first group of 137 prisoners was sent to the Alcatraz Federal Penitentiary, a maximum-security prison on Alcatraz Island in the San Francisco Bay, USA.

1929 Baseball legend

US baseball player George Herman Ruth, Jr, also known as Babe Ruth, hit his 500th home run at League Park, Cleveland, USA, becoming the first player to do so in Major League Baseball.

2019 Zooming ahead

Winning two out of six races, British racing driver Jamie Chadwick earned 110 points to win the first-ever W Series championship, a women-only Formula 3 racing competition held in Europe.

Born this day

1965 Viola Davis, Black American actor. The first Black American to win the trio of a Tony Award, an Emmy Award, and an Academy Award, she has starred in many plays, TV series, and films.

Total eclipse 1999

Seen by 350 million people around the world, the last solar eclipse of the 20th century lasted 2 minutes and 23 seconds.

August 12

1883

Lost species

The last living quagga, a type of South African zebra hunted to extinction in the wild, died at the Natura Artis Magistra zoo in Amsterdam, Netherlands.

Also on this day

1990 One of the largest-ever *Tyrannosaurus rex* fossils, nicknamed "Sue", was discovered in South Dakota, USA.

2016 Scientists declared they had found the longest-living vertebrate animal – a nearly 400-year-old Greenland shark.

2018 NASA's *Parker* Solar Probe was launched to study the Sun. Travelling to the Sun at a speed of 690,000 kph (428,746 mph), it became the fastest human-made object in history.

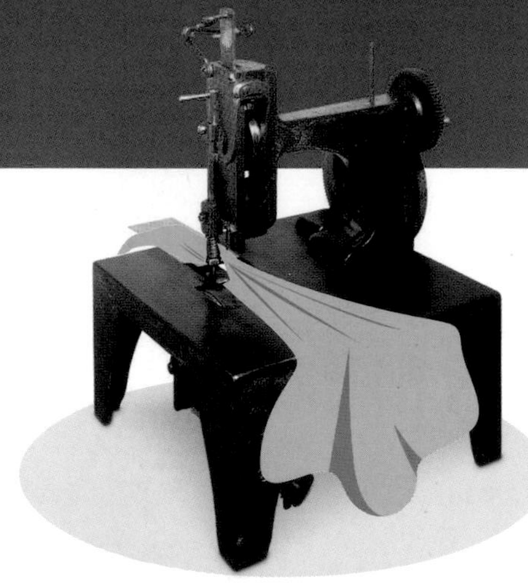

1851 Smart sewing

US inventor Isaac Merritt Singer received a patent for his sewing machine, which improved upon existing designs. It held the fabric in place and had a needle that moved up and down very quickly.

Born this day

1911 Mario Moreno, Mexican actor. Better known by his stage name Cantinflas, he was one of Latin America's most popular comedians.

1865 Antiseptic revolution

British surgeon Joseph Lister sprayed a chemical called carbolic acid on his patient's wounds during surgery, preventing infection by harmful airborne microorganisms. Lister's first antiseptic was soon widely used, and death rates dropped dramatically.

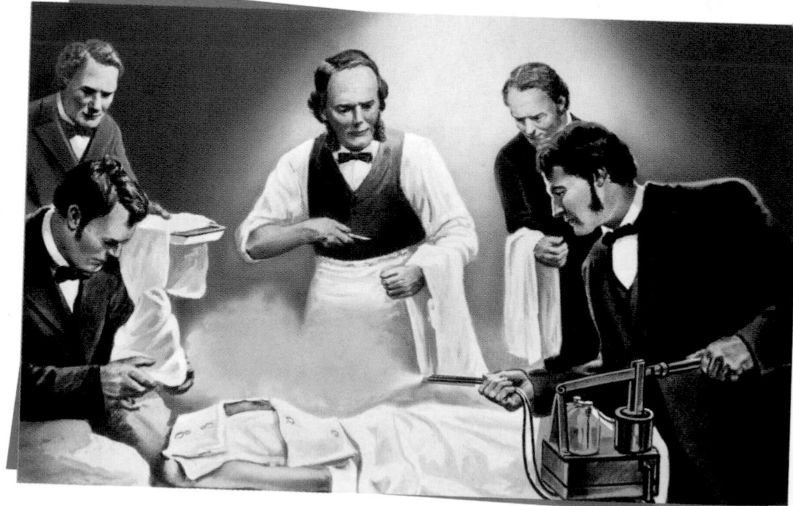

August

13

1961 Berlin Wall

To prevent people from leaving Soviet-controlled East Berlin for West Berlin (controlled by the UK, USA, and France), Soviet forces began to build a wall around West Berlin. It became a symbol of the Cold War, until it fell in 1989.

Also on this day

1512 The Spanish army conquered the capital city of the Aztec Empire, Tenochtitlán (in present day Mexico), leading to Spanish rule in the region.

1918 Opha May Johnson of Indiana, USA, became the first woman to join the US Marine Corps when she enlisted during World War I.

2003 Canadian stunt artist Scott Hammell escaped from a straitjacket while hanging from a hot-air balloon 2,195 m (7,200 ft) above ground.

1976 Left-handers united

US soldier Dean R Campbell established International Left-Handers Day. This annual celebration of left-handed people is an occasion to raise awareness about the challenges they may face in their daily lives.

Olympic champion 2016

At the Olympic Games in Rio de Janeiro, Brazil, US swimmer Michael Phelps won his 23rd Olympic gold medal. He has won more Olympic gold medals than any other athlete.

Born this day

1860 Annie Oakley, US sharpshooter. She travelled across the USA with the *Wild West* show, entertaining audiences with her shooting skills.

1899 Alfred Hitchcock, British film director, producer, and screenwriter. He directed more than 50 thrillers, gripping audiences worldwide.

August 14

1880 Cologne Cathedral

The construction of this cathedral, the world's tallest twin-spired church, was finished after 632 years of work. This German landmark attracts nearly 20,000 visitors a day.

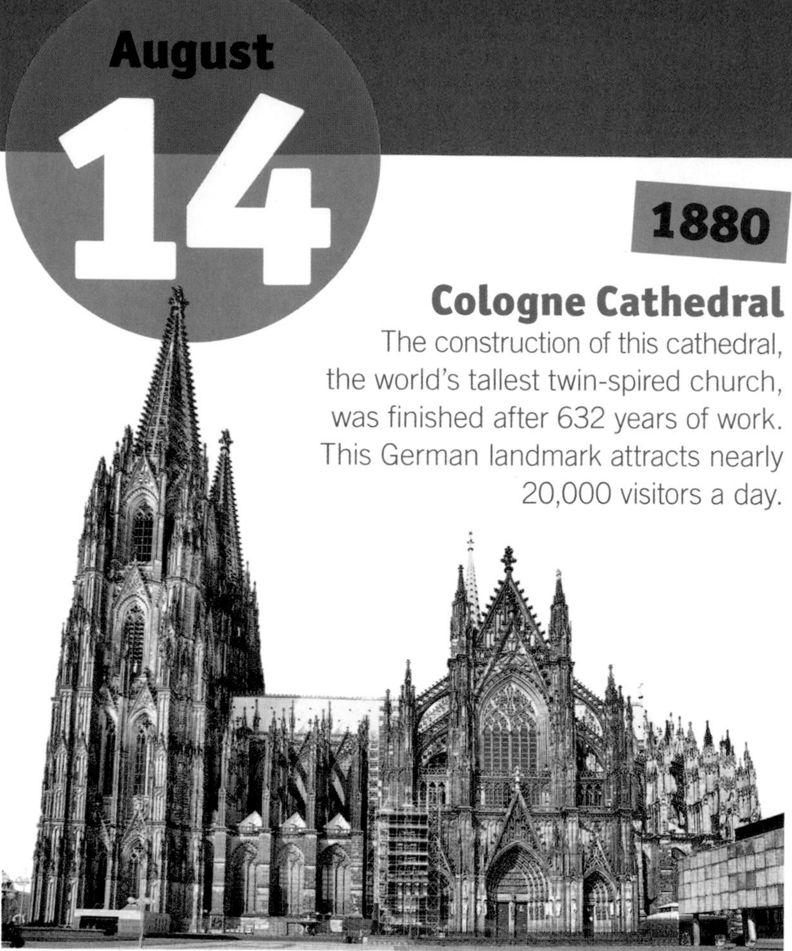

2019 Plastic raindrops

Scientists reported that they had found tiny plastic particles called microplastics in rainfall in Boulder, Colorado, USA. Less than 5 mm (0.2 in) in size, microplastics are harmful to humans and animals if eaten.

Born this day

1959 Earvin "Magic" Johnson, Black American basketball player. During his 13-year career, he played for the Los Angeles Lakers, and won gold at the 1992 Olympic Games.

Golden sprint 2016

At the Olympic Games in Rio de Janeiro, Brazil, Jamaican sprinter Usain Bolt won the 100 m event in just 9.81 seconds. It earned him his third consecutive gold medal for the 100 m sprint after wins at the 2008 and 2012 Olympics.

Also on this day

1281 While invading Japan, Mongol forces led by Kublai Khan faced a typhoon at sea, losing most of their ships. The Japanese believed that the invading fleet was destroyed by divine winds, or *kamikaze*.

1945 Japan surrendered to the Allied forces, ending World War II, following the US bombings of the cities of Hiroshima and Nagasaki.

August

15

1947 The partition of India

When granting independence to the Indian subcontinent, the British partitioned (divided) the region into two countries based on religion – Muslim-majority Pakistan and Hindu-majority India. Millions were forced to leave their homes and move to the newly formed countries, with many travelling in jam-packed trains.

Born this day

1964 Melinda French Gates, US humanitarian. As a co-founder of the Bill and Melinda Gates Foundation, she has worked to improve gender equality and health care.

Small carnivore 2013

Scientists at the Smithsonian in the USA announced the discovery of a meat-eating mammal called the olinguito. This relative of the raccoon uses its large eyes and sharp claws to hunt prey in the forests of Colombia and Ecuador.

Also on this day

1914 The Panama Canal, a 77 km (48 mile) waterway, opened to ships. The canal connected the Pacific and Atlantic oceans by cutting across Panama. Previously, ships had to sail all the way around South America.

1948 The first elected government of South Korea was formed, led by President Syngman Rhee, ending a period of US military rule.

1969 Woodstock Festival

More than 400,000 music fans gathered in a farm in Bethel, New York, USA, to watch rock 'n' roll stars such as Jimi Hendrix (above), The Who, the Grateful Dead, and Janis Joplin. This festival is remembered as one of the greatest moments in music history.

August

16

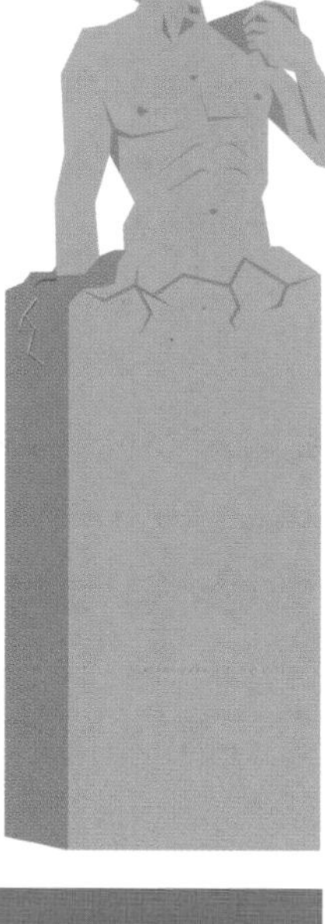

1501

Marble masterpiece

Italian Renaissance artist Michelangelo was asked to carve a statue from a 5.2 m (17 ft) tall block of marble in Florence, Italy. The sculpture, called *David*, took him three years to complete.

Also on this day

1858 The first transatlantic telegram was sent from the UK to the USA via 4,000 km (2,500 miles) of cable under the Atlantic Ocean.

1896 Three men discovered gold in a tributary of the Klondike River in Yukon, Canada, setting off the Klondike Gold Rush.

2007 Chinese officials reported that a couple had named their baby "@" (at), which translates as "love him" in Chinese.

Born this day

1958 Madonna, US singer, songwriter, and actor. Known for frequently changing her image, the "queen of Pop" has sold more than 300 million records worldwide.

1994

First smartphone

A personal digital assistant (PDA) called "IBM Simon" was launched by US tech company IBM. It could make phone calls, send and receive emails and faxes, and take notes. This PDA is now considered the world's first smartphone.

2018

Gollum fish

After severe flooding in Kerala, India, locals discovered a new species of fish that had been flushed out of its underground habitat. The Gollum snakehead was named after the underground-dwelling character from the fantasy book *The Lord of the Rings*.

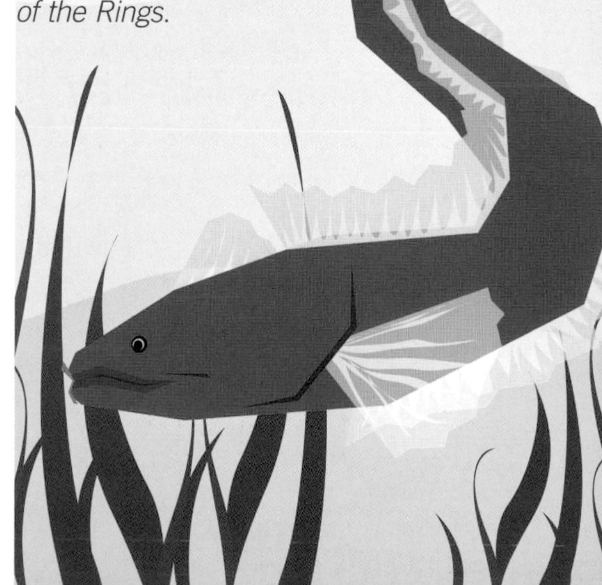

August 17

Also on this day

1612 One of the most famous witch trials in England began in Pendle, Lancashire, UK. Of the 10 people accused of witchcraft, all but one were found guilty and executed.

2015 A study of the fossils of *Montsechia vidalii*, a prehistoric plant, revealed that it grew 125 million years ago, making it one of the world's oldest flowering plants.

1908 Early animation

Fantasmagorie – the world's first hand-drawn animated film – was released. Created by French cartoonist and animator Émile Cohl, it featured a stick figure that interacted with different objects and characters.

1807 Full steam ahead!

A steam-powered boat called the *Clermont*, built by US engineer Robert Fulton, set out from New York City, USA, to ferry passengers along a 64 km (40 mile) stretch of the Hudson River to Albany, USA. This was the first commercial use of a steamboat.

1959 Road safety

Nils Bohlin of Swedish car company Volvo filed a patent for his three-point seatbelt design. Instead of charging their competitors money to use the design, Volvo made the patent free for all, which made it a standard safety feature in cars today.

Born this day

1992 Saraya Jade-Bevis, British wrestler. Known as Paige, she is the youngest winner of the WWE Divas Championship and the NXT Women's Championship.

August

18

1805

Taking to the skies

French aviator Sophie Blanchard began her career as the first female professional hot-air balloonist when she flew by herself for the first time, over Toulouse, France.

1931

New rose

Henry Bosenberg of New Jersey, USA, was granted the first plant patent for the new variety of rose he had created, called New Dawn. This plant produces silvery pink roses that bloom throughout the year.

Born this day

1911 Amelia Boynton Robinson, Black American civil rights activist. She led three protest marches from Selma, Alabama, USA.

1988 Kwon Ji-yong, South Korean rapper and producer. Known by his stage name G-Dragon, he found fame with the band Big Bang, before releasing his first solo album in 2009.

Also on this day

1590 On returning to Roanoke, USA, colonist John White discovered that everyone in the English settlement had mysteriously disappeared.

2005 A massive power outage on the Indonesian islands of Java and Bali left nearly 120 million people in darkness.

2019 A memorial service was held for the Okjökull glacier in Iceland, after it melted away following the country's warmest summer on record.

1920

Last tug of the rope

Tug-of-war was played as an Olympic sport for the last time at the Antwerp Olympics in Belgium, with Great Britain winning against the Netherlands.

August 19

1934

Soap Box Derby

The first All-American Soap Box Derby was held in Dayton, USA, with children driving homemade cars propelled only by gravity. First down the hill to become championship winner was 11-year-old Robert Turner, in a wooden vehicle running on buggy wheels.

Also on this day

1839 French photographer Louis Daguerre showcased his invention of daguerreotypes – camera images produced by chemical reactions on silver plates.

1887 Russian chemist Dmitri Mendeleev flew solo in a hot-air balloon to watch a solar eclipse in the skies over Russia.

1931 Water levels reached a height of 16 m (53 ft) during devastating floods in China, which affected millions.

Olympic cricket

The only cricket match played at the Olympics took place at the Vélodrome de Vincennes stadium in Paris, France. Great Britain beat France by 158 runs.

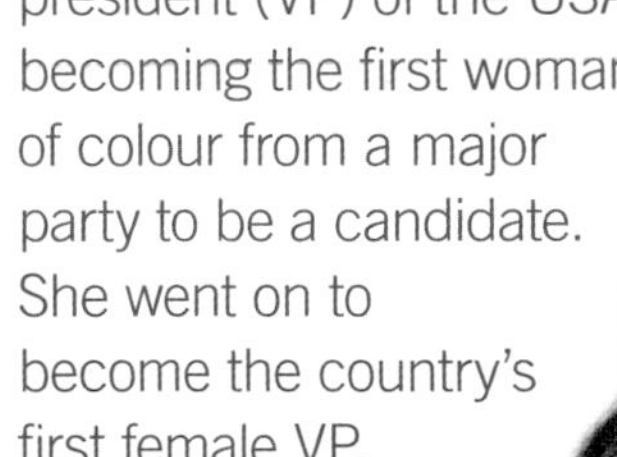

Born this day

1883 Coco Chanel, French fashion designer. She founded the Chanel brand, and is famous for her designs of handbags, perfumes, and clothing, including the "little black dress".

Harris for vice president

2020

Following a successful career as a lawyer and politician, Kamala Harris accepted the nomination for vice president (VP) of the USA, becoming the first woman of colour from a major party to be a candidate. She went on to become the country's first female VP.

August

20

1999 Off the danger list

The peregrine falcon was removed from a list of endangered species by the US Fish and Wildlife Service. Its formerly declining populations had recovered thanks to protection provided by the Endangered Species Act and a ban on harmful pesticides.

Born this day

1992 Demi Lovato, US singer and actor. They began their career on television before topping the charts as a pop singer. Lovato is a campaigner for the LGBTQ+ community.

1922 Women's World Games

The first international competition in track and field sports for women was held in Paris, France. About 15,000 spectators gathered to watch the female athletes in action.

Also on this day

636 The Battle of Yarmouk resulted in victory for Arab forces, bringing an end to the Byzantine Empire in Syria.

1619 The first group of enslaved people from Africa arrived at the British colony of Virginia in North America.

1897 British doctor Ronald Ross found the parasite that causes the disease malaria in the stomach of a female *Anopheles* mosquito.

Climate strike 2018

Fifteen-year-old Greta Thunberg skipped school to sit outside the Swedish parliament in Stockholm, with a homemade placard announcing a "school strike for climate". Her campaigns seeking action to tackle climate change have sparked a global movement.

August

21

1961 Kenyan freedom leader

After nine years in prison, Jomo Kenyata was released by British authorities. The leader of the Kenyan independence movement, he was instrumental in freeing his country from British rule.

Also on this day

1968 The Prague Spring in Czechoslovakia (present-day Czechia) – a series of mass demonstrations for political reform – came to an end when Soviet forces invaded and took back control.

1986 Lake Nyos in Cameroon suddenly released a dense gas cloud of carbon dioxide, known as a limnic eruption, suffocating people and farm animals in nearby villages.

2018 Scientists confirmed that the Indian spacecraft ***Chandrayaan-1*** had detected the first water ice on the Moon.

Calculating machine 1888

US inventor William S Burroughs patented the first successful calculator. Although adding machines were already available, this device was more accurate, consistently giving correct answers.

Missing Mona Lisa 1911

The world-famous painting by Renaissance artist Leonardo da Vinci was stolen from the Louvre Museum in Paris, France. Spanish artist Pablo Picasso was suspected after he was found buying items stolen from the museum. He was later cleared of the charges.

Born this day

1986 Usain Bolt, Jamaican athlete. He is considered one of the greatest sprinters of all time, winning numerous Olympic gold medals in the 100 m and 200 m events.

August

22

Cadillac cars

1902

One of the first car makers, the Cadillac Motor Company, was founded by US engineer Henry Leland. The luxury car company was the first to sell vehicles with lights and an electric ignition to start the engine.

Also on this day

1642 English king Charles I raised his flag above Nottingham Castle, UK. It was an act of war against Parliament and triggered the first English Civil War.

1963 NASA's *X-15* rocket plane set a world record by reaching an altitude of 108 km (67 miles).

1993 Jeanne-Marie Ruth-Rolland of the Central African Republic became the first woman to run for president in an African country.

Haitian hero

1791

A revolt by enslaved people of colony of Saint-Domingue marked the start of the Haitian Revolution. Gifted military general Toussaint Louverture led the struggle for the country's independence from French rule.

Legendary pirates

1720

Irish pirate Anne Bonney, together with British pirate Mary Read, took part in capturing the sailing boat *William* in the Caribbean islands. Both women found fame with their swashbuckling adventures during the Golden Age of Piracy.

Born this day

980 Ibn Sina/Avicenna, Muslim thinker and scientist. He wrote The *Canon of Medicine*, which medical students used for centuries.

1898

Southern Cross Expedition

Led by Anglo-Norwegian explorer Carsten Borchgrevink, the first British expedition to Antarctica set sail on a ship called *Southern Cross*. Its crew was the first to spend winter on the Antarctic mainland.

Also on this day

1942 The Battle of Stalingrad began as Soviet forces fought the Nazis for control of the Russian city of Stalingrad.

1966 The first photograph of Earth taken from orbit around the Moon was captured by NASA's robotic spacecraft *Lunar Orbiter 1*.

1991 The World Wide Web was opened to the public by its inventor, Tim Berners-Lee.

Born this day

1769 Georges Cuvier, French naturalist. He made important contributions to the study of fossils and proved that it was possible for species to become extinct.

1988 Jeremy Lin, US basketball player. He is the first Asian American to win a National Basketball Association (NBA) championship.

2007

Hashtag tweet

The hashtag (#) symbol was first used in a tweet when US blogger Chris Messina posted "#barcamp" on the social media site Twitter.

1989

Baltic chain

About 2 million people sang and held hands to form a human chain stretching more than 600 km (373 miles) through the countries of Estonia, Latvia, and Lithuania. The protest demonstrated their shared goal of independence from Soviet rule.

August

24

Egyptian hieroglyphs

394 CE

To celebrate Osiris – the ancient Egyptian god of the dead – an inscription was carved into a wall at the Temple of Isis in Egypt. Called the Graffito of Esmet-Akhom, it is the last known inscription written in hieroglyphics.

Also on this day

410 CE The Germanic Visigoths sacked the city of Rome. It was the first time in 800 years Rome had fallen to an enemy.

1821 The signing of the Treaty of Córdoba led to the end of Spanish rule in Mexico.

2006 Pluto was reclassified as a dwarf planet rather than a planet after the official definition of a planet was changed.

Born this day

1945 Marsha P Johnson, Black American drag queen. She led many campaigns fighting for equal rights for the LGBTQ+ community.

1957 Stephen Fry, British actor and mental health activist. An award-winning performer, he voiced all seven of the audiobooks for the *Harry Potter* series of novels.

1967 Cool customers

As temperatures soared during summer in London, UK, two penguins from Chessington Zoo – Rocky the Rockhopper penguin and his friend – enjoyed a day trip to a nearby ice rink to cool down.

August 25

1609 Telescope on show

Italian astronomer Galileo Galilei demonstrated his first telescope to Venetian merchants. He pointed his telescope up to the sky, using it to study the Sun, the Moon, and other objects in space.

1958 Fast food

Branded as Chikin Ramen, instant noodles in a packet were launched by Taiwanese-Japanese entrepreneur Momofuku Ando. About 13 million packets were sold within the first year.

Born this day

1927 Althea Gibson, Black American tennis player. She was the first Black American to win the French Open, Wimbledon, and the US Open.

1958 Tim Burton, US director and writer. He is known for the quirky characters in his fantasy films, and has revamped many classic stories, such as *Alice in Wonderland*.

2006 Tallest tree

Two US biologists found the world's tallest living tree – later named Hyperion – in Redwood National Park, USA. The location of this 116 m (379 ft) tall tree is secret. It is thought to be between 600 and 800 years old.

Also on this day

1944 The city of Paris, France, was freed by Allied forces during World War II, ending four years of Nazi occupation.

2012 NASA space probe *Voyager 1* became the first human-made object to reach interstellar space.

2017 Hundreds of thousands of Rohingya Muslims began to flee Myanmar, crossing the border into Bangladesh, to escape persecution by the Myanmar military.

August 26

1346

Battle of Crécy

In one conflict of the Hundred Years' War, the French army launched an attack on invading English troops travelling through northern France. English soldiers made the fast-loading longbow their weapon of choice at the Battle of Crécy, resulting in a convincing victory.

Born this day

1918 Katherine Johnson, Black American mathematician. Among the first Black women to work at NASA, she made calculations that were crucial to the flights of the *Friendship 7* craft, the *Apollo* spacecraft, and the Space Shuttle.

Also on this day

1789 ***The Declaration of the Rights of Man and of the Citizen*** was published by the French Assembly to establish universal equality and liberty in the country.

1914 In the Battle of Tannenberg, which began on this date, German troops defeated the Russian army to achieve their greatest victory of World War I.

2018 British explorer Ash Dykes set off to walk the entire length of the Yangtze River in China, completing the journey of 6,437 km (3,999 miles) almost a year later.

1959

Mini moment

The Morris Mini-Minor was officially shown to the public by the British Motor Corporation. Nicknamed the Mini, this compact car proved a hit with its attractive design, affordable price, and room for four passengers.

August 27

1869 Racing boats

The first international boat race took place on the River Thames in England. The UK's Oxford University beat the USA's Harvard University to the finish line. The race was widely reported in US newspapers.

Born this day

1908 Don Bradman, Australian cricketer. During his career, he racked up an incredible batting average of 99.94 runs per inning.

1958 Sergei Krikalev, cosmonaut (Russian astronaut). He has undertaken six space flights and spent 803 days in Earth's orbit.

1914 Modern zip

Swedish-American engineer Gideon Sundback filed an application to patent his invention of the zip. This was the first metallic fastener suited to everyday use and it transformed clothing, shoes, and bags in the years to come.

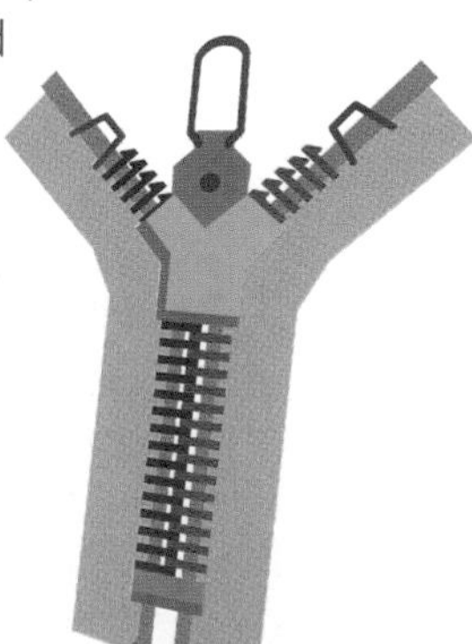

1883 Violent volcano

One of the most destructive volcanic eruptions reached its peak on the small Indonesian island of Krakatoa. More than 36,000 people died from the eruption and the tsunamis that followed.

Also on this day

1689 The Treaty of Nerchinsk was signed by Russia and China. It opened trade links to exchange goods between the two nations.

1896 The Anglo-Zanzibar War ended within just 45 minutes, making it the shortest war on record.

1964 A fantastical film about a magical nanny, ***Mary Poppins***, premiered in Los Angeles, USA.

August

28

1963 Civil rights speech

Black American civil rights leader Martin Luther King, Jr gave his most important speech to 250,000 people. His passionate "I have a dream..." speech called for an end to racial discrimination.

2020 Flying car

Japanese technology company SkyDrive completed the first test flight of its new flying car. The electric vehicle was flown by a pilot over the Toyota Test Field.

Born this day

1965 Shania Twain, Canadian singer and songwriter. She brought country music to the masses, selling more than 100 million records.

Steam power 1830

A steam locomotive named *Tom Thumb* raced a horse-drawn railway car in the USA. The locomotive broke down and was overtaken by the horse, but onlookers were still impressed. The local railway company replaced its horses with locomotives within a year.

Also on this day

1859 The Carrington Event, the strongest solar storm ever to hit Earth, disrupted power supplies and telegraph networks.

1980 An MRI (magnetic resonance imaging) machine was first used to scan the body of a patient, at the Aberdeen Royal Infirmary in Scotland.

2017 Kenya introduced the world's strictest measure against plastic pollution – with anyone found using plastic bags facing four years in prison or a US $40,000 fine.

August 29

1854 Revolutionary windmill

The Self-Governing Windmill was patented by US inventor Daniel Halladay. His efficient design could turn itself automatically to face the changing winds and control how fast the blades rotated.

Born this day

1993 Liam Payne, British singer and songwriter. He rose to fame as a member of the successful pop band One Direction.

1997 Netflix launch

US entrepreneurs Reed Hastings and Marc Randolph founded Netflix. At first, the company rented out movies, sending them by post to film fans, but it's now an online video streaming service with more than 200 million subscribers.

Food fight! 1945

Now the world's biggest food fight, the annual festival of *La Tomatina* was first held in Buñol, Spain, when people at a fancy dress parade started throwing tomatoes. Each year, thousands of people travel to Buñol to hurl millions of tomatoes at each other.

Also on this day

1833 The Factory Act in Britain set new rules to improve the conditions for children working in factories and reduce their working hours.

1949 The Soviet Union successfully detonated RDS-1, the country's first atomic bomb, at a test site in Kazakhstan.

2005 With winds topping 200 kph (125 mph), Hurricane Katrina caused destruction and flooding in New Orleans, USA, and along the Louisiana coastline.

August 30

1983

Space success

When US Air Force pilot and astronaut Guion S Bluford, Jr launched into orbit aboard Space Shuttle *Challenger*, he became the first Black American to go into space.

1906

Expert explorer

Norwegian explorer Roald Amundsen became the first person to sail through the Arctic waterway called the Northwest Passage after searching for the route for three years. Five years later, he would lead the first successful expedition to the South Pole.

Also on this day

1835 The city of Melbourne was founded by European settlers in Australia. This date is now celebrated annually as Melbourne Day.

1941 World War II code breakers at Bletchley Park in the UK, intercepted a message that helped break the cipher used by Germany's Lorenz machine, giving Allied forces access to the Nazis' secret information.

Born this day

1797 Mary Shelley, British author. She wrote the classic novel *Frankenstein*, which has been adapted into many films and plays.

1972 Cameron Diaz, US actor. She has starred in many comedies and dramas, including *Charlie's Angels*, and voiced the part of Princess Fiona in *Shrek*.

1904

Marathon secret

US runner Fred Lorz crossed the finish line first to win the Olympic marathon in St Louis, USA. Soon after, he admitted cheating by catching a lift in his manager's car for about 18 km (11 miles) of the race, so he was disqualified.

August 31

Moving pictures 1897

US inventor Thomas Edison patented a device called the kinetoscope, which was an early version of the film projector. It created moving pictures visible through an eyepiece.

Born this day

1975 Sara Ramirez, Mexican-American actor. They have starred in Broadway musicals and TV dramas, and have campaigned for the LGBTQ+ community.

Princess's day 1885

The fifth birthday of Princess Wilhelmina was celebrated as the first Princess's Day in the Netherlands. This national holiday changes date according to the ruling monarch's birthday. On this day, people wear orange clothes to celebrate the royal family.

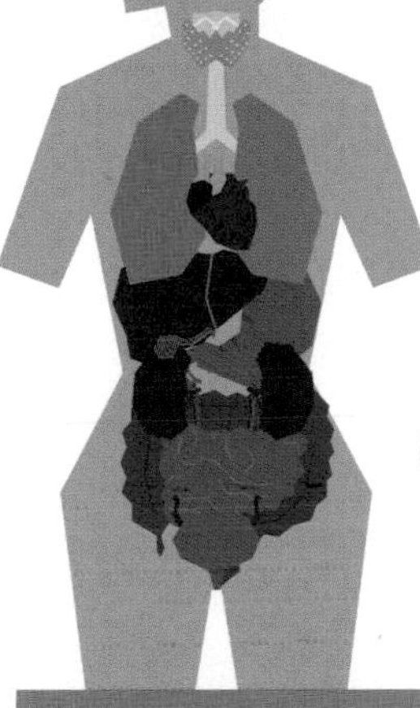

1968 Breakthrough surgery

In the world's first multi-organ transplant, US surgeon Michael DeBakey used the heart, a lung, and two kidneys from a single donor to help four different patients.

Also on this day

1943 US Navy ship USS *Harmon* was commissioned, taking its name from heroic wartime sailor Leonard Roy Harmon. It was the first navy vessel named after a Black American.

1955 The Sunmobile, the world's first solar-powered car, was demonstrated by car manufacturer General Motors at a show in Chicago, USA.

1997 A car crash in a tunnel in Paris, France, killed Diana, Princess of Wales, her partner, and the driver.

September 1

The great evacuation

1939

Days before Britain entered World War II, millions of people, mostly children, began to be evacuated from British towns and cities to the countryside to save them from anticipated German bombings.

Born this day

1996 Zendaya, US actor. She became a famous Disney star before playing Michelle Jones (or MJ) in *Spider-Man: Far From Home*.

Spring Temple Buddha

2008

After more than 10 years of construction, the Spring Temple Buddha was completed in Henan, China. With a height of 128 m (420 ft), it was the tallest statue in the world until 2018.

Turin race

1946

A Grand Prix motor race, held in Turin, Italy, was the first to follow a new set of rules that would later define Formula 1 (F1) racing.

Also on this day

1939 Germany invaded Poland. This act prompted Britain and France to declare war against Germany, starting World War II.

1941 In Nazi-occupied Europe, Jews were ordered to identify themselves by wearing a yellow, star-shaped badge on their clothes.

1985 The wreckage of the RMS *Titanic* was found at the bottom of the Atlantic Ocean.

A flying tank? 1942

The Soviet Union claimed to have carried out the first test flight of a flying tank called the Antonov A-40. Designers hoped that it could be dropped from an aircraft and glide down onto the battlefield.

Born this day

1948 Christa McAuliffe, US teacher and astronaut. She was the first teacher chosen to travel to space, but died when the Space Shuttle *Challenger* exploded after take-off.

1964 Keanu Reeves, Canadian actor. He rose to fame with starring roles in films such as *Bill & Ted's Excellent Adventure*, *Speed*, and *The Matrix*.

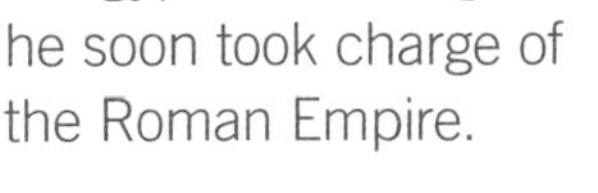

31 BCE Battle of Actium

In a naval battle off the coast of Actium, Greece, Roman leader Octavian defeated the joint forces of his rival Mark Antony and Queen Cleopatra of Egypt. Renaming himself Augustus, he soon took charge of the Roman Empire.

Space toys 2015

The first Danish astronaut to go to space, Andreas Mogensen, took 20 LEGO® figurines to the International Space Station (ISS), to be awarded as a competition prize to schoolchildren at the end of his mission.

Also on this day

1666 The Great Fire of London began at a bakery. It destroyed most of the city before it was put out.

1945 Vietnam declared its freedom from French colonial rule, after defeating the occupying Japanese forces at the end of World War II.

2013 US swimmer Diana Nyad became the first person to cross the shark-infested waters between Cuba and Florida, USA, without a shark cage for protection.

September 3

1838

Escape to freedom

Frederick Douglass, an enslaved Black American, escaped from a plantation in Maryland, USA, and made his way to freedom, travelling by train and boat to New York City. He became an important figure in the anti-slavery movement.

Born this day

1875 Ferdinand Porsche, Austrian-German automobile engineer. He founded the car company Porsche.

2010 Tanitoluwa Adewumi, Nigerian-American chess player. He was eight when he won the 2019 K-3 New York State chess championship.

1935 Record-breaking drive

At the Bonneville Salt Flats in Utah, USA, British racing driver Malcolm Campbell became the first person to hit the land speed milestone of 300 miles an hour when he reached a top speed of 485 kph (301 mph) in his custom-built car, the Campbell-Railton *Blue Bird*.

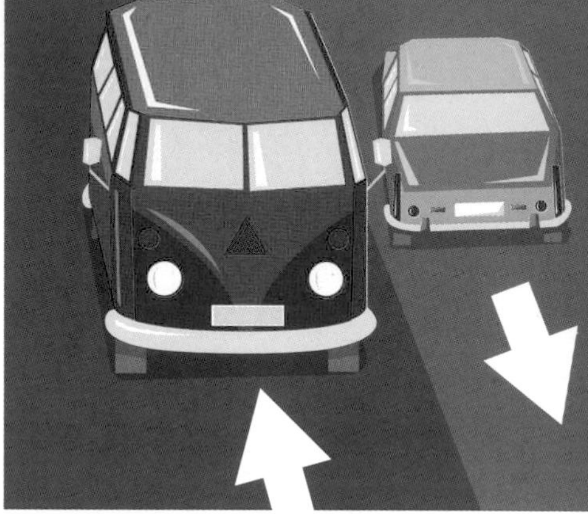

1967 Swedish switch

At 4:50 a.m., drivers in Sweden switched from driving on the left-hand side of the road to the right-hand side. This switch was followed by the massive task of changing road signs, traffic signals, street lights, and intersections across the country.

Also on this day

301 CE The world's oldest republic, the small nation of San Marino, was founded by Saint Marinus.

1260 The Mongol Empire was defeated in the Battle of Ayn Jalut in western Asia by the Mamluk Dynasty of Egypt.

1939 Britain and France declared war on Nazi Germany, officially kickstarting World War II, after Adolf Hitler invaded Poland.

September 4

476 CE Fall of Rome

Led by the Germanic soldier Odoacer, the Roman army revolted against Emperor Romulus Augustus and overthrew him, bringing an end to the Western Roman Empire.

Born this day

1913 Kenzō Tange, Japanese architect. He was known for combining traditional Japanese architectural styles with the modernism of the 20th century.

1886 End of a long struggle

Apache leader Geronimo finally surrendered to US military forces after a 30-year-long battle to protect the homelands of the Apache people. He had gained a fearsome reputation for being able to repel invasions of Apache land.

Also on this day

1957 The governor of Arkansas, USA, ordered the Arkansas National Guard to prevent a group of nine Black American students from attending Little Rock High School.

1998 The founders of Google officially listed the search engine as a company.

2002 Kelly Clarkson from Texas, USA, won the first season of the singing contest *American Idol*. She went on to become a bestselling artist.

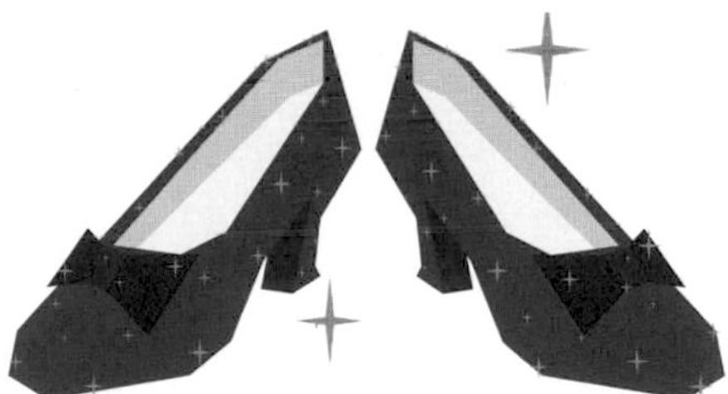

2018 Ruby slippers

The FBI announced that they had recovered the ruby red shoes worn by the character Dorothy in the film *The Wizard of Oz*. The shoes had been stolen from the Judy Garland Museum in Minnesota, USA, in 2005.

2014

Fiery stunt

South African stuntmen Enrico Schoeman and André de Kock drove through a 120 m (395 ft) long tunnel of fire in Parys, South Africa, setting a death-defying world record.

Also on this day

1882 In the USA's first Labor Day parade, 10,000 workers marched from City Hall to Union Square in New York City.

1972 At the Olympic Games in Munich, Germany, Palestinian terrorists took nine members of the Israeli team hostage.

1991 The Indigenous and Tribal Peoples Convention, an international treaty defending the rights of these marginalized groups, came into force.

1885 Petrol pump

US inventor Sylvanus Bowser sold a new device for dispensing kerosene (a type of fuel) to a grocery store owner in Fort Wayne, USA. By 1905, after cars began to be built, it had been converted into a petrol pump.

2007

Going to space

Yi So-yeon was selected for a South Korean space mission, beating more than 36,000 applicants. After completing her training, she set off in 2008 on board a Soyuz spacecraft to become the first Korean astronaut in space.

Born this day

1847 Jesse James, US criminal. He robbed several banks and trains, becoming a legendary outlaw.

1946 Freddie Mercury, British rock singer and songwriter. Known for his powerful voice, he found fame as the lead vocalist of the rock band Queen.

September 6

1593 Pirate queen

Queen Elizabeth I of England met Grace O'Malley (left), the Irish "pirate queen", and agreed to release her son from an English prison if she stopped attacking English vessels off Ireland.

1776 First submarine attack

During the American Revolutionary War, a submarine called *Turtle* set out to attack the British ship HMS *Eagle* in New York Harbor, USA, but failed in its mission.

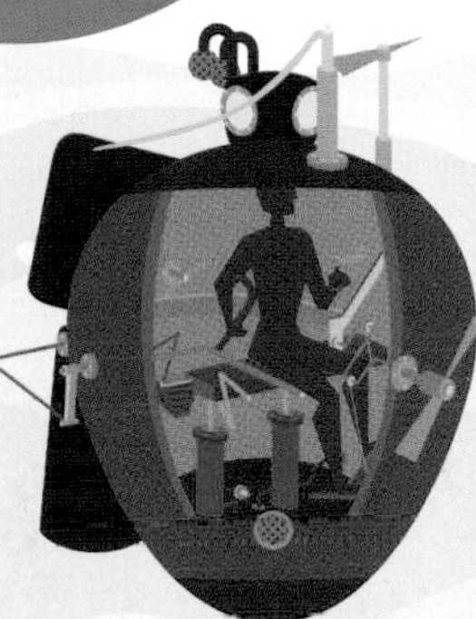

Also on this day

1620 A group of English families set sail on the *Mayflower* from Plymouth, England, on a voyage across the Atlantic Ocean to set up a new colony in North America.

1916 The world's first supermarket, Piggly Wiggly, opened in Memphis, USA.

1997 A huge crowd of more than a million people lined the streets of London, UK, during the funeral of Diana, Princess of Wales.

Born this day

1860 Jane Addams, US social reformer. She was the first US woman to win the Nobel Peace Prize for promoting international peace.

1972 Idris Elba, British actor. He has starred in many action and animation films.

1522 Sailing home

The ship *Victoria* returned to Spain after completing the first round-the-world trip in search of a western sea route to the Spice Islands of Indonesia.

September 7

1695 Pirates ahoy!

Notorious English pirate Henry "Long Ben" Every raided the *Ganj-i-Sawai*, the Mughal flagship loaded with treasures on its way to Surat, India. Every and his crew looted items equivalent to millions of pounds in today's currency, and were never heard from again.

1822 Emperor of Brazil

Defying the decision of Portugal's parliament, Portuguese prince Dom Pedro supported Brazil's desire for freedom and declared the country independent of Portugal. Pedro would become Brazil's emperor. Brazilians celebrate this date as their independence day.

Born this day

1943 Gloria Gaynor, Black American singer. One of the most prominent singers of the disco era, she is known for many hits, including the classic *I Will Survive*.

Also on this day

1812 French emperor Napoleon Bonaparte's army defeated Russian forces in the bloody Battle of Borodino in Russia.

1923 The International Criminal Police Organization, commonly known as INTERPOL, was founded in Vienna, Austria. It is the world's largest police organization and serves as a link between police departments around the world.

The Blitz begins 1940

During the early years of World War II, the Luftwaffe (German air force) began swift and targeted bombing of major cities in the UK, including London (below), Liverpool, and Portsmouth. The attack was called the Blitz, short for Blitzkrieg, the German word for "lightning war".

1966

Star Trek

The first episode of the science-fiction TV show *Star Trek* aired on US television. The show ran for only three seasons, but grew in popularity in the following years, leading to several spin-off shows and films.

Also on this day

1504 The statue of David, a masterpiece by Michelangelo, was unveiled outside the Palazzo Vecchio in Florence, Italy.

2020 The world's first lightsaber, resembling the fictional weapon from the *Star Wars* series, was created by Canada's Hacksmith Industries.

1916

Riding for a cause

Sisters Augusta and Adeline Van Buren completed an 8,900 km (5,500 mile) ride across the USA on their motorcycles to promote the idea that women could be employed as military riders during the ongoing World War I.

2013

Sporting champion

After winning the women's singles at the 2013 US Open, Black American tennis player Serena Williams became the world's highest-earning sportswoman, with prize money totalling more than US $50 million. This was her 17th career Grand Slam title.

Born this day

1979 Alecia Beth Moore, US singer and songwriter. Known by her stage name P!nk, she has sold more than 90 million records worldwide.

September 9

2009 Dubai Metro

The first urban rail system in the Arabian peninsula was launched in Dubai, UAE. Its first train ran through the city's business district.

2018 Legendary moment

US singer John Legend won an Emmy award to become the first Black American entertainer to achieve the celebrated EGOT – wins at the Emmy, Grammy, Oscar, and Tony awards.

Also on this day

1739 The Stono Rebellion, one of the largest uprisings of enslaved people in the British American colonies, began in South Carolina.

1940 US researcher George Stibitz, who coined the term "digital", demonstrated his new invention, the electrical digital computer.

1945 The second Sino-Japanese War ended with Japan's surrender to China at 9 a.m. on this date, the ninth day of the ninth month of this year. The Chinese character for nine means "long-lasting" – Japan hoped the peace between the nations would last for ever.

Battle of Svolder 1000

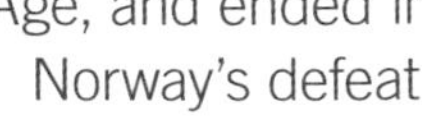

A combined fleet, which included Danish and Swedish ships, ambushed the warships of Norway's king Olaf Tryggvason in the Baltic Sea. The battle that followed was the largest naval conflict of the Viking Age, and ended in Norway's defeat.

Born this day

1969 Shane Warne, Australian cricketer. He was the first bowler to take 700 wickets in Test match cricket.

2008 Colliding particles

Scientists at CERN, in Geneva, Switzerland, switched on the Large Hadron Collider (LHC) for the first time. It is the world's largest particle accelerator, a machine that makes high-energy particles collide with one another so that scientists can study the fundamental forces of the Universe.

Born this day

1852 Alice Brown Davis, Indigenous American leader. She was the first female chief of the Seminole Nation of Oklahoma, USA.

1946 Mother Teresa

On a train ride in India from Kolkata to Darjeeling, Albanian Catholic nun Mother Teresa decided to devote her life to helping the poor and sick.

210 BCE First Emperor

Qin Shi Huang, an emperor of the Qin Dynasty and the first ruler of a united China, died. He had assumed the title of First Emperor after his army had defeated all other warring states.

Also on this day

1960 Ethiopian marathon runner Abebe Bikila became the first African athlete to win gold in the Olympic Games.

1984 British geneticist Alec Jeffreys discovered that DNA can be used to identify a person. His techniques helped develop forensic science.

September

11

2001 9/11 attacks

In the deadliest terror attack on record, members of the terrorist group al-Qaeda hijacked US passenger planes, crashing two of them into the World Trade Center's twin towers in New York City, USA (right), a third one into the Pentagon, and a fourth in Pennsylvania. Nearly 3,000 people were killed and around 25,000 suffered serious injuries.

1942 Famous Five

British author Enid Blyton published *Five on a Treasure Island*, the first book in her *Famous Five* series. These books, featuring the adventures of four children and their dog, would go on to sell more than 100 million copies.

Born this day

1945 Franz Beckenbauer, German footballer. One of the best players in footballing history, he helped Germany win the FIFA World Cup in 1974 as a player and in 1990 as the team manager.

Also on this day

1297 Scottish forces led by William Wallace and Andrew Moray defeated a larger English army during the First War of Scottish Independence.

1903 The Milwaukee Mile, a motor racetrack in Wisconsin, USA, held its first automobile race.

1973 Military officers led by General Augusto Pinochet seized control of Chile from the elected government, establishing a military dictatorship that lasted for 17 years.

September 12

1992 Black astronaut

Mae Jemison became the first Black American woman to travel to space when she was selected to be part of NASA's seven-person crew for the Space Shuttle *Endeavour*.

Born this day

1931 Ian Holm, British actor. Starting out in theatre, he went on to star in many films, including *The Lord of the Rings*.

1957 Hans Zimmer, German film score producer. One of the best-known composers in film, he has written music for more than 150 movies, including *The Lion King*.

490 BCE First marathon

After the first Persian invasion of Greece, the invaders were defeated at the Battle of Marathon. The best runner in the Greek camp, Pheidippides, ran 41 km (26 miles) from Marathon to Athens non-stop to deliver news of the victory. This run gave the modern-day marathon its name.

1940 Accidental discovery

While looking for hidden treasure in Montignac, France, a group of teenagers found a series of caves – now known as Lascaux – with ancient paintings on their walls. These paintings are nearly 17,000 years old.

Also on this day

1942 A German submarine sank the British ship RMS *Laconia* during World War II, killing more than 1,400 people.

2010 Tony Gonzalez became the first player in the USA's National Football League (NFL) to catch 1,000 passes in the "tight end" position.

2017 A 250 m (820 ft) long mass of solidified oil, grease, and plastics, nicknamed a "fatberg", was found blocking an underground sewer in London, UK.

September

13

1898

Photographic patent

The patent for camera film on celluloid rolls was given to US priest Hannibal Goodwin. This flexible, transparent film would later be used in movie-making machines.

1848

Shocking accident

US construction worker Phineas Gage was speared in the head by a metal rod in a workplace accident. Though Gage survived, his personality changed so dramatically afterwards that he became a case study for doctors researching the human brain.

Born this day

1857 Milton S Hershey, US chocolatier. He began his career in a sweet shop before setting up his own hugely successful company selling milk chocolate bars.

1916 Roald Dahl, British author. He ranks among the world's most popular writers, selling more than 250 million copies of his books, which include *Charlie and the Chocolate Factory.*

Also on this day

1940 During World War II, Italy invaded Egypt with the aim of expanding the Italian Empire, but it was defeated by the British.

1993 Ministers from Israel and Palestine signed a peace agreement in the White House, USA, following decades of conflict.

2004 US talk show host Oprah Winfrey gave away 276 new Pontiac G-6 cars to her studio audience.

2016

Turtle conservation

More than 200 royal turtles arrived at the Koh Kong Reptile Conservation Centre in Cambodia, as part of a breeding programme to increase their numbers. The species is almost extinct in the wild.

September 14

American chopper

1939

The first helicopter with rotor blades to successfully fly took off in Connecticut, USA. Invented and flown by Russian-American aircraft designer Igor Sikorsky, the pioneering VS-300 design was tethered to the ground for its first flight.

Born this day

1973 Nasir bin Olu Dara Jones, Black American rapper and songwriter. Known by his stage name Nas, he has sold more than 25 million records.

1975

Māori march

With the support of 50 followers, Māori leader Whina Cooper (centre right) began the Māori Land March on the North Island of New Zealand to protest against the sale of Māori land. Thousands of people joined Cooper during the month-long march to Parliament in Wellington.

Also on this day

786 Harun al-Rashid took charge as ruler of the Abbasid Caliphate, an Islamic empire that stretched across South Asia, North Africa, and Spain. His reign is considered the start of the Islamic Golden Age.

1814 Inspired by the War of 1812, US lawyer Francis Scott Key wrote a poem, which later became the *Star-Spangled Banner*, the USA's national anthem.

Golden toilet

2019

Thieves stole a fully functioning 18-carat solid gold toilet from Blenheim Palace in Oxfordshire, UK. Named *America*, the unique object was part of an art exhibition where visitors were each allowed three minutes to use the extravagant toilet.

September 15

1916 Tank fight

The Battle of Flers-Courcelette in France during World War I was the first conflict in which tanks were used. British forces deployed 49 Mark I tanks in the fight against German forces.

Born this day

1890 Agatha Christie, British crime author. She is the creator of the famous fictional detectives Hercule Poirot and Miss Marple.

1984 Prince Harry, Duke of Sussex and member of the British Royal Family. The second son of Prince Charles and Princess Diana, he served in the British Army in Afghanistan.

1830 Inter-city railway

Crowds watched the official opening of the steam-powered Liverpool and Manchester Railway, built to carry raw materials, goods, and passengers between the two cities. It was the world's first inter-city railway.

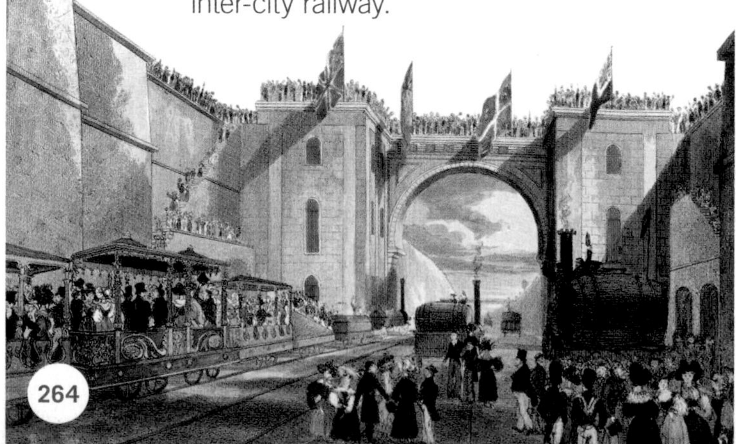

1983 Achoo!

British schoolgirl Donna Griffiths finally stopped sneezing after two years and 246 days. Her epic sneezing session saw her sneeze about a million times in the first year alone.

Also on this day

1821 The Act of Independence of Central America made Guatemala, Nicaragua, El Salvador, Costa Rica, and Honduras independent of Spain.

1935 The Nuremberg Laws were introduced by the Nazi Party, stripping German Jews of citizenship and taking away their rights.

1835 Galápagos trip

British naturalist Charles Darwin arrived at the Galápagos Islands near to South America to study the local plants and animals. He found that the tortoises there looked different depending on which island they lived – an observation that later led him to formulate his theory of evolution.

Born this day

1948 Julia Donaldson, British author. Her rhyming children's stories introduced popular characters such as the Gruffalo and Stick Man.

1992 Nick Jonas, US singer and actor. A member of the pop band The Jonas Brothers, he has also had success as a solo artist.

1979 Balloon escape

Against all odds, two families escaped the communist regime in East Germany using a homemade hot-air balloon. They flew over the border in the middle of the night and landed safely in West Germany.

1810 Cry of Dolores

Mexican priest Miguel Hidalgo asked the people of his parish in Dolores, Mexico, to fight against Spanish rule. His rallying call became known as *Grito de Dolores*, meaning "Cry of Dolores", and it triggered Mexico's War of Independence.

Also on this day

1400 Owain Glyndŵr was announced as the Prince of Wales, marking the start of the Welsh Revolt, which tried to end English rule in Wales.

1963 Malaysia was created by the merging of Malaya, Sabah, Sarawak, and Singapore.

1976 Armenian hero Shavarsh Karapetyan saved 20 people when he swam down to the bottom of Yerevan Lake, Armenia, after a bus fell into the water.

Red Baron

1916

German pilot Manfred von Richthofen shot down a British fighter plane over France, winning his first aerial combat. Nicknamed the Red Baron, the flying ace went on to win 80 dog fights during World War I.

Born this day

1960 Kevin Clash, US puppeteer. He provided the voice and actions for the furry red monster Elmo on the US TV show *Sesame Street*.

Swedish victory

1631

At the first Battle of Breitenfeld in Germany, Swedish king and military mastermind Gustavus Adolphus defeated the Holy Roman Emperor and his army. It was the first Protestant win during the Thirty Years' War – a period of religious conflict in Europe.

Also on this day

1683 Dutch scientist Antonie van Leeuwenhoek wrote to the Royal Society in London, UK, describing tiny "animalcules" – later understood to be the first microorganisms ever observed.

1978 The Camp David Accords were signed by the US president, Egyptian president, and Israeli prime minister to bring peace to the Middle East.

1787

New constitution

The US Constitution, detailing the nation's laws and principles, was signed by representatives from 12 states in Philadelphia, USA. This date is now remembered in the USA as Constitution Day.

We the People of the United
insure domestic Tranquility, provide for the common defence, promote
and our Posterity, do ordain and establish this Constitution for the United
Article. I.
Section. 1. All legislative Powers herein granted shall be vested in a
of Representatives.
Section. 2. The House of Representatives shall be composed of Members
in each State shall have the Qualifications requisite for Electors of the most numerous
No Person shall be a Representative who shall not have attained to
and who shall not, when elected, be an Inhabitant of that State in which he shall
Representatives and direct Taxes shall be apportioned among the several
Numbers, which shall be determined by adding to the whole Number of free Per
not taxed, three fifths of all other Persons. The actual Enumeration shall be

September 18

1960 Paralympic Games

In Rome, Italy, 400 disabled athletes from 23 countries gathered to compete in eight sports, including basketball and archery, at the ninth Stoke-Mandeville Games, now recognized as the first Paralympic Games.

Born this day

1976 Ronaldo, Brazilian footballer. One of the greatest strikers of all time, he was awarded FIFA Player of the Year three times.

Also on this day

1850 The US Congress passed the Fugitive Slave Act, requiring escaped enslaved people to be returned to their enslavers if captured.

1980 Cuban astronaut Arnaldo Tamayo Méndez became the first Latin American person to go into space.

2020 Archaeologists found ancient footprints in Saudi Arabia's Nefud Desert and dated them as 120,000 years old, providing the earliest evidence of humans in the Arabian Peninsula.

324 CE Constantine the Great

After defeating his rival Licinius at the Battle of Chrysopolis, Constantine I became emperor of the Roman Empire. He built a new capital city called Constantinople (modern-day Istanbul, Turkey), which flourished for centuries.

1793 Capitol cornerstone

George Washington, the first president of the USA, laid the foundation stone of the Capitol building in Washington, DC. It took nearly a century to complete, and is now where the US House of Representatives and Senate meet.

September 19

1783

Balloon experiment

A sheep, a rooster, and a duck took to the skies in the first hot-air balloon flight to carry living things. Launched by French aviators Joseph and Jacques Montgolfier, the balloon floated in the air for about eight minutes before landing safely.

1946

Council of Europe

Following World War II, Winston Churchill gave a speech in Zurich, Switzerland, calling for Europe to unite. It set off a series of events that, in 1949, led to the formation of a council to promote unity, democracy, and human rights throughout the continent.

Born this day

1965 Sunita Williams, US astronaut. On her first two missions, she spent 322 days in space and made seven spacewalks.

Unlikely winner

2000

Despite being the lowest-ranked swimmer at the Sydney Olympics, Eric Moussambani of Equatorial Guinea won his qualifying event for the 100 m freestyle when his fellow competitors were disqualified for false starts.

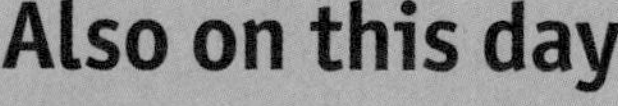

Also on this day

1893 A new electoral act was signed into law in New Zealand, making it the first country in the world to allow women voting rights for parliamentary elections.

1940 Polish officer Witold Pilecki allowed himself to be captured and held at Auschwitz concentration camp to uncover information about the conditions inside.

1991 The frozen body of a prehistoric human, now called Ötzi the Iceman, was discovered in the Ötztal Alps.

2014 HeForShe

British actor and UN Women Goodwill Ambassador Emma Watson delivered an inspiring speech to give a public face to the HeForShe campaign, which encourages men and boys to join the fight for gender equality for women.

1973

King vs Riggs

In a famous tennis match, top women's singles player Billie Jean King beat Bobby Riggs, a former No. 1 men's singles player, who had claimed he could defeat any female player.

Born this day

1934 Sophia Loren, Italian actor. She starred in many Italian and Hollywood films, and was the first to win an Oscar for Best Actress for a non-English film.

2019 Polar expedition

The German ship *Polarstern* set sail from Norway with a team of researchers from 20 countries for the MOSAiC expedition. The goal was to stay trapped in the polar ice and drift across the Arctic Ocean for a year to study the impact of climate change.

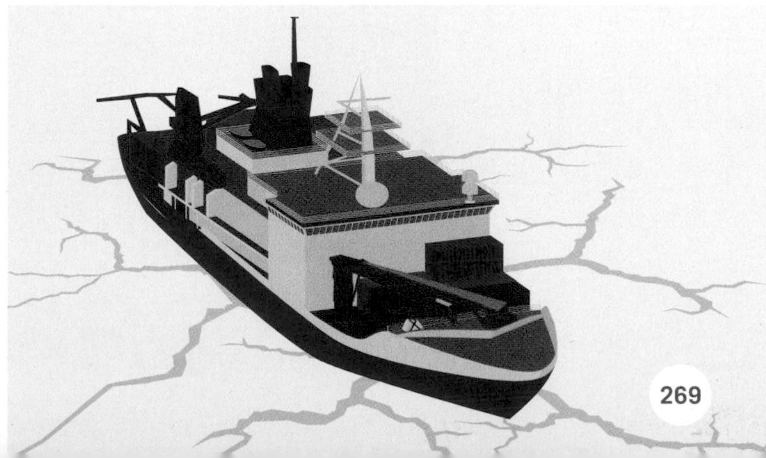

Also on this day

1857 The army of the East India Company recaptured Delhi, suppressing the Indian Rebellion, the first major uprising against British colonial rule.

2001 Following the 9/11 terrorist attacks in the USA, President George W Bush announced a "War on Terror".

2019 Ahead of a UN summit on climate change, about 4 million people – led by schoolchildren – took part in a global climate strike.

September 21

1937

The Hobbit

British fantasy writer J R R Tolkien's novel *The Hobbit* was published. It introduced readers to Middle Earth and Bilbo Baggins's quest for treasure guarded by the dragon Smaug.

1912

Incredible stunt

Hungarian-American illusionist Harry Houdini first performed his Chinese Water Torture Cell stunt in Berlin, Germany. To the astonishment of those watching, he escaped a water tank after being lowered into it upside down with his feet locked.

Born this day

1979 Chris Gayle, West Indian cricketer. He was the first to score centuries in all three forms of the game.

1898

Empress Dowager

Chinese emperor Guangxu's adoptive mother, the Empress Dowager Cixi, opposed his Hundred Days of Reform, which sought to modernize China. She imprisoned him and took charge of the Qing Dynasty.

Also on this day

1522 The New Testament of the Bible was translated from Latin into German by German reformer Martin Luther, making it more accessible.

1792 The French legislative assembly voted to abolish the monarchy one year after most of King Louis XVI's powers had been taken away.

2018 Japan became the first country to land robots on an asteroid. These tiny rovers took pictures to send back to Earth.

September

22

1762

Russian coronation

After seizing power from her husband, Catherine II was crowned empress of Russia at a grand ceremony in Moscow. Catherine the Great ruled for 34 years, expanding her empire so that it became the largest in the world.

1968

Abu Simbel

A UNESCO-led team of engineers completed reassembling the massive Abu Simbel temple in Egypt. It was raised 64 m (210 ft) above its original location to save it from the waters of the human-made Lake Nasser.

Born this day

1791 Michael Faraday, British scientist. He discovered how electrical currents could be created using magnets, and invented the electric motor.

2000

World Car-Free Day

To draw attention to the impact of cars on the environment, people in more than 700 cities across the world cycled, walked, or took public transport instead of driving their cars on the first World Car-Free Day.

Also on this day

1948 US pilot Gail Halvorsen made his first flight to drop bundles of sweets in tiny parachutes made from handkerchiefs over West Berlin after being given permission by the US Air Force. The packages were meant for children affected by the Berlin Blockade that had been put in place by the Soviet Union.

1991 Photographs of the Dead Sea Scrolls, religious manuscripts dating to Biblical times, were made public for the first time.

Discovering Neptune 1846

German astronomer Johann Gottfried Galle spotted Neptune using a telescope at the Berlin Observatory in Berlin, Germany. He had used mathematical calculations made by French astronomer Urbain Jean Joseph Le Verrier and British astronomer John Couch Adams to locate the planet.

2018 Sign Language Day

Following a request by the World Federation of the Deaf, the United Nations (UN) declared this date the International Day of Sign Languages, recognizing the need to preserve languages used by the Deaf to communicate.

Born this day

1930 Ray Charles, Black American singer and musician. After being blinded in childhood, he turned to music and went on to pioneer soul music in the USA.

1889 Nintendo founded

Entrepreneur Fusajiro Yamauchi founded a company called Nintendo in Kyoto, Japan. It began by producing playing cards for the Japanese game *Hanafuda*, but eventually became a computer game giant, creating some of the world's most successful video games, such as *Super Mario*.

Also on this day

1338 The first naval battle using artillery was fought between an English ship and a French fleet during the Hundred Years' War.

1884 US inventor Herman Hollerith filed a patent for a machine that could process data, long before the first computer was invented.

2000 With his win in Sydney, Australia, British athlete Steve Redgrave became the first rower to win a gold medal in five consecutive Olympic Games.

September

24

1957 Little Rock Nine

In Arkansas, USA, after racial segregation had been prohibited by the US Supreme Court, US Army soldiers stepped in to protect nine Black American students who were being prevented from attending the previously white-only Little Rock High School by a white mob.

Test of endurance 1974

The first modern-day triathlon was held in California, USA. Contestants ran 8.5 km (5.3 miles), then cycled for 8 km (5 miles), and finally swam 548 m (1,800 ft) in the Pacific Ocean to complete the race.

Born this day

1936 Jim Henson, US puppeteer and filmmaker. He created the popular TV puppet characters called the Muppets, including Kermit the Frog, Miss Piggy, and Cookie Monster.

Also on this day

1852 A steam-powered airship, built by French engineer Henri Giffard, took its first flight from Paris to Elancourt, France, travelling 27 km (17 miles) at a speed of 10 kph (6 mph).

1948 Japanese industrialist Soichiro Honda founded The Honda Motor Company.

2014 India's *Mangalyaan* space probe entered orbit around Mars after a 298-day journey, making India the first country in the world to achieve this feat on its first attempt.

1906 First national monument

US president Theodore Roosevelt declared Devils Tower, a 1,558 m (5,112 ft) tall igneous rock formation in Wyoming, USA, as the first US national monument, now protected by the US National Park Service.

September 25

2020

Scanning faces

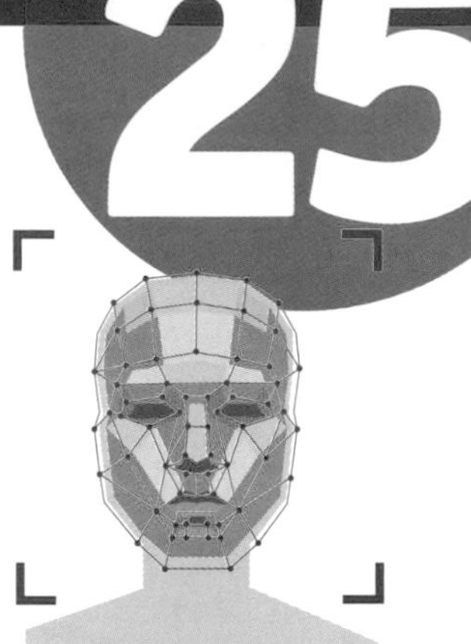

The government of Singapore announced plans to begin using facial recognition software to verify the identities of its citizens.

1790

Peking opera

Four opera troupes from China's Anhui province performed a style of musical theatre called Hui opera for the 80th birthday of the Qianlong Emperor, the fifth ruler of the Qin Dynasty. It developed to become Peking opera, which combines music, speech, dance, and acrobatics performed by costumed actors.

Born this day

1968 Will Smith, Black American actor and rapper. He found fame in the TV series *The Fresh Prince of Bel-Air*, before starring in a string of action and drama films.

Sprinting record

2000

At the Sydney Olympics, Indigenous Australian sprinter Cathy Freeman raced to victory in the 400 m final in 49.11 seconds, becoming the first Indigenous Australian to win an Olympic gold medal in an individual sport.

Also on this day

1956 The world's first transatlantic telephone call via cable was made between North America and the UK over 3,584 km (2,226 miles) of deep-sea cable laid at the bottom of the Atlantic Ocean.

2016 The world's largest radio telescope, called FAST, began operating in Guizhou, China. Its reflector dish, which is as large as 30 football pitches, is used to search for signs of alien life in outer space.

September 26

Aerial feat 2008

Dropping from an aircraft above Calais, France, Swiss pilot Yves Rossy used one of his inventions – a set of carbon-fibre wings powered by four jet engines – to fly 35 km (22 miles) across the English Channel, landing in the British town of Dover.

2009 Bottle ban

Stores in the town of Bundanoon, Australia, stopped selling bottled water, making the town the first place in the world to enforce a ban on plastic bottles, which harm the environment.

Also on this day

1887 US journalist Nellie Bly entered an asylum as an undercover patient to reveal the harsh treatment of people suffering from mental illnesses.

1905 German-born US physicist Albert Einstein published a research paper introducing his theory of special relativity, which is concerned with the nature of space and time.

1969 ***Abbey Road***, the final studio album recorded by British band The Beatles, was released.

Born this day

1981 Serena Williams, Black American tennis player. She has won 23 women's singles Grand Slams, the second-highest number of titles in tennis history.

2018 Feathered giants

A research paper in the *Royal Society Open Science* journal confirmed that the elephant birds of Madagascar were the largest birds ever to have lived. These flightless birds, which died out more than 1,000 years ago, were 3 m (10 ft) in height.

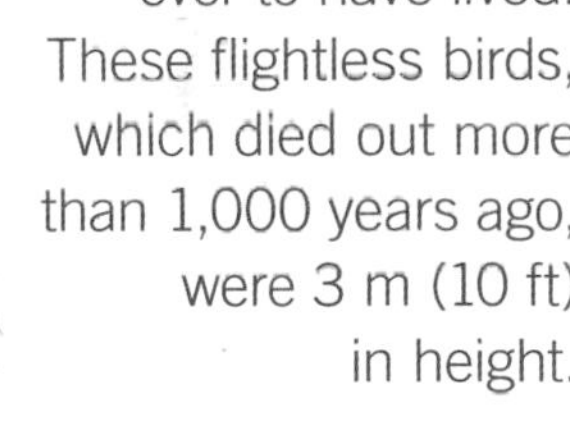

September 27

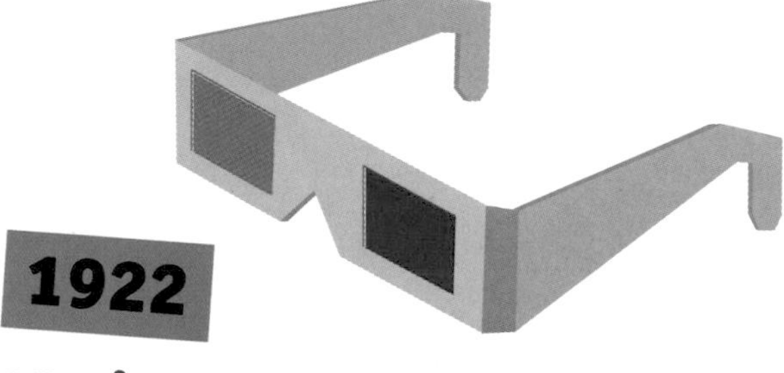

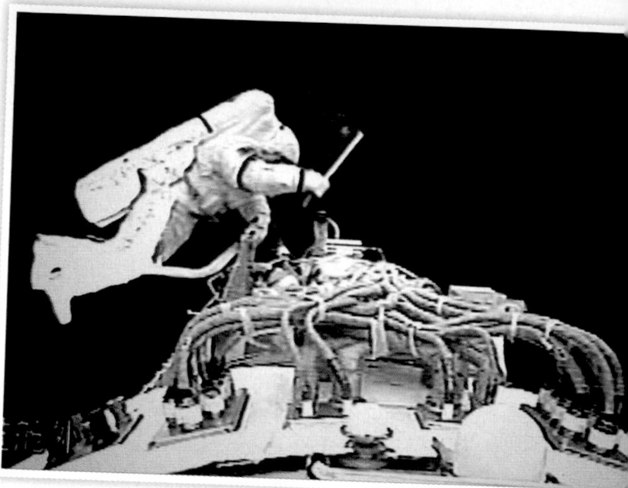

1922

3D cinema

The Power of Love, the world's first 3D film, premiered at the Ambassador Hotel Theater in Los Angeles, USA. Special glasses with one red lens and one green one enabled the audience to see in 3D.

Born this day

1972 Gwyneth Paltrow, US actor. She won an Oscar for Best Actress in 1999 and has played the role of Pepper Potts in several Marvel films.

Also on this day

1825 The Stockton and Darlington Railway, the world's first public railway system with steam engines, opened to the public in England.

1940 Germany, Italy, and Japan signed the Tripartite Pact, forming the World War II alliance called the Axis powers.

1962 US conservationist Rachel Carson published *Silent Spring*. The book highlighted the environmental damage caused by pesticides.

Walking in space

2008

Taikonaut (Chinese astronaut) Zhai Zhigang became the first person from China to perform a spacewalk. He was the commander of the craft *Shenzhou 7*, which was the third Chinese human spaceflight mission.

1937

Extinct tiger

The Balinese tiger was declared extinct when the last living member of its species – an adult female – was killed in Bali, Indonesia. The reasons for it dying out were excessive hunting and the loss of its forest habitat due to human activities.

Also on this day

1889 The length of a metre was officially established by the General Conference on Weights and Measures (CGPM) in France.

2008 The Formula One motorsport race hosted its first-ever night race at the Singapore Grand Prix.

2018 The melting of ice caps in the Arctic Ocean made it possible for a container ship, the *Venta Maersk*, to pass through Arctic waters for the first time.

1924 World flight

Four US Army Air Service aircraft returned to Seattle, USA, after completing the first flight around the globe. The mission was accomplished in 175 days, with the crew braving extreme weather conditions along the way.

1928 Making antibiotics

When Scottish scientist Alexander Fleming noticed a type of mould killing bacteria in a Petri dish, he realized he could use it for medical purposes. He called the substance it produced "penicillin", which became the first antibiotic.

Born this day

551 BCE Confucius, Chinese philosopher. A celebrated thinker, he set up schools to teach young scholars, and his teachings came to be known as Confucianism.

1538 Fierce warrior

At the Battle of Preveza, Turkish admiral Hayreddin Barbarossa commanded a victorious fleet, defending the Ottoman Empire against Christian forces. Also known as Redbeard, he was feared throughout the Mediterranean.

September

29

Bobby's peelers

1829

Dressed in blue suits and top hats, the first police officers in the world took to the streets of London, UK, after British politician Robert Peel launched his crime-fighting team – the Metropolitan Police Force.

Seeing the Pacific

1513

While hunting for gold in South America, Spanish explorer Vasco Núñez de Balboa crossed a strip of land called the Isthmus of Panama on foot and became the first European to see the Pacific Ocean. He claimed it for Spain, calling it the South Sea.

Born this day

1758 Horatio Nelson, British Navy commander. He led his ships to victory in a number of battles, most notably in the Battle of Trafalgar against France and Spain.

Also on this day

1916 US oil tycoon John D Rockefeller became the first-ever US dollar billionaire.

2004 Asteroid 4179 Toutatis passed by Earth at a distance of about 1.5 million km (961,000 miles) – just four times the distance between Earth and the Moon.

2020 Scientists discovered three underground lakes on Mars using radar on the orbiting *Mars Express* spacecraft. They think these lakes must be very salty, as salt prevents water from freezing at low temperatures.

September 30

2004

Sea monster!

A rare, gigantic squid known as *Architeuthis* was photographed in its natural habitat for the first time by scientists in Tokyo, Japan.

Also on this day

1935 The Boulder Dam – the largest concrete structure in the world at the time – was opened in the USA by President Franklin D Roosevelt.

1949 The Berlin airlift ended after 15 months. This military operation during the Cold War saw US and British troops delivering rations to needy citizens in Soviet-surrounded West Berlin, Germany.

1960 *The Flintstones*, an animated TV show set in the Stone Age, premiered in the USA.

1520

Suleiman the Magnificent

Suleiman I began his reign as sultan of the Ottoman Empire, which was ruled from what is now Turkey. A notable leader in 16th-century Europe, he promoted the development of the arts, architecture, and law in his vast dominion.

Born this day

1980 Martina Hingis, Swiss tennis player. She competed in her first tournament aged four and has won more than 90 Women's Tennis Association (WTA) titles.

1968

Boeing 747

The first jumbo jet was revealed to the public in Washington, USA, kickstarting a new era in commercial air travel. With a tail as high as a six-storey building and a wing area bigger than a basketball court, the Boeing 747 was the largest airliner at the time.

October

1

1908

Ford Model T

The Ford Model T was introduced by US industrialist Henry Ford. It would become the world's first car to be made on an assembly line, resulting in fast and cheap production.

Also on this day

331 BCE At the Battle of Gaugamela (in modern-day Iraq), the Macedonian forces of Alexander the Great defeated the Persian army, led by King Darius III.

1982 The compact disc (CD), developed by multimedia companies Philips and Sony to store and play audio, was first released in Japan.

1989 Denmark became the first country to allow same-sex couples to register themselves as domestic partners.

Born this day

1959 Youssou N'Dour, Senegalese singer, songwriter, and musician. He helped develop a style of popular Senegalese music called *mbalax*.

1990

Giant explosion

Satellites recorded a 90 tonne meteor exploding over the Pacific Ocean, with a blast force greater than 900 tonnes of powerful explosives.

Bullet train

1964

The Tōkaidō Shinkansen, Japan's first high-speed train, started running. Popularly called the "bullet train", it could travel at a speed of 220 kph (137 mph), covering the distance between Tokyo and Osaka in just four hours.

1949 Modern China

The Chairman of the Chinese Communist Party (CCP), Mao Zedong, declared the creation of the People's Republic of China.

October 2

Also on this day

1870 The city of Rome was made a part of the Kingdom of Italy, ending nearly 1,000 years of rule by the Roman Catholic Church.

1967 Thurgood Marshall was sworn in as the first Black American US Supreme Court Justice.

2018 US scientist Arthur Ashkin was pronounced the winner of the Nobel Prize in Physics for his invention of optical tweezers, microscopic devices with "arms" made of lasers, which can grab tiny particles such as atoms, viruses, or cells.

1866

Open it up

At a time when most canned goods were sold in iron cans that had to be opened with a hammer and chisel, US inventor J Osterhoudt patented a tin can with a tab, which could be opened simply by rolling back the lid.

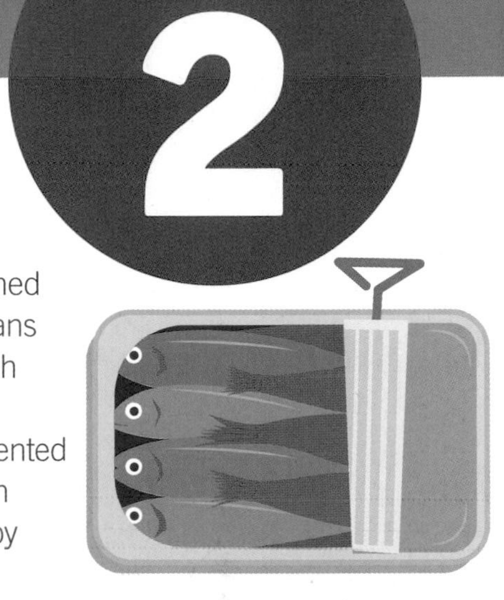

1925

Artist on the rise

Josephine Baker, a Black American dancer, performed for the first time in the La Revue Nègre, a dance show in Paris, France. It made her an instant celebrity.

1608

Early telescope

German-Dutch eyeglass maker Hans Lipperhey applied for a patent for an early model of a telescope, a device that enabled distant objects to be seen clearly.

Born this day

1869 Mohandas Karamchand Gandhi, Indian activist. Known as Mahatma Gandhi, he led a movement of non-violent resistance against British colonial rule in India.

October 3

1888

The Haka

Wearing all black, the New Zealand Native rugby team performed the haka (a traditional ceremonial dance of the Māori people) for the first time before an international match. The impressive ritual continues to this day.

Also on this day

42 BCE To avenge the death of Roman general Julius Caesar, his supporters fought his assassins in the first Battle of Philippi.

1904 Black American civil rights activist Mary McLeod Bethune opened her first school for Black American girls in Daytona Beach, Florida, USA.

Born this day

1969 Gwen Stefani, US singer and songwriter. She found fame in the band No Doubt, with hit singles such as *Don't Speak*, before launching a successful solo career.

1983 Tessa Thompson, Black American actor. She is known for playing Valkyrie in the Marvel movies.

1990

A nation reunited

Following the collapse of the Soviet Union, East and West Germany, which had been separated for 45 years, came together to form a united German nation.

Ancient kingdom

1949

The Republic of Korea celebrated Gaecheonjeol (National Foundation Day) for the first time. It honoured the legendary founding of the ancient Korean kingdom of Gojoseon by the king Dangun Wanggeom in 2333 BCE.

1883 Luxury travel

The *Orient Express*, a long-distance luxury rail service, made its first journey from Paris, France, to Istanbul, Turkey. Considered a glamorous way to travel, the train became the setting of many books, films, and TV shows.

1957

Space Age begins

The Soviet Union launched the world's first human-made satellite, *Sputnik I*, into Earth's orbit, kickstarting the Space Age – a new era of space exploration.

Also on this day

1853 The Crimean War began when the Ottoman Empire, joined by its allies, declared war on Russia over control of the Middle East.

1986 The Oosterscheldekering, a 9 km (5.5 mile) long dam that forms part of Delta Works, was inaugurated by Queen Beatrix of the Netherlands. The Delta Works is a large system of dams and sea walls designed to protect the low-lying Netherlands from being flooded by seawater.

Born this day

1946 Susan Sarandon, US actor and social activist. She has starred in many award-winning drama films, and is known for her charity work in fighting world hunger.

1927 National monument

The faces of four of the USA's most honoured presidents – George Washington, Thomas Jefferson, Theodore Roosevelt, and Abraham Lincoln – began to be carved on the peak of Mount Rushmore in South Dakota, USA. It took 12 years for the monument to be completed.

October 5

2006

Prehistoric hunter

Researchers announced the discovery of the first-ever complete skeleton of a fossilized plesiosaur, an ancient short-necked marine reptile. They had found the remains of this 10 m (33 ft) long predator on Norway's Svalbard Islands in the Arctic Ocean.

Born this day

1975 Kate Winslet, British actor. In a TV and film career that has spanned more than two decades, she has won an Oscar, an Emmy, three BAFTAs, and four Golden Globes.

1789

March on Versailles

Angered by how expensive and rare bread had become, the women in the markets of Paris, France, marched to the Palace of Versailles in protest. It became one of the most important events of the French Revolution.

Tasmanian devil

A news article announced that 26 Tasmanian devils had been successfully reintroduced into the wild on mainland Australia. For nearly 3,000 years, the species had only been found on the island of Tasmania.

Also on this day

1910 The Portuguese Republican Party seized power, overthrowing the country's monarchy and forming the First Portuguese Republic.

1962 British rock band The Beatles released their first single *Love Me Do* in the UK. It debuted at number 17 on the UK music charts.

1962 ***Dr No*, the first movie in the *James Bond* film series**, was released. Scottish actor Sean Connery starred as the famous spy.

October 6

Also on this day

2001 Thirty students in Nelspruit, South Africa, set a world record when they pushed a soapbox cart across 2,061 km (1,280 miles) to Cape Town, the country's capital.

2010 Scientists revealed they had discovered more than 200 new species of animals and plants on the islands of Papua New Guinea.

2010 The social media platform Instagram launched, with more than 25,000 users signing up on the first day.

2007 Incredible journey

When he returned to Greenwich, UK, British explorer Jason Lewis became the first person to circumnavigate (travel all the way around) the globe using only human muscle power – by skating, cycling, walking, and kayaking. Starting at Greenwich, he had travelled nearly 75,000 km (46,600 miles) in 4,833 days.

1829 Revolutionary Rocket

British engineer Robert Stephenson's steam-powered locomotive – the *Rocket* – won the Rainhill Trials, a competition to decide the type of engine to be used on the Liverpool and Manchester Railway. It had wheels that ran on railway tracks.

Born this day

2000 Jazz Jennings, US transgender activist and YouTube personality. One of the youngest people to publicly identify as transgender in the USA, Jazz faced struggles growing up as a transgender teenager, documented in the reality show *I Am Jazz*. She champions the rights of LGBTQ+ youth.

October 7

1959 Dark side of the Moon

The Soviet Union's *Luna 3* space probe took the first photographs of the Moon's far side, which is not visible from Earth.

2018 A new Doctor

British actor Jodie Whittaker appeared on screen for the first time as the 13th Doctor in the British science-fiction TV series *Doctor Who*. She was the first female actor to portray the famous Time Lord.

Born this day

1991 Zhang Yixing, Chinese singer and actor. Known by his stage name Lay Zhang, he found fame as a member of different pop groups before having a successful solo career.

Also on this day

2000 The first annual World Cyber Games, a global e-sports competition, began in Yongin, South Korea.

2001 Following the 9/11 attacks in the USA, US and British forces began bombing targets in Afghanistan to weaken the terrorist group called the Taliban.

2010 Researchers announced that the *Paris japonica* flower has the world's longest genetic code, 50 times longer than that of a human.

Battle of Lepanto 1571

An alliance of Spanish and Italian forces defeated the Ottoman Empire in a naval battle off the coast of Lepanto, Greece. One of the largest naval conflicts in history, it was also one of the last to be fought almost entirely using rowing vessels.

2004

Peace prize

It was announced that Kenyan activist Wangari Maathai would be awarded the Nobel Peace Prize for sustainable development in Kenya through her Green Belt Movement.

1906

Making waves

In London, UK, German hairdresser Karl Nessler showed off his new invention – a device that could make a person's hair wavy. It worked by heating the hair wrapped around its brass rollers, resulting in wavy or curly hair.

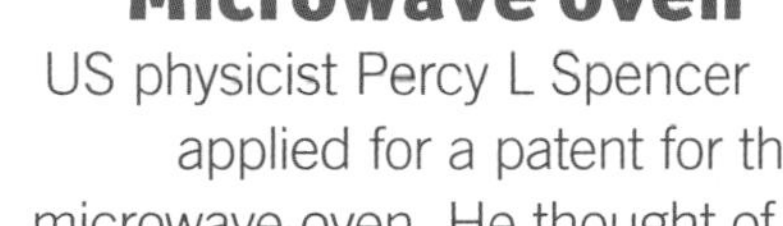

Microwave oven

1945

US physicist Percy L Spencer applied for a patent for the world's first microwave oven. He thought of cooking food with microwaves after seeing a chocolate bar melt near a radar machine.

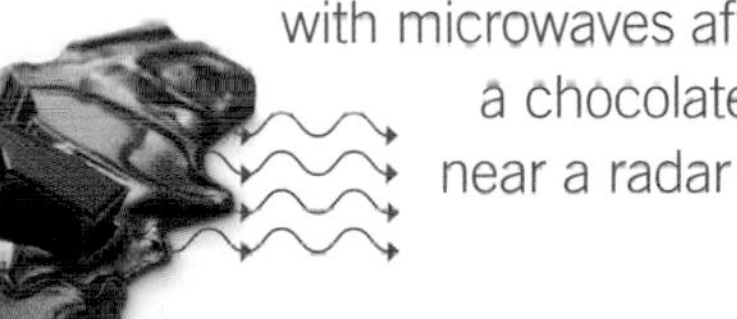

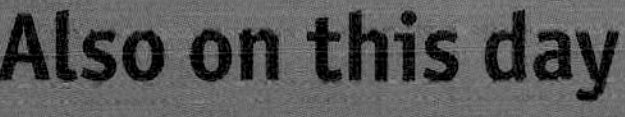

Also on this day

1871 The Peshtigo fire – the deadliest forest fire on record – burned around 1.2 million acres (490,000 hectares) of land in Wisconsin, USA.

1978 Using a speedboat, Australian motorboat racer Ken Warby became the first person to travel at 483 kph (300 mph) on water.

2008 Scientists revealed the discovery of around 270 new marine species near Tasmania.

Born this day

1910 Kirk Alyn, US actor. He was the first actor to play Superman on screen for a live-action film.

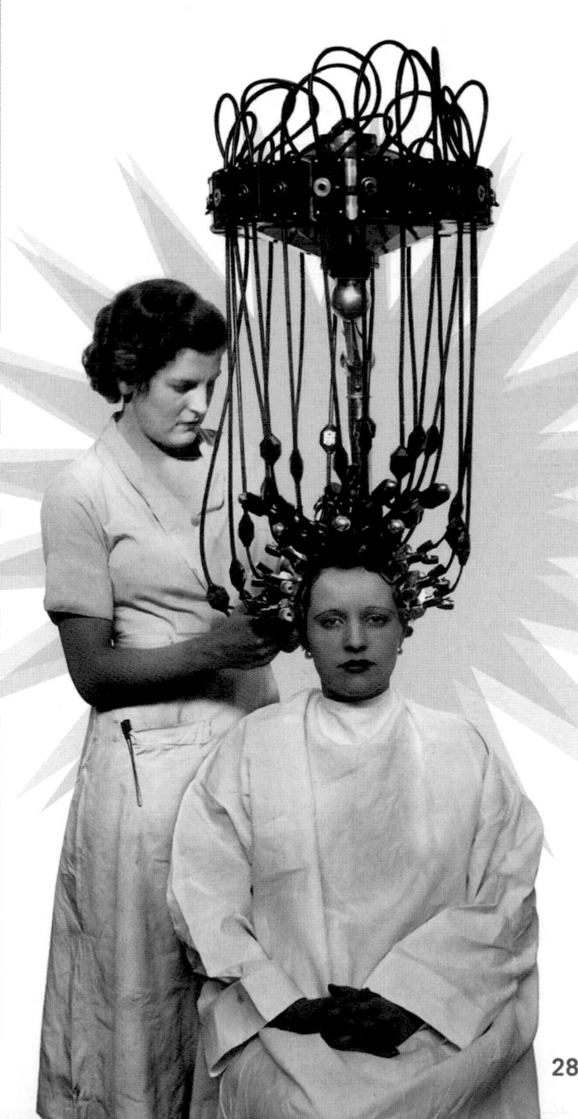

October 9

1945

Celebrating Hangeul

Hangeul Day was observed as a national holiday in South Korea for the first time to celebrate the creation of Hangeul, the Korean alphabet, by medieval king Sejong of the kingdom of Joseon.

Also on this day

768 Charlemagne was crowned the ruler of a large medieval kingdom in western Europe inhabited by Germanic tribes called the Franks.

2005 Stanley the Volkswagen, a self-driving Volkswagen Touareg car designed by Stanford University's racing team, was awarded a US $2 million prize for winning a race against four other driverless vehicles in the Mojave Desert in Nevada, USA.

1000

Finding Vinland

Viking explorer Leif Erikson landed on the shores of what is now Canada, becoming the first European explorer to set foot on the North American mainland. He named the region "Vinland" after the local grapevines.

Old clock

1410

Construction finished on the Prague Astronomical Clock in Czechia. Designed by clockmaster Mikuláš and scientist Jan Šindel, it is the world's oldest working clock.

Born this day

1823 Mary Ann Shadd Cary, Black American-Canadian teacher, anti-slavery activist, publisher, and lawyer. She was North America's first Black female publisher.

October 10

Also on this day

1967 An international agreement called the Outer Space Treaty – originally signed by the USA, the UK, and the Soviet Union – came into force. According to the treaty, the Moon and other bodies in space can be used for peaceful purposes, including space exploration, by all countries. It doesn't allow any country to claim ownership over anything in outer space.

2013 The world's first drone that could be activated and flown by winking was unveiled in St Andrews, Scotland. It was developed by Peruvian inventor Katia Vega.

1964 An Olympic first

The 1964 Summer Olympic Games began in Tokyo, Japan. This was the first time an Olympic event was held in an Asian country.

1903 Suffrage for all

British activist Emmeline Pankhurst founded the Women's Social and Political Union (WSPU) in Manchester, England. The organization fought for women's right to vote through demonstrations, marches, and strikes.

Off with their heads! 1789

French physician Joseph-Ignace Guillotin proposed that death penalties for criminals should be carried out painlessly. His idea led to the creation of the guillotine – a device with an angled blade that, when dropped on someone's neck, killed them instantly.

Born this day

1970 Matthew Pinsent, British rower. In his 17-year career, he won 10 rowing world championships and four Olympic gold medals.

October 11

1919

In-flight meals

Passengers on a flight from London, UK, to Paris, France, became the first to receive an in-flight meal, which included fruit and sandwiches.

Born this day

1821 George Williams, British humanitarian. He founded the Young Men's Christian Association (YMCA) to help young people.

AIDS memorial quilt

1987

A team of 48 volunteers unfolded 1,920 AIDS quilt panels at the National Mall in Washington, DC, USA. They had been crafted to honour loved ones lost to the AIDS epidemic.

Kitesurfing

1977

Dutch surfer and inventor Gijsbertus Adrianus Panhuise received the patent for kitesurfing, a water sport in which a person on a surfboard is pulled by a parachute.

Also on this day

1745 The Leyden Jar, a type of early battery to store electric charge, was invented by German cleric Ewald Georg von Kleist. Dutch scientist Pieter van Musschenbroek independently came up with the same idea at around the same time.

1984 US astronaut Kathryn Sullivan became the first US woman to perform a spacewalk, on a mission in the Space Shuttle *Challenger*.

2010 At the Commonwealth Games in New Delhi, India, discus thrower Krishna Poonia won India's first gold in athletics since 1958.

October 12

1492 Columbus Day

Italian explorer Christopher Columbus arrived in North America, landing in the Bahamas. This began centuries of European exploration and colonization of the continent. The date is annually observed by many American countries as Columbus Day.

Also on this day

1979 Typhoon Tip became the largest and most intense tropical storm ever recorded, with a diameter greater than 2,200 km (1,360 miles) and wind speeds of 300 kph (187 mph).

1992 The first Indigenous People's Day was celebrated in the USA to remember the loss of Indigenous communities and identities with the arrival of Columbus and European colonial forces.

Born this day

1864 Kamini Roy, poet and social worker in the Indian subcontinent. At a time when few women in this part of the world were allowed an education, she became the first female honours graduate.

1968 Hugh Jackman, Australian actor. Known for his work in many different action films and musicals, he is best known for playing the mutant Wolverine in the *X-Men* movies.

Oktoberfest 1810

Citizens of Munich, Germany, gathered to celebrate the marriage of Crown Prince Ludwig. The celebrations became annual, gradually turning into the modern-day folk festival Oktoberfest.

2019 Record run

Kenyan athlete Eliud Kipchoge completed a marathon in Vienna, Austria, 20 seconds before the two-hour mark. However, it was not deemed a record as this event wasn't an official competition.

October

13

Ada Lovelace Day 2009

Named after the British mathematician who wrote the first computer program, Ada Lovelace Day was celebrated for the first time. It highlights the achievements of women in science, technology, engineering, and mathematics (STEM). This day is now observed each year on the second Tuesday of October.

Also on this day

1943 The Italian government declared war on Nazi Germany to liberate central and northern Italy from German control after signing a truce with the Allied forces.

1958 Written by British author Michael Bond, the tale *A Bear Called Paddington* was first published.

Born this day

1989 Alexandra Ocasio-Cortez, US politician. At 29 years of age, she became the youngest woman ever to serve in the US Congress.

Dino discovery 2005

Palaeontologists announced the discovery of the fossils of a birdlike dinosaur in Patagonia, South America. The fossils suggest that this species, called *Buitreraptor gonzalezorum*, lived around 98 million years ago.

Crystal clear 1986

Off the Antarctic coast, the Weddell Sea was discovered to have the clearest water of any sea on Earth. Scientists from the Alfred Wegener Institute in Bremerhaven, Germany, compared its purity to that of distilled water.

October 14

1947 Speed of sound

With US pilot Charles "Chuck" Yeager at the controls, the experimental Bell X-1 rocket-powered plane reached a speed of 1,127 kph (700 mph), flying faster than the speed of sound. It was the first crewed aircraft to achieve this feat.

Also on this day

1962 In the build-up to the Cuban Missile Crisis, a US aircraft took photographs of Soviet ballistic missiles installed in Cuba, confirming the threat of a potential Soviet nuclear attack on the USA.

1968 Black American athlete Jim Hines ran the 100 m in 9.95 seconds, becoming the first person to do this in less than 10 seconds.

2012 Space skydive

Austrian Felix Baumgartner became the first skydiver to break the speed of sound when he jumped from a balloon 39 km (24 miles) above Earth. He opened his parachute and landed near Roswell in New Mexico, USA, nine minutes later.

Born this day

1978 Usher, Black American singer and songwriter. One of the biggest names in modern R&B music, he has sold more than 100 million records worldwide.

1066 Battle of Hastings

Duke William of Normandy killed King Harold II of England at the Battle of Hastings, defeating the Anglo-Saxon army. This victory allowed William's Norman-French soldiers to take over England.

October 15

1952 Charlotte's Web

US author E B White's children's book *Charlotte's Web* was published. It tells the story of the friendship between Wilbur the pig and Charlotte, the barn spider. The book went on to sell more than 45 million copies worldwide.

1997 Faster than sound

When British driver Andy Green hit a top speed of 1227.9 kph (763 mph) in the *ThrustSuperSonicCar* (*ThrustSSC*) in Nevada's Black Rock Desert in the USA, it became the first land vehicle to break the sound barrier.

1989 Hockey record

In the final moments of a game against the Edmonton Oilers, Canadian ice hockey player Wayne Gretzky scored a goal for the Los Angeles Kings, winning them the game. It made him the all-time top points scorer in North America's National Hockey League (NHL), with 1,851 career points.

Born this day

1938 Fela Kuti, Nigerian musician and composer. He blended American and West African musical influences to invent a new style of music called Afro-beat.

Also on this day

1582 Catholic countries in Europe were the first in the world to adopt the Gregorian calendar, which was more accurate than the previously used Julian calendar.

2003 China's *Shenzou 5* spacecraft carried Yang Liwei, the first Taikonaut (Chinese astronaut), into space.

2011 The world's fifth LEGOLAND® opened in Florida, USA, with displays made up of 50 million LEGO® bricks.

October 16

1950

Adventures in Narnia

The children's classic *The Lion, the Witch and the Wardrobe*, by British author C S Lewis, was published. This was the first title in a seven-part fantasy series called *The Chronicles of Narnia*.

Born this day

1997 Naomi Osaka, Japanese tennis player. She has won four Grand Slams, and in 2019, became the first Asian player in history to be ranked world number one.

1793

Royal beheading

Queen Marie Antoinette of France was executed by guillotine during the French Revolution. She and her husband, King Louis XVI, were blamed for indulging in an expensive and carefree lifestyle while the country's people suffered.

1384

Female king

As a nine-year-old girl, Jadwiga was crowned king of Poland in the capital city of Kraków, becoming the kingdom's first female monarch. During her reign, she made religious work and charity her main priorities.

Also on this day

1968 Black American athletes Tommie Smith and John Carlos gave the Black Power salute on the winners' podium at the Mexico City Olympics to protest against racial discrimination.

2001 Construction began on the Millau Viaduct in France, a miracle of engineering that when completed stood 343 m (1,125 ft) high and remains the world's tallest bridge.

October

17

Empress of China 690

China's only female ruler, Empress Wu Zetian was the power behind the throne of both her husband and her son until she took control in her own right. Her reign was marked by economic success and the expansion of China's empire.

Born this day

1914 Jerry Siegel, US comic book writer. Along with comic book artist Joe Schuster, he created the world-famous character Superman.

2008 Snack attack

A hungry crowd in Tehran, Iran, foiled a record-breaking attempt to make the world's longest sandwich, taking bites before judges could measure it.

2014 Climate warriors

To raise awareness of the dangers of fossil fuels, protestors from 12 low-lying Pacific island nations threatened by rising sea levels sailed into Australia's Newcastle Coal Port in canoes and blocked coal ships from leaving.

Also on this day

1604 German astronomer Johannes Kepler observed SN 1604, the last supernova (exploding star) in our galaxy to be seen without a telescope.

1931 After a lifetime of crime, US gangster Al Capone was imprisoned for 11 years. He had been charged with failing to pay his taxes.

2009 British footballer Darren Bent scored a win for his team when his shot hit a beach ball thrown onto the pitch by fans and bounced straight into the net.

October 18

Also on this day

1565 Japanese and Portuguese ships clashed at the Battle of Fukuda Bay, in the first recorded sea battle between Japan and a western country.

2011 Spaceport America, the world's first purpose-built spaceport, opened in New Mexico, USA.

2019 Tasked with fixing a battery unit on the International Space Station, US astronauts Christina Koch and Jessica Meir teamed up in the first all-woman spacewalk.

1921

Toast is ready!

Charles P Strite patented his new electric toaster. It was the first design to heat both sides of a piece of bread at the same time. Once ready, the toast popped up automatically.

Born this day

1926 Chuck Berry, Black American singer and songwriter. Known as the Father of Rock 'n' Roll, he was a pioneering figure in developing the popular 1950s music genre.

1984 Freida Pinto, Indian actor. She rose to fame with the film *Slumdog Millionaire*.

1851

The Whale

Moby Dick by US writer Herman Melville was published under its original title *The Whale*. This classic novel tells the story of a sea captain who seeks revenge against a white whale that bit off his leg.

New Qing ruler

1735

Emperor Qianlong took the throne, becoming the fifth emperor of the Qing Dynasty in China. During his 60-year reign, he secured and enlarged his empire through a series of military campaigns.

October 19

British surrender

1781

After losing at the Battle of Yorktown, British general Charles Cornwallis surrendered to US general George Washington. The defeat marked the end of the Revolutionary War and set a course towards American independence.

The Santos-Dumont No. 6

1901

In his newly designed airship, Brazilian aviator Alberto Santos-Dumont became the first person to fly from Parc Saint Cloud in Paris, France, to the Eiffel Tower and back – a distance of 11.3 km (7 miles) – in less than 30 minutes.

1872

The Holtermann Nugget

Gold miners in New South Wales, Australia, led by mine manager Bernhardt Holtermann, struck it rich when they unearthed the largest mass of reef gold ever discovered. The precious metal was found embedded in a large piece of quartz rock.

Born this day

1926 Marjorie Tallchief, ballet dancer. A member of the Osage Nation, she was the first Indigenous American to receive the title of principal dancer at the Paris Opera Ballet.

Also on this day

1469 King Ferdinand II of Aragon and Queen Isabella I of Castile were married, uniting the kingdoms of Aragon and Castile into a single country called Spain.

1914 Allied and German forces started to fight for control of the city of Ypres in Belgium during World War I.

1972 At Stanford University, USA, 24 gamers battled to win *Spacewar!* at the world's first video-game tournament.

October 20

1968 Fosbury flop

US student Dick Fosbury transformed the sport of high jumping for ever when he tried out a never-before-seen technique at Mexico's Olympic Games, leaping backwards over the bar. He easily won gold.

2010 Sloth celebration

The first International Sloth Day took place to celebrate this slow-moving, leaf-eating mammal and raise awareness of the threats it faces in its native Central and South America.

Born this day

1882 Bela Lugosi, Hungarian-American actor. Following his move from Hungary to the USA, he became a Hollywood star after being cast as the title character in the 1931 horror film *Dracula*.

Sydney Opera House 1973

Fourteen years after construction began, the Sydney Opera House was opened to the public by Queen Elizabeth II. The building, located on the water's edge, was designed to resemble the sails of a ship.

Also on this day

1818 The USA and the UK signed a treaty setting out the border between US territory and British-controlled Canada.

2017 ***Coco***, the first nine-figure-budget animated film to have a cast formed entirely of Latin American actors, was released in Mexico.

2019 An image was released to the public showing an 8,000-year-old pearl found by archaeologists on Marawah Island in the UAE.

October 21

1879

Light bulb

US inventor Thomas Edison made an application to patent his design for a light bulb, which had a burning carbon filament inside. Practical and affordable, his invention could light a space for more than 13 hours.

Born this day

1833 Alfred Nobel, Swedish chemist. He donated his wealth to create the Nobel Prize, which is awarded to leading figures who have contributed to the benefit of humankind.

New art gallery 1959

In New York City, USA, the Solomon R Guggenheim Museum opened to visitors. The building's unusual modern design was unlike any art gallery seen before.

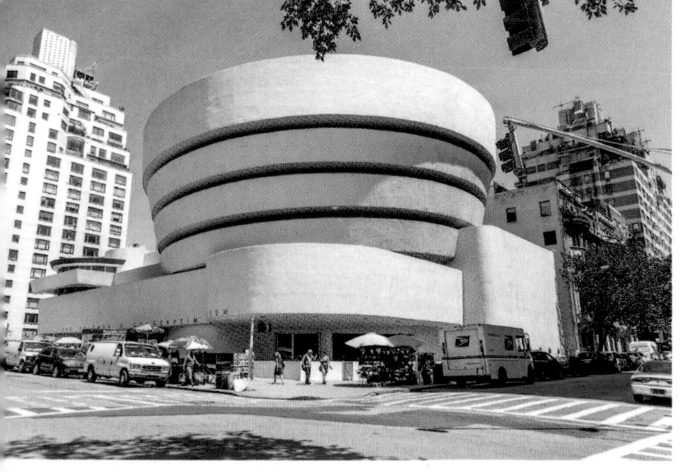

Tokugawa victory 1600

In the Battle of Sekigahara, the forces of Tokugawa Ieyasu defeated the ruling Toyotomi clan. This victory led to the establishment of the Tokugawa Shogunate, a military government that ruled Japan for the next two and a half centuries.

1854 Champion nurse

British nursing pioneer Florence Nightingale left England for Constantinople (modern-day Istanbul, Turkey), where she introduced new standards of cleanliness in disease-ridden hospitals filled with soldiers wounded in the Crimean War.

Also on this day

1520 Portuguese explorer Ferdinand Magellan's ships began to navigate a narrow waterway in southern Chile that linked the Atlantic and Pacific oceans.

1805 British ships defeated the French and Spanish fleets at the Battle of Trafalgar, off the Spanish coast.

October 22

Also on this day

1884 The Royal Observatory in Greenwich, UK, was established as the prime meridian or 0° longitude. It is an imaginary line used as the basis for the world's time zones.

2009 To help train medical staff, Japanese engineers revealed a robot that simulated the symptoms of a person sick with the H1N1 flu virus.

1850 Early Olympics

The Much Wenlock Olympian Games, an annual sporting competition that helped to inspire the modern Olympic Games, was launched in Shropshire, England. Local athletes competed in sports such as penny farthing cycling and blindfold wheelbarrow racing.

Justin Fashanu 1990

Black British striker Justin Fashanu came out as gay, becoming the first professional footballer worldwide to do so. Also the first player to command a transfer fee of £1 million, he is remembered as a pioneer on and off the pitch.

Born this day

1913 Robert Capa, Hungarian-American war photographer. He risked his life to report on conflicts such as World War II.

1952 Jeff Goldblum, US actor. He has starred in a number of huge Hollywood blockbusters, including *Jurassic Park* and *Independence Day*.

Sky-high pioneer 1797

French balloonist André-Jacques Garnerin became the first person to successfully parachute. Using a hot-air balloon, he rose to a height of 1,000 m (3,280 ft), before letting go of the balloon and parachuting down to Parc Monceau in Paris, France, landing shaken but safe.

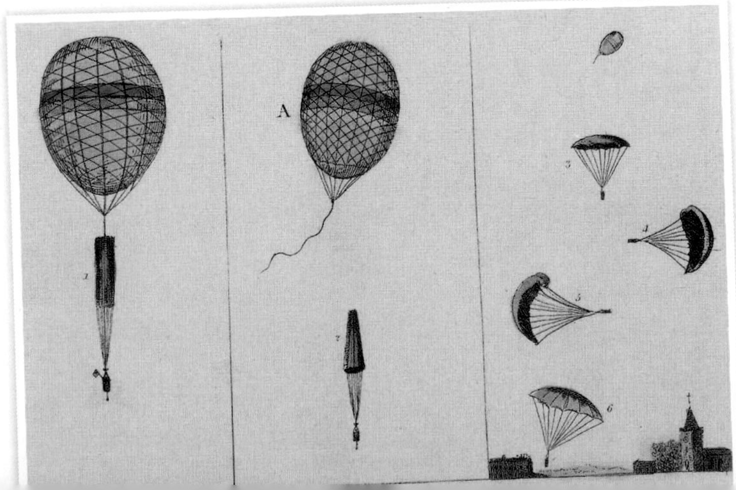

October 23

Going fast

1970

US racing driver Gary Gabelich set a new land speed record of 1,001.667 kph (622.407 mph) in a special rocket-powered vehicle called *Blue Flame* at the Bonneville Salt Flats in Utah, USA.

Battle of Leyte Gulf

1944

The largest naval battle of World War II began as Japan fought the Allied forces near the Philippine islands. Over the next four days, the Japanese navy was defeated, allowing the Allies to gain power in the Pacific Ocean.

Also on this day

1958 Fictional little blue people named the Smurfs first featured in the comic series *Johan and Peewit* by Belgian cartoonist Peyo.

1991 The Paris Peace Agreements were signed in France in an official declaration of peace marking the end of the decade-long Cambodian–Vietnamese War.

Born this day

1940 Edson Arantes do Nascimento, Brazilian footballer. Popularly known as Pelé, he played for his country from the age of 16, and is considered the greatest footballer of all time.

Crossing the sea

2018

After nine years of construction, the Hong Kong-Zhuhai-Macau Bridge was opened by Chinese leader Xi Jinping. Spanning 55 km (34 miles), it is the world's longest sea bridge-tunnel system and connects the islands of Hong Kong to mainland China.

October 24

2014 Space skydive

US engineer Alan Eustace travelled into space in a gas-powered balloon, before skydiving 40 km (25 miles) back down to Earth, parachuting to the ground moments before landing. The journey lasted 15 minutes and set a new world record for the highest and longest freefall.

Also on this day

1945 The United Nations (UN) was officially established, with 50 countries agreeing to maintain international peace, prioritize human rights, and promote progress and prosperity.

1975 Most women in Iceland went on strike for the day to protest against inequality in the workplace. It led to a new law that ensured equal pay for women and men.

1929 Black Thursday

The New York stock market crashed, triggering the collapse of the US economy. This led to the Great Depression, a period of worldwide economic hardship that lasted through the 1930s.

Born this day

1632 Antonie van Leeuwenhoek, Dutch scientist. Known as the Father of Microbiology, he built hundreds of microscopes to study tiny bacteria in great detail.

1986 Drake, Canadian actor, rapper, and singer. He began his career on a teen television programme before moving into music. One of the biggest names in hip-hop today, he has sold more than 170 million records worldwide.

1901 Daring drop

On her 63rd birthday, US teacher Annie Edson Taylor climbed into a barrel and plunged 51 m (167 ft) down Niagara Falls in Canada. She was the first person to survive the drop, escaping with only minor cuts and bruises.

October

25

1917

October Revolution

During World War I, a revolution swept through Russia, brought about by the Bolshevik Communists under leader Vladimir Lenin. They took control of major government buildings and transport links, with opposition to their actions resulting in civil war.

2001

Colossal crocodile

Experts at the University of Chicago in the USA revealed that they had been studying the 110-million-year-old fossils of *Sarcosuchus*, among the largest crocodile species on Earth at a length of about 12 m (40 ft).

Born this day

1881 Pablo Picasso, Spanish sculptor and painter. He invented Cubism, a form of abstract art where the subject is shown in the form of geometric shapes and designs.

1984 Katy Perry, US singer. She stormed the global pop music charts, selling more than 125 million singles.

Motorbike stunt

1975

US stunt performer Evel Knievel successfully jumped 40 m (133 ft) over 14 buses on his Harley-Davidson motorbike in Ohio, USA. This was his longest successful jump in a career of 75 nail-biting stunts.

Also on this day

1415 Despite being outnumbered by French forces at the Battle of Agincourt, the English army emerged victorious.

2000 Fossils of a 6-million-year-old human species, known as Millennium Man, were discovered in the Tugen Hills of Kenya.

2001 US computer software giant Microsoft released its Windows XP operating system.

Also on this day

1881 The Gunfight at the OK Corral in Tombstone, Arizona, was one of the most infamous shootouts in the American Wild West.

1917 Brazil declared its decision to support the Allied forces in World War I, becoming the only South American nation to enter the war.

2020 US space agency NASA reported finding water on the sunlit surface of the Moon.

Oldest football body

1863

The Football Association was set up at the Freemasons' Tavern in London, UK. Team captains and representatives from 11 local football clubs gathered in the pub to agree shared rules for the game.

1985

Winning back Uluru

The Australian government returned ownership of the sacred red sandstone formation called Uluru to the First Australians. It was a hard-earned victory for their land rights movement.

2005

Mali musicians

Blind musical duo Amadou & Mariam from Mali received a French platinum sales disc for selling 300,00 copies of their Afro-blues album *Dimanche à Bamako*.

Born this day

1947 Hillary Clinton, US politician. She was the First Lady while her husband Bill Clinton was president. She served as senator and then secretary of state, and later campaigned to become the country's first female president in 2016.

October

27

2019 Historic win

When actor Wes Studi was given the Governors Award, an Academy Award for a lifetime of achievements in film, he became the first Indigenous American actor to win an Oscar.

Skiing on water 1925

Water skis were patented by US film producer Fred Waller, who also publicized the thrilling new sport in advertisements.

Born this day

1858 Theodore Roosevelt, 26th US president. He served two terms in office, and won the Nobel Peace Prize for his part in ending the Russo-Japanese War.

1917 Oliver Tambo, South African anti-apartheid activist. He set up the first Black law firm in South Africa alongside Nelson Mandela before becoming president of the African National Congress for 24 years.

2014 Pop classic

US music star Taylor Swift released her groundbreaking pop album entitled *1989*, which documents her life and loves. It won Swift the Album of the Year Grammy and has sold more than 10 million copies worldwide.

Also on this day

1962 Nuclear war between the Soviet Union and the USA was narrowly avoided during the Cuban Missile Crisis when Soviet naval officer Vasili Arkhipov refused to fire a nuclear torpedo at a US warship.

2010 Details about a new species of snub-nosed monkey named *Rhinopithecus strykeri*, discovered in northern Myanmar (Burma), were published.

October 28

Gulliver's Travels

1726

Irish author Jonathan Swift's satirical adventure novel, *Gulliver's Travels*, was first published. It describes the fictional travels of Lemuel Gulliver, including his journey to the islands of Lilliput and Blefuscu, which are populated by tiny people.

Born this day

1955 Bill Gates, US technology entrepreneur. He established the global software giant Microsoft and became one of the world's wealthiest people. He runs a charity foundation with his former wife, Melinda Gates.

A new capital

1420

Beijing, which means "Northern Capital", was declared the capital city of the Ming Dynasty in China. At its centre was the Forbidden City, the imperial palace complex of the emperor, accessible only to the royal family and their servants.

1793

Cotton gin

US inventor Eli Whitney applied for a patent for the cotton gin, a machine that quickly and easily removed cotton fibres from their seeds. The device boosted the harvesting of cotton in the country, especially in the Southern states.

Also on this day

1886 The Statue of Liberty, given to the USA as a gift from France, was dedicated in New York Harbor at a special ceremony attended by US president Grover Cleveland.

1982 The largest census in history confirmed that China was home to more than a billion people, making up almost a quarter of the world's population at that time.

October 29

1923

New moves

A new dance trend called the Charleston, which included high kicks and twisting steps, took the US by storm after it appeared in the musical comedy show *Runnin' Wild* on Broadway in New York City, USA.

Born this day

1971 Ma Huateng, Chinese entrepreneur. His global media and technology business Tencent created the social media platform WeChat, which has more than a billion users.

1904 Champion gymnast

German-American disabled gymnast George Eyser won six medals, including three golds, in just one day at the 1904 Olympics in Missouri, USA. Eyser had lost his left leg after being run over by a train as a child, and had competed in the sporting events with a wooden prosthetic leg.

539 BCE A vast empire

Cyrus the Great, founder of the Achaemenid Empire, arrived in the city of Babylon (near modern-day Baghdad, Iraq) after conquering the Babylonians. His empire would eventually span more than 5.5 million sq km (2.1 million sq miles).

Also on this day

1847 British mathematician George Boole published a new system of using 0s and 1s to make calculations. It is still used to program computers today.

2013 The Marmaray rail tunnel, the world's first underwater tunnel between two continents, opened beneath the Bosphorus Strait. The tunnel links Europe and Asia.

October 30

1938 Alien alert

When an adaptation of British writer H G Wells's science-fiction novel *The War of the Worlds* aired on US radio, confused listeners supposedly panicked, fearing that news reports of an alien invasion were true.

Born this day

1960 Diego Maradona, Argentinian footballer. He was named FIFA's Player of the 20th century. His extraordinary technical skill and creativity made him one of history's greatest footballers.

Also on this day

1961 The most explosive nuclear bomb ever, the *Tsar Bomba*, was detonated by the Soviet Union in a test on Severny Island, north of Russia.

1991 At a peace conference in Madrid, Spain, representatives from Israel, Palestine, and the Arab states met those from the USA and the Soviet Union to plan how to achieve peace in the Middle East.

Sunglasses on! 2013

Residents in the town of Rjukan, Norway, celebrated the town's first-ever day of winter sun. Located deep in a valley, Rjukan is in darkness for half the year, so giant mirrors were installed to reflect sunlight down to the town's centre.

October 31

1517

The Reformation

German priest Martin Luther wrote a letter accusing the Catholic Church of corruption and questioning its practices and he may have nailed a copy of his 95 questions to a church door. In doing so, he sparked the Reformation, a movement that led to the establishment of Protestantism.

2000

Humanoid robot

Standing at 120 cm (3 ft 11 in) tall, humanoid robot ASIMO was introduced to the world by its Japanese engineers. ASIMO could run, climb stairs, recognize faces, and answer questions.

Also on this day

1950 In the first Trick-or-Treat for UNICEF, five US children dressed up for Halloween and visited neighbours to request charity donations.

2002 In protest against what they thought was unfair refereeing in a previous game, Madagascan football team Stade Olympique de L'Emyrne scored 149 own goals, intentionally losing a match.

2011 Earth's human population reached a milestone of 7 billion people.

Born this day

1875 Vallabhbhai Patel, Indian politician. He played an important role in India's struggle for independence and was the first deputy prime minister of an independent India.

1961 Peter Jackson, New Zealand film director. He has directed blockbuster film series, including *The Lord of The Rings* and *The Hobbit*.

2018

Climate activists

In London, UK, 1,000 people gathered for the launch of the Extinction Rebellion movement. This international group, formed of climate activists, uses non-violent protest methods to raise awareness about environmental threats.

November 1

A spectacular ceiling

1512

The ceiling of the Sistine Chapel in Rome, Italy, was officially opened. Italian painter Michelangelo had spent four years painting frescoes of scenes from the Old Testament of the Bible across the 460 sq m (5,000 sq ft) ceiling.

Born this day

1990 Simone Giertz, Swedish inventor. Her inventions include a robot that applies lipstick. She demonstrates them to her fans on her YouTube channel.

2014

Day of the Dead

During the annual Day of the Dead festivities in Mexico, more than 500 women came together in Mexico City to set a world record for the greatest gathering of women dressed as La Catrina, the celebration's symbolic female skeleton figure.

Also on this day

1478 The Spanish Inquisition was established by Catholic monarchs King Ferdinand and Queen Isabella, who used it to find those who did not believe in Christianity.

1755 Tsunami waves and local fires caused by the Great Lisbon Earthquake devastated the capital city of Portugal, leading to huge loss of life.

1994 The first World Vegan Day was celebrated to bring attention to veganism.

1938

Kahlo exhibition

The first solo exhibition of Mexican painter Frida Kahlo opened at the Julien Levy Gallery in New York City, USA, to rave reviews from art critics.

November 2

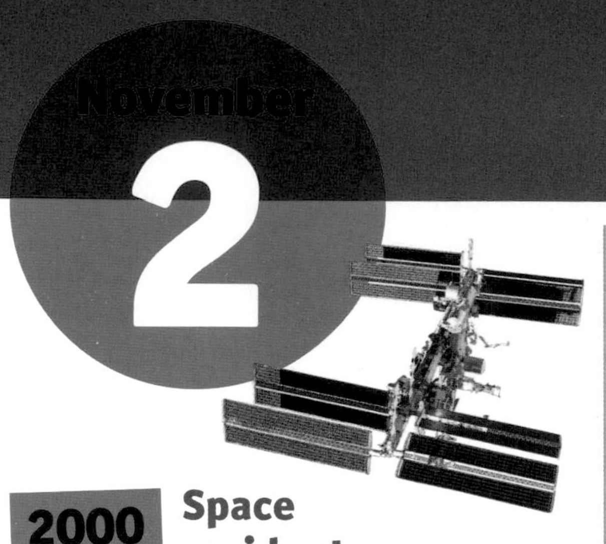

2000 Space residents

The first long-term residents of the International Space Station (ISS) arrived for a four-month mission. The three astronauts made themselves at home by switching on the lights and joining a communications link with mission control.

Born this day

1966 David Schwimmer, US actor. He rose to fame as Ross Geller in the TV show *Friends*, and later provided the voice of Melman the giraffe in the *Madagascar* film series.

Also on this day

1936 The British Broadcasting Corporation (BBC) launched the world's first high-definition TV service in London, UK.

1988 An early computer malware, named the Morris worm, was released over the internet to disable computer systems, resulting in criminal charges against its US inventor, Robert Morris.

2017 Scientists revealed the discovery of a secret chamber inside the Great Pyramid of Giza in Egypt.

1789 Late fees

Two library books borrowed by US president George Washington from the New York Society Library were due back on this date, but were never returned. By 2010, the late fees totalled a staggering US $300,000!

2012 Talking elephant

Some news agencies around the world reported that an elephant named Koshik at Everland Zoo in Yongin, South Korea, could make human sounds by placing his trunk in his mouth. The animal could supposedly recreate five words – *annyeong* ("hello"), *anja* ("sit down"), *aniya* ("no"), *nuwo* ("lie down"), and *joa* ("good").

November 3

Caribbean heroes

1915

The British West Indies Regiment (BWIR) was set up to create a support regiment during World War I. These volunteers from British colonies in the Caribbean helped Britain's war effort in Europe, Africa, and the Middle East.

1975

Tennis ace

US tennis player Chris Evert became the first person to receive the No. 1 ranking from the Women's Tennis Association (WTA). She remained in the top spot for 25 weeks.

Also on this day

1838 ***The Times of India***, the world's largest circulated English-language daily newspaper, published its first edition.

1954 **The epic monster movie *Godzilla*** was released to packed cinema audiences in Japan, becoming an instant box-office smash.

1973 **US space agency NASA launched *Mariner 10***, the first space probe to reach Mercury.

Born this day

1900 **Adolf Dassler**, German cobbler. He founded the sportswear company Adidas, which grew into a global business empire.

1949 **Anna Wintour**, British-born US journalist. The editor-in-chief of the US magazine *Vogue*, she is recognized as an influential fashion icon and media powerhouse.

1911

Chevrolet founded

US car manufacturer Chevrolet was founded. In 1912, it released its first car, the Chevrolet Series C Classic Six, which would challenge Ford's dominant Model T.

November 4

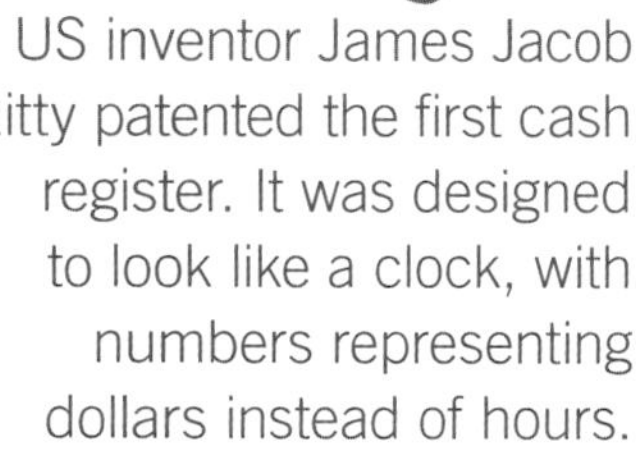

1879 Cash register

US inventor James Jacob Ritty patented the first cash register. It was designed to look like a clock, with numbers representing dollars instead of hours.

1961 Clever chimps

British primate expert Jane Goodall realized that chimpanzees could make tools, like humans. She made this breakthrough discovery while observing two chimpanzees using branches to remove termites from mounds.

Born this day

1993 Elisabeth Seitz, German gymnast. She won a bronze medal at the 2018 Artistic Gymnastics World Championships, and has created her own tricky twist, called the Seitz.

Oldest opera house 1737

The Teatro di San Carlo was inaugurated in Naples, Italy, and financed by King Charles VII of Naples. It remains the oldest continuously active opera house.

Also on this day

1847 Chloroform was found to be an effective anaesthetic for medical operations, following research by Scottish physician James Young Simpson.

1952 The Kamchatka earthquake in Russia triggered tsunami waves that reached the islands of Hawaii, USA, more than 5,000 km (3,100 miles) away.

2001 *Harry Potter and the Philosopher's Stone* premiered in London, UK. It was the first of many films in the *Harry Potter* series.

1605 Bonfire night

The Gunpowder Plot failed to set off explosives hidden under the English parliament in London, which were intended to kill King James I. The government eventually made this day an annual celebration of the plot's failure, with bonfires and fireworks.

Born this day

1984 Eliud Kipchoge, Kenyan long-distance runner. At the 2018 Berlin Marathon, he ran the 42.2 km (26.2 mile) stretch in just over 2 hours and 1 minute.

1988 Virat Kohli, Indian cricket player. He captains the national team and is one of the best batsmen in India.

Longest-serving president 1940

Franklin D Roosevelt became the only US president to be elected for a third term in office, ultimately serving a total of 12 years in four terms. An amendment to the Constitution was later passed so that a president could serve a maximum of two terms.

Also on this day

1811 Legend has it that Catholic priest José Matías Delgado rang the bells of the Church of La Merced San Salvador in El Salvador to mark the launch of the country's independence movement.

2013 India launched the Mars Orbiter Mission, with the *Mangalyaan* probe arriving in the orbit of Mars almost a year later.

2019 The scientific journal *BioScience* published an article warning that global warming is causing an emergency on Earth. It was signed by more than 11,000 scientists.

Screenwriters' strike 2007

When discussions with studio representatives failed to agree on a better deal for royalty payments, nearly 12,000 screenwriters staged a strike in Hollywood, protesting outside film studios.

November 6

1991

Burning oil

The last burning oil well in Kuwait was put out after about 700 oil wells blazed for 10 months. They had been lit by Iraqi military troops at the end of the Gulf War.

Born this day

1814 Adolphe Sax, Belgian musician. He invented the saxophone, a brass woodwind instrument, which would transform jazz music.

1988 Emma Stone, US actor. She has played a variety of characters in Hollywood films, including Gwen Stacy in *The Amazing Spider-Man*.

1913

Jailed abroad

Indian lawyer Mohandas Karamchand Gandhi (known later as Mahatma Gandhi) was arrested for leading a march of thousands of Indian miners and their families in South Africa. They were protesting peacefully against a tax on workers, which was abolished as a result.

1869 American football

The first game of a new sport called American football was played between Princeton and Rutgers colleges in New Jersey, USA. It started out as a combination of football and rugby but developed into its own game, becoming the nation's most popular sport.

Also on this day

1975 The Green March, a demonstration by 350,000 Moroccan people, began. They crossed Morocco's border into the Spanish-occupied region of the Sahara and called for the land to be returned.

1998 The journal *Science* reported that US biologist James Thomson had removed multiple stem cells from a human embryo. Stem cells can grow into any type of cell in the body, and can potentially help in treating many disorders.

November 7

1905 Remote control

The Telekine, the earliest example of a machine that could control a distant object wirelessly, like a remote control, was demonstrated by Spanish inventor Leonardo Torres y Quevedo in Bilbao, Spain.

1492 Ensisheim meteorite

A 127 kg (280 lb) meteorite fell to Earth, leaving a deep hole in a wheat field near the village of Ensisheim in France. It is the oldest meteorite with an exact recorded date of impact.

Also on this day

1885 The final spike of the Canadian Pacific Railway was banged into place, completing the new transcontinental railway route.

1907 Mexican hero Jesús García drove a burning train, full of dynamite, a safe distance away from the mining town of Nacozari de García before it exploded.

2019 For the first time, scientists observed the Solar System's plasma shield, a protective bubble around it that stops high levels of cosmic radiation from entering.

Melbourne Cup 1861

A crowd of 4,000 people watched the first-ever race of the Melbourne Cup at the Flemington Racecourse in Melbourne, Australia. This competition is now an annual event.

Born this day

1867 Marie Curie, Polish physicist. She won two Nobel Prizes for her pioneering work on the discovery of new elements and understanding radioactivity.

1895 Using X-rays

The first X-ray scan, produced by German physicist Wilhelm Röntgen using electromagnetic radiation, showed his wife Bertha's hand. This invention enabled doctors to look inside the human body.

Born this day

1656 Edmond Halley, English astronomer. Halley expanded scientific knowledge of comets and worked out that Halley's Comet, the famous comet named after him, orbited the Sun every 76 years or so.

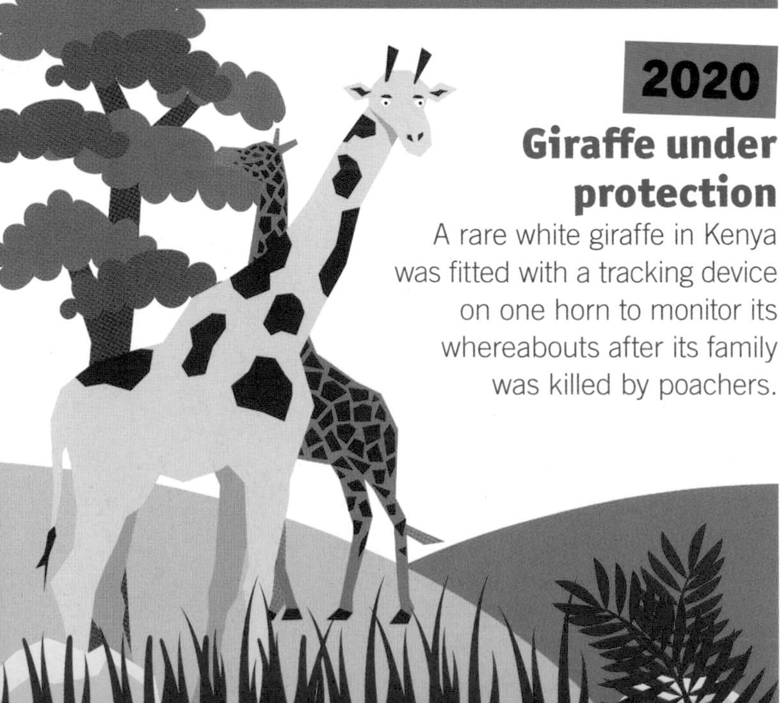

2020 Giraffe under protection

A rare white giraffe in Kenya was fitted with a tracking device on one horn to monitor its whereabouts after its family was killed by poachers.

Also on this day

1519 Spanish soldier Hernán Cortés arrived in the city of Tenochtitlán (in modern-day Mexico) where he was greeted by the Aztec emperor Moctezuma II.

1644 The Shunzhi Emperor, a monarch of the Qing Dynasty, was enthroned in Beijing as the first Qing emperor to rule over China.

1939 Nazi dictator Adolf Hitler survived an assassination attempt when a bomb exploded in a Munich building after he had already departed.

2016 Trump's term

Republican Donald J Trump was elected president of the USA when he beat the Democrat nominee, Hillary Clinton, in the race for the White House. He served four years as president.

November 9

1620 Pilgrim Fathers

A group of 102 people sighted land at Cape Cod on the North American continent from aboard the ship *Mayflower*. The travellers, later known as the Pilgrim Fathers, had set out from Plymouth, England, looking for a better life and religious freedom.

Born this day

1984 Delta Goodrem, Australian singer and actor. Her first album, *Innocent Eyes*, is among the bestselling Australian albums of all time.

Fall of the Berlin Wall 1989

Five days after half a million people in East Berlin staged a protest at the ban on entering West Berlin, a restless crowd of thousands pushed through the border gates and began tearing down the Berlin Wall. Communism had begun losing its stronghold in Eastern Europe.

Also on this day

1938 Across Germany, Nazis damaged Jewish schools, businesses, and synagogues, smashing their windows, and arrested 30,000 Jews. This violent anti-Semitic campaign was known as *Kristallnacht*, meaning "The Night of Broken Glass".

2016 The Sub1 Reloaded became the fastest robot to solve a Rubik's cube puzzle, in 0.637 seconds, at an electronics fair in Munich, Germany.

2020 The Virgin Hyperloop, a system of travelling in a pod within a vacuum tube at high speed, carried its first passengers in Nevada, USA.

November

10

2011

Extinct rhino

Africa's western black rhinoceros was declared extinct in the wild by the International Union for Conservation of Nature (IUCN). Poaching had wiped out this vulnerable species.

1958

Hope Diamond

US diamond merchant Harry Winston donated the Hope Diamond to the Smithsonian Institution in Washington, DC, USA. Discovered in a mine in India in the 17th century, this stone is one of the world's most recognizable jewels.

Born this day

1483 Martin Luther, German monk. He stood against the corrupt practices of the Roman Catholic Church and helped kickstart the Protestant Reformation.

1960 Neil Gaiman, British author. He is a prolific writer of popular graphic novels and books, including *Sandman* and *Good Omens*.

Also on this day

1903 US inventor Mary Anderson received the patent for her invention – the windscreen wiper.

1969 The children's TV show *Sesame Street* was first shown by the National Educational Television network in the USA.

2005

Telescopic titan

The Southern African Large Telescope (SALT), near Sutherland, South Africa, began operating. The largest telescope in the Southern Hemisphere, it attracts astronomers from around the world because it faces no light pollution in its remote location, at an altitude of more than 1,500 m (5,000 ft) above sea level.

1942

Fighting in Egypt

During World War II, the second Battle of El Alamein ended with the Allies defeating Axis forces at El Alamein in Egypt. This marked a turning point in the war as German forces began to surrender to the Allies in northern Africa.

1918

War is over

World War I ended on this date, the 11th day of the 11th month, when Germany signed an armistice with the Allied forces. Every year on this day – known as Armistice Day – people wear poppies and observe a two-minute silence to remember the soldiers who died in the conflict.

Born this day

1914 Daisy Bates, Black American activist and newspaper publisher. She campaigned against racial segregation using her newspaper, the *Arkansas State Press*.

1974 Leonardo DiCaprio, US actor and environmental activist. He has starred in many popular Hollywood films, such as *Titanic*, *The Aviator*, and *Inception*.

1926

Route 66

The famous highway Route 66 in the USA was completed, spanning 3,940 km (2,448 miles) from Chicago to Los Angeles. Road signs were put in place a year later to mark the route for the ultimate American road trip across the west.

Also on this day

2017 The Louvre Abu Dhabi opened in Abu Dhabi, United Arab Emirates, a result of the first partnership between France and the UAE. It soon became the most visited museum in the Arab world.

November

12

1859 High-flyer

At the Cirque Napoléon in France, daredevil acrobat Jules Léotard first performed a flying trapeze act. He later invented (and gave his name to) the leotard – a stretchy, tight-fitting outfit worn by gymnasts.

Also on this day

1956 The biggest iceberg on record, larger than Belgium, was spotted off Antarctica by a US Navy ship.

1970 The Bhola tropical cyclone, the most lethal ever, hit East Pakistan (modern-day Bangladesh) and West Bengal, India, killing at least 500,000 people.

1980 The NASA probe *Voyager I* made its closest approach to Saturn and took detailed images of the planet's rings.

Box-kite flight 1894

Australian Lawrence Hargrave proved that a machine heavier than air could fly. He joined four large box kites (his own invention) to a sling seat, and floated 5 m (16 ft) above the ground, anchored by piano wire.

Born this day

1980 Ryan Gosling, Canadian actor and musician. He won a Golden Globe Best Actor award for his role in the musical film *La La Land*.

1966 Space selfie

US astronaut Buzz Aldrin took the first space selfie, outside the spacecraft on the *Gemini 12* mission. These spacewalks paved the way for the first Moon landing.

November 13

Let it snow

1946

The first artificial snow was produced in Massachusetts, USA, after a plane dropped ice crystals into a natural cloud. Unfortunately, the snow evaporated before it could hit the ski slopes below.

Born this day

1715 Dorothea Christiane Erxleben, German doctor. She was the first woman to be licensed to practise medicine.

1955 Whoopi Goldberg, Black American actor. She has won an Emmy, a Grammy, an Oscar, and a Tony award.

1856

Big Ben bongs

The gigantic bell now known as Big Ben struck its first notes in a test exercise. Made for the new tower beside the Palace of Westminster in London, UK, its booming chimes attracted quite a crowd.

Statue in a sewer

2020

A bust dating from 300 BCE of the ancient Greek god Hermes was found in a sewer in Athens, Greece. The sculpture was in good condition, despite its murky surroundings.

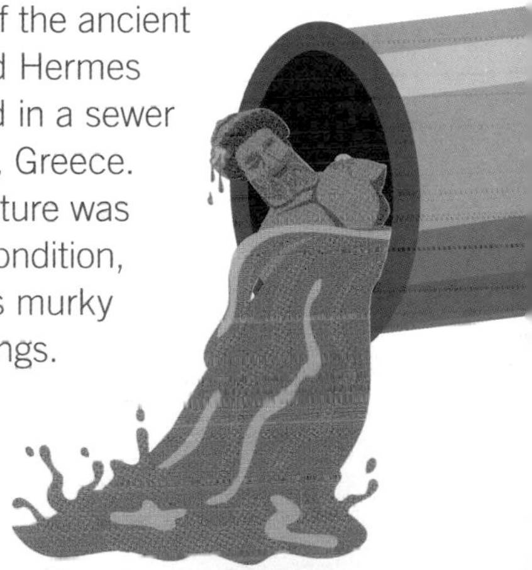

Also on this day

1956 Segregation on buses in Alabama, USA, was declared illegal by the US Supreme Court, ending the Montgomery bus boycott.

1985 A volcanic eruption in Colombia destroyed the town of Armero, killing 25,000 people – the deadliest lahar (mud flow) ever.

2010 Burmese politician Aung San Suu Kyi was released after seven years of house arrest.

November 14

1883

Ahoy, Matey!

An adventure novel that popularized treasure hunts and one-legged pirates, *Treasure Island*, by Scottish author Robert Louis Stevenson, was published for the first time.

Born this day

1907 Astrid Lindgren, Swedish author. Her children's books have sold millions internationally.

1998 Vanessa Hudgens, US actress. She is best known for her role in the *High School Musical* film series.

1960

School for all

Six-year-old Black American Ruby Bridges shaped history when she made her way into an all-white primary school. She became the first Black child to do so in the state of Louisiana, USA.

Also on this day

1152 BCE Ancient Egyptian labourers walked out of work in the first strike in history.

1967 The first "Day of the Colombian Woman" was celebrated in honour of the independence leader, Policarpa Salavarrieta.

2018 The jewellery of French queen Marie Antoinette, not seen in public for 200 years, was sold at an auction in Switzerland.

1889

From fiction to reality

Inspired by a famous novel, trailblazing US journalist Nellie Bly set off from Hoboken Pier in New Jersey, USA, to circle the globe in less than 80 days. She achieved her aim with time to spare – in 72 days!

November 15

1533

Taking over

Spanish *conquistador* "conqueror" Francisco Pizarro entered Cuzco, the Inca capital. He soon captured Inca leader Atahualpa, which marked the end of the Inca Empire. He later formed the first Spanish settlement in Peru.

1887

Power up!

The first dry cell battery was patented by German inventor Carl Gassner. A commercial success, it didn't spill its chemicals as previous types did. This reliable battery is similar to the carbon-zinc combination used today.

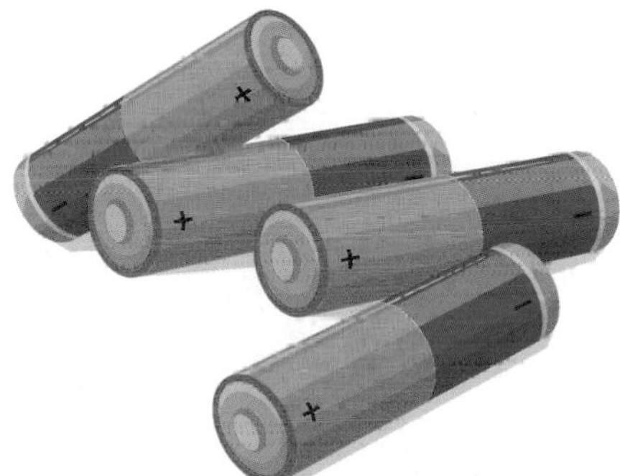

Born this day

1981 Lorena Ochoa, Mexican golfer. Considered the best Mexican golfer of all time, she was ranked highest in the world for 158 weeks from 2007 to 2010.

1971

Pioneering processor

The world's first microprocessor – the Intel 4004 – was released in the USA. As a crucial "building block" in electronic devices, it revolutionized the way people used computers.

Also on this day

2001 The gaming console Xbox was first released by Microsoft in the USA, changing the world of online gaming.

2010 Al Boraq, Morocco's first high-speed train line, was inaugurated, linking the cities of Tangiers and Casablanca.

2019 Pakistan became the first country in the world to introduce a vaccine against typhoid.

November

16

1807 Fierce pirate

When Chinese pirate Zheng Yi died, his wife Ching Shih took command of the Guangdong pirate confederation. Roaming the South China Sea with up to 80,000 followers, she was the world's most feared pirate.

Born this day

1892 Tazio Nuvolari, Italian racing driver. He won 150 races during his career, including 24 Grand Prix titles.

1963 Meenakshi Seshadri, Indian actor. She starred in many successful Hindi, Tamil, and Telugu films.

Protestant victory 1632

The Battle of Lützen took place between the Protestant Swedish Empire and the Catholic forces of the Holy Roman Empire. It was a Protestant victory, but Swedish king Gustavus Adolphus was killed in battle.

Also on this day

1879 Children took turns to meet Santa Claus at the first-ever Santa's Grotto in a shop in Liverpool, UK.

1928 Australian polar explorer Hubert Wilkins and US pilot Carl Ben Eielson made the first powered flight over Antarctica.

1965 The first space probe to land on another planet, the *Venera 3*, left Earth for Venus.

1974 Space message

In Puerto Rico, astronomers sent a message into space using the Arecibo Radio Telescope. It will take almost 25,000 years for the Arecibo message to reach its destination – the M13 star cluster on the edge of our galaxy.

2020 Whale discovery

While searching for a hard-to-find whale species deep in the waters off the coast of Mexico, unexpected clicking noises led researchers to discover another previously unknown beaked species of whale.

Born this day

1944 Danny DeVito, US screenwriter, actor, and director. He has starred in films such as *Matilda* and *Batman Returns*.

1960 RuPaul Charles, Black American drag queen and television star. He presents the globally successful TV show *RuPaul's Drag Race*.

1869 Suez Canal

The 193 km (120 mile) long Suez Canal in Egypt officially opened in front of spectators, with feasts and firework displays. The waterway allows ships to pass between the Mediterranean and Red seas.

1970 Computer mouse

US inventor Douglas Engelbart received a patent for his computer mouse. The handheld device made it possible for a computer user to guide a pointer to different places on a screen.

Also on this day

1989 The Velvet Revolution began when students in Prague, Czechoslovakia (present-day Czechia), gathered to protest against the communist government.

2003 Former bodybuilder and actor Arnold Schwarzenegger became governor of California, USA.

2011 Australian scientists found sunken sections of an ancient supercontinent called Gondwana in the Indian Ocean.

November

18

1761

Telling time

British inventor John Harrison's M4 marine chronometer finally cracked the longitude problem – the measure of how far east or west you are – after his son William tested the device on a voyage to Jamaica.

Butterfly effect

1962

US mathematician Edward Lorenz wrote a paper that lay the groundwork for a theory that he later called the "butterfly effect". It states that small changes, such as the air moved by the flap of a butterfly's wings, can start a chain of events that ends with something big happening, such as a tornado.

Also on this day

1803 Haitian revolutionaries inflicted a huge defeat on their colonial overlords, France. Haiti declared independence the following year.

1910 Suffragettes – women campaigning for the right to vote – were attacked at what the media later called the Black Friday protest.

2011 *Minecraft* was released. It went on to become the biggest-selling video game ever.

Born this day

1968 Owen Wilson, US actor. He starred in the *Night at the Museum* series, and voiced Lightning McQueen in the *Cars* animated films.

Battle of the Somme

1916

The Battle of the Somme, one of the major battles of World War I, ended after 140 days. It was one of the deadliest battles ever – more than 3 million soldiers died and about 1 million more were wounded.

November 19

Gettysburg Address

1863

As the US Civil War raged, President Abraham Lincoln delivered a short speech in Gettysburg, Pennsylvania, that explained the importance of the conflict for the freedom of all Americans.

Motorcycle record

2017

The world record for the most people on one moving motorcycle was broken by 58 members of the ASC Tornadoes Motorcycle Team of Bangalore, India. Surprisingly, no injuries were reported in the record-breaking attempt!

Born this day

1828 Lakshmibai, Indian queen. She defended her state, Jhansi, against British forces, but was eventually defeated.

Also on this day

1274 The Mongols began their ultimately unsuccessful attempt to conquer Japan. The battles featured an early use of hand-thrown bombs.

1969 Pelé, the Brazilian football star, scored his 1,000th goal on his way to a world-record 1,279 goals.

2018 A 4,000-year-old underground termite "city", larger than the island of Great Britain, was described in a biology publication.

Toilet day

2001

The first World Toilet Day was held. The day is aimed at bringing international awareness to the fact that billions of people around the world live without hygienic toilets – a massive crisis that can cause serious illnesses.

1866 Whirligig wonder

The patent was granted for the whirligig, better known as the yo-yo. This popular spinning toy was invented by Americans James L Haven and Charles Hettrick, but basic variations had existed since ancient times.

Born this day

1889 Edwin Hubble, US astronomer. He discovered galaxies beyond the Milky Way and devised a way to classify them based on their shape.

Medal of Freedom 2013

Award-winning US activist and journalist Gloria Steinem received the Medal of Freedom from US president Barack Obama in recognition of her role in the women's liberation movement and campaigns for women's rights.

Sherlock Holmes 1886

A Study in Scarlet, the first book to feature the fictional detective Sherlock Holmes, was accepted by London-based publishers Ward, Lock & Co. British author Arthur Conan Doyle wrote 60 stories featuring this beloved character.

Also on this day

1969 Indigenous American activists gathered on Alcatraz Island, a former US prison base in San Francisco Bay, to protest against their unfair treatment by the US government and demand the return of their former land, including this island.

2019 A scientific study based on fossil findings revealed that for 70 million years, prehistoric snake species had lived with back legs.

1963

Rocket launch

India's first rocket blasted off from the Thumba Equatorial Rocket Launch Station (TERLS). Supplied by NASA, the *Nike-Apache* sounding rocket carried out in-flight experiments, marking the start of the country's space programme.

2019

Shatterproof shocker

Tesla chief executive Elon Musk launched the car company's electric pick-up truck, Cybertruck, at a special event in Los Angeles, USA. However, his demonstration did not go to plan when the vehicle's shatterproof windows smashed on stage.

Also on this day

1783 The first untethered hot-air balloon with people on board took off from Paris, France, and flew 8 km (5 miles) before landing safely.

2017 Cheers greeted the reading aloud of Robert Mugabe's resignation letter in the Zimbabwean parliament after his controversial 37 years as the country's leader.

1843

Vulcanized rubber

British engineer Thomas Hancock patented his invention of tough vulcanized rubber, made by placing natural rubber in molten sulphur. It transformed the automobile industry as tyres made of vulcanized rubber could withstand extreme heat and cold, making them last longer.

Born this day

1965 Björk, Icelandic singer and songwriter. She is known for her innovative musical style, which blends influences from many genres.

1987 Eesha Karavade, Indian chess player. She made her mark on the world stage by winning the titles of International Master and Woman Grandmaster.

November 22

Capturing Blackbeard

British Navy lieutenant Robert Maynard and his crew fought the infamous British pirate Blackbeard (below) in an effort to capture him. In the battle, the pirate took five musket shots and 20 cuts by sword before he fell.

Born this day

1984 Scarlett Johansson, US actor. She is well known for playing Black Widow in the Marvel films, and is one of the highest-earning female actors of all time.

Popular leader

Angela Merkel was sworn in as Germany's first female chancellor. She was re-elected to this position in 2009, 2013, and 2018.

Also on this day

1975 Prince Juan Carlos I of the Spanish royal family was declared king of Spain following the death of military dictator Francisco Franco. He transformed Spain into a democracy, and later a constitutional monarchy.

1995 ***Toy Story***, the first feature-length computer-animated film, was released by Walt Disney Pictures and Pixar Animation Studio.

1963 National tragedy

As he travelled through Dealey Plaza in Dallas, Texas, USA, John F Kennedy – the 35th president of the USA – was fatally shot by a man named Lee Harvey Oswald.

November 23

Also on this day

543 BCE In ancient Greece, Thespis of Icaria became the first person on record to act as a character in a play on stage.

1868 French inventor Louis Ducos du Hauron filed a patent for a process that added colour to photographs, marking the beginning of colour photography.

1963 The first episode of the British science-fiction TV show *Doctor Who* went on air.

Born this day

1805 Mary Seacole, British-Jamaican nurse. During the Crimean War, she set up the "British Hotel", where wounded soldiers could be treated for their injuries.

1915 Anne Burns, British aeronautical engineer and glider pilot. She was the first woman to cross the English Channel in a glider.

Queen Wilhelmina

1890

When King William III of the Netherlands died without a male heir, a law was passed to allow his daughter, Princess Wilhelmina, to take the throne. She became queen at the age of 10, and would later keep her country out of World War I.

Deep dive

French diver Jacques Mayol attempted a free dive from a boat off the coast of the island of Elba, Italy. He was able to reach a depth of 100 m (330 ft) without any breathing equipment, making him the first diver to achieve this extraordinary feat.

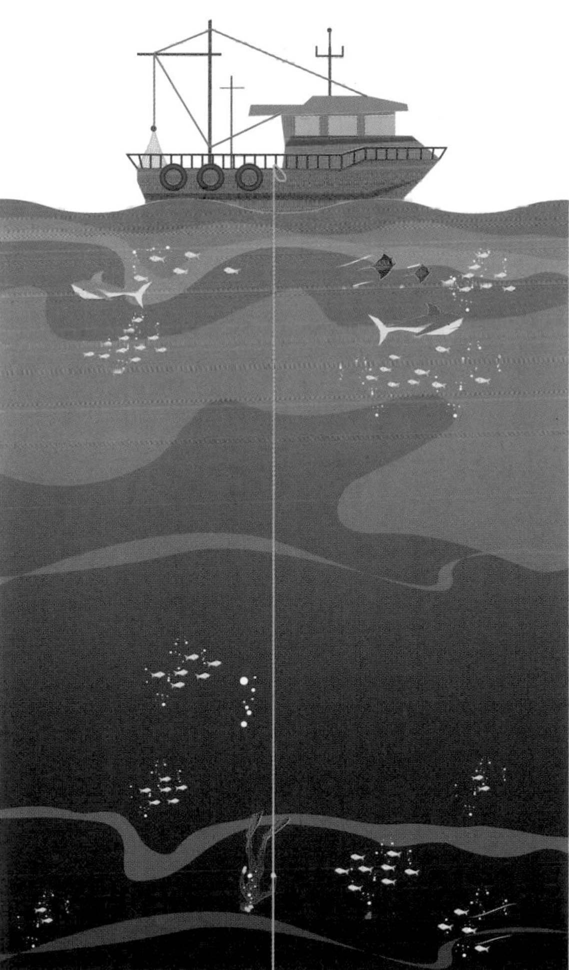

November 24

1974 Finding Lucy

US scientists Donald Johanson and Tom Gray discovered the skeleton of *Australopithecus afarensis*, a human ancestor, in Ethiopia. They nicknamed it "Lucy" after The Beatles' song *Lucy in the Sky with Diamonds*.

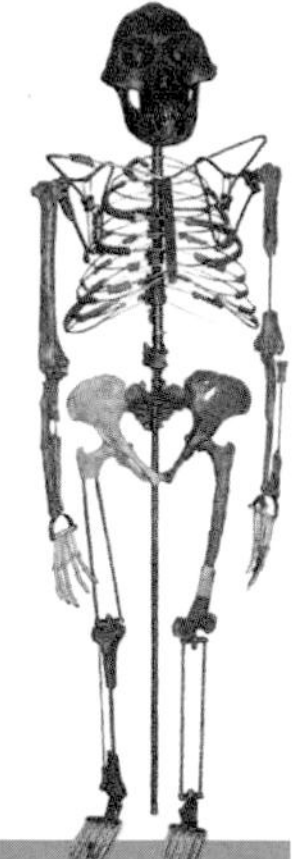

Born this day

1849 Frances Hodgson Burnett, British-American novelist and playwright. One of her most popular books is *The Secret Garden*.

1971 Parachuting hijacker

A hijacker calling himself Dan Cooper parachuted from a plane over the state of Washington, USA, with US $200,000 in ransom money. The mystery of his whereabouts has never been solved.

Also on this day

1859 British biologist Charles Darwin's book *On the Origin of Species* was published, outlining his groundbreaking theory of evolution.

1877 *Black Beauty*, a bestselling novel about a horse by British author Anna Sewell, was published.

2016 In Colombia, a peace deal was signed between the government and the Revolutionary Armed Forces, ending the country's 50-year-long civil war.

2020 K-pop sensation

After smashing YouTube records, with their hit song *Dynamite* achieving 100 million views in one day, Korean sensation BTS became the first K-pop band to receive a Grammy Award nomination. This was a major boost for diversity within the pop music industry.

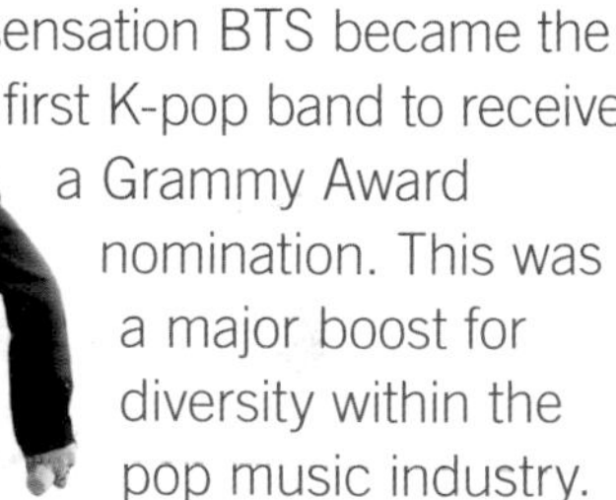

November

25

2019

Jewel theft

Dazzling royal jewellery from one of Europe's finest treasure collections was stolen from the Dresden Green Vault Museum, Germany. The items, said to be worth 1 billion euros, have never been recovered.

Also on this day

1915 German-born US physicist Albert Einstein announced his theory of general relativity, describing the nature of gravity. The theory states that the bigger an object is, the greater gravitational pull it has.

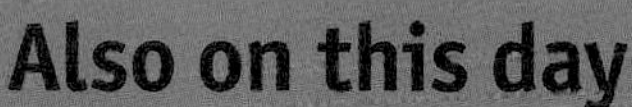

1975 Suriname gained independence from the Netherlands, becoming the last country in South America to free itself from colonial rule.

2011

Skiing solo

British explorer Felicity Aston set out to become the first person to ski alone across Antarctica using only her own muscle power. It took her 59 days to cover a distance of 1,744 km (1,084 miles).

2020

A new species

Scientists discovered a new type of Loricifera – a microscopic marine invertebrate – in the seas surrounding Japan. Living in the tiny spaces between mud and sand, its head is covered in more than 200 spines.

Born this day

1914 Joe DiMaggio, US baseball player. Considered one of the greatest players of all time, he spent his entire 13-year career in Major League Baseball playing for the New York Yankees.

November 26

1789 Thanksgiving holiday

During his presidential speech, George Washington declared "a day of public thanksgiving and prayer" across the USA. The thanksgiving tradition, which began with farming families giving thanks for their annual harvests, became an annual holiday in the USA, celebrated on the fourth Thursday of November with a feast.

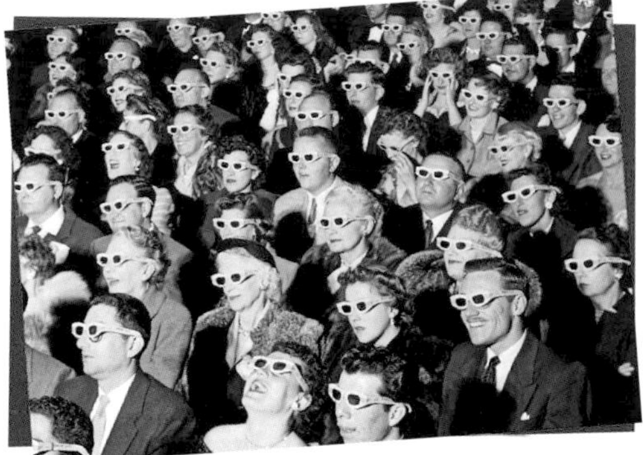

3D film 1952

Bwana Devil, the first feature-length 3D film, was released in the USA. Audiences wore 3D glasses to see lifelike hungry lions on the loose on the cinema screen.

Born this day

1922 Charles M Schulz, US cartoonist. Nicknamed "Sparky", he created the comic strip *Peanuts*, featuring the beloved characters Charlie Brown and Snoopy the Dog.

1865 Alice in Wonderland

The children's classic *Alice's Adventures in Wonderland* by British author Lewis Caroll was published in London, UK. The fictional account of a young girl's experiences in a fantasy world of peculiar characters became an international bestseller.

Also on this day

1922 British archaeologist Howard Carter entered Pharaoh Tutankhamen's tomb in Egypt, which was full of ancient treasures.

1949 The Constitution of India was adopted, with the country's laws and principles documented in the world's longest written constitution.

2008 A series of terrorist attacks began in Mumbai, India, killing 174 people.

Also on this day

1924 The first annual Macy's Thanksgiving Day Parade took place in New York City, USA.

2013 Disney's fantasy film *Frozen* was released to packed cinemas, becoming one of the highest-earning animated films of all time.

2019 The president of Ghana gave 126 people Ghanaian citizenship to commemorate the 400-year anniversary of the first enslaved people from Africa landing in Jamestown, USA.

1890 Football nets

Goal nets for football matches were patented by British engineer John Alexander Brodie, making it easier to spot when a goal was scored. In 1891, nets were made compulsory for all league matches.

Wartime hero 1939

Despite losing his legs in a plane crash, British Royal Air Force (RAF) pilot Douglas Bader returned to duty in World War II wearing a pair of prosthetic legs to fly a fighter plane.

2015 Circus festival

The first African Circus Arts Festival opened in Ethiopia. More than 100 artists from around the continent showcased their talents to visitors, who were given free entry. The festival helped promote the circus arts in Africa.

Born this day

1701 Anders Celsius, Swedish astronomer. He built the Uppsala Astronomical Observatory in Uppsala, Sweden, and invented the Celsius temperature scale.

1940 Lee Jun-fan, Chinese-American martial artist. Better known as Bruce Lee, he starred in about 30 films, bringing kung fu to the masses.

November

28

1862

Notts County FC

The world's first professional football team Notts County Football Club was founded in Nottingham, UK. With their black and white striped kit, they have since been nicknamed The Magpies.

Also on this day

1814 A steam-powered printing press was used to print a newspaper for the first time. The press was designed by German engineers.

1895 The first US automobile race was won by engineer Frank Duryea in about 10 hours.

2012 A film adaptation of the first part of J R R Tolkien's classic fantasy novel *The Hobbit* was released in cinemas.

1893

Women at the polls

In New Zealand, 90,290 women queued up to cast their ballot in the country's national election. New Zealand was the first country in the world to grant all women the right to vote, following years of campaigning.

Pulsar discovery

1967

Astrophysicist Jocelyn Bell Burnell from Northern Ireland discovered the first pulsar in space – a very small, very dense, fast-spinning star that emits regular beams of radiation, like a flashing lighthouse.

Born this day

1943 Randy Newman, US film composer. He created the music for many of Pixar's animated films, such as *Toy Story* and *Monsters, Inc.*

Also on this day

1947 The United Nations voted to separate Palestine into an Arab state and a Jewish one (Israel), despite protests by Arab countries.

1949 New Zealand's first female Māori Member of Parliament, Iriaka Rātana, was elected.

1998 A record-breaking ensemble of 1,013 cello players came together in Kobe, Japan, to perform at the first Concert of 1,000 Cellists.

Born this day

1832 Louisa May Alcott, US author. She wrote the novel *Little Women*.

1976 Chadwick Boseman, Black American actor. In *Black Panther*, he became the first Black actor to take the lead role in a Marvel Cinematic Universe film.

1935 Schrödinger's famous cat

Austrian physicist Erwin Schrödinger published his thought experiment about a cat in a box with radioactive material, arguing that it's impossible to know if the cat is alive, dead, or both, if you can't see it.

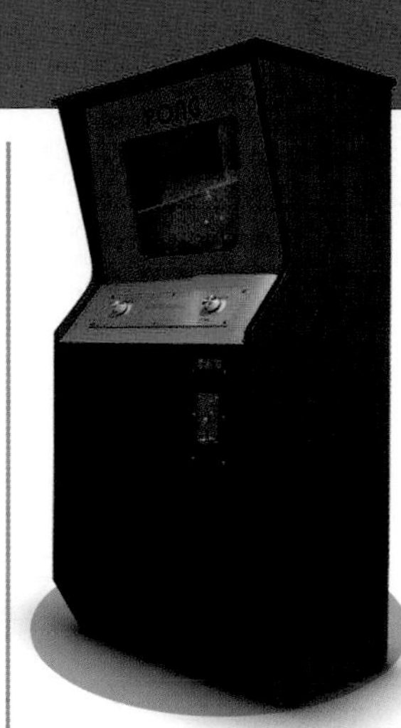

The birth of video gaming 1972

Inspired by table tennis, the first commercial hit arcade game *Pong* was launched by US video-game company Atari. Players competed by knocking a ball (a dot) back and forth using a paddle (a line). They won points when their opponent missed.

South Pole flight 1929

Richard E Byrd, a US Navy admiral, and his crew of three, became the first to fly over the South Pole. The round trip, setting out from their base on Antarctica's Ross Ice Shelf, took just over 17 hours.

November

30

2017 Over the rainbow

Students from the Chinese Culture University in Taiwan witnessed the longest-lasting rainbow on record. The keen observers produced more than 10,000 images to prove that it lasted exactly 8 hours and 58 minutes.

1872 Global kick-off

The first official international football game was played on a cricket ground in Glasgow, Scotland. The England versus Scotland match was watched by 4,000 spectators, and ended in a draw.

Also on this day

1803 The Balmis expedition, a Spanish health care mission, set off to vaccinate millions of people around the world against smallpox.

1954 Ann Hodges was hit by a meteorite when it crashed into her home in Alabama, USA. She walked away with just bruises.

2006 South Africa became the first country in Africa to legalize same-sex marriage when the Civil Union Act of 2006 came into effect.

Born this day

1874 Winston Churchill, British politician. He led the UK as prime minister in World War II.

1924 Shirley Chisholm, Black American politician. In 1968, she became the first Black woman to join the US Congress.

Bold boycott 1955

Black American activist Rosa Parks refused to give up her seat to a white passenger, and was arrested. Her protest led to the Montgomery Bus Boycott and the ban of racial segregation on US public buses.

Born this day

1761 Madame Tussaud, French artist. She made lifelike wax sculptures of famous people, and founded her own museum in 1835.

Also on this day

1640 The House of Bragança came into power in Portugal, ending the Iberian Union and 60 years of rule by the Spanish crown.

1959 Twelve countries signed the Antarctic Treaty, which banned military activity on the continent.

1990 Workers met midway under the English Channel as they dug the Channel Tunnel, which links the United Kingdom to France.

1988

HIV awareness

World AIDS Day was first established on this day to raise awareness of the millions of people living with HIV around the world. People wear a red ribbon on World AIDS Day each year to show their support.

1920

Straight off the line

The world's first moving assembly line in the car industry was introduced by US entrepreneur Henry Ford. This improvement slashed the time taken to make each Model T, so they became cheaper to produce, and therefore more affordable for ordinary families.

December 2

2017 Space pizza!

One of the world's favourite dishes finally reached orbit as astronauts in the International Space Station held a pizza party in space. The crew threw pizzas about in zero gravity before devouring them.

1988 Female leader

Pakistani politician Benazir Bhutto was sworn in as the prime minister of Pakistan. She was the first woman to lead the country, and served for five years over two terms.

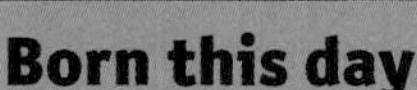

Born this day

1898 Indra Lal Roy, Indian aviator. An ace flyer, he was the only Indian pilot to see combat in World War I.

1946 Gianni Versace, Italian fashion designer. He founded the successful Versace fashion house.

Also on this day

1766 The Swedish parliament passed a law that guaranteed freedom of speech, making Sweden the first country in the world to do so.

1959 A film enhanced by aromas piped into the cinema, *Behind the Great Wall*, was shown for the first time. It was the first movie to use smells as part of the experience.

1805 Battle of Austerlitz

One of French general Napoleon's greatest victories occurred at Austerlitz, in modern-day Czechia. His army of 68,000 French troops managed to defeat the opposing 90,000 Austrian and Russian soldiers.

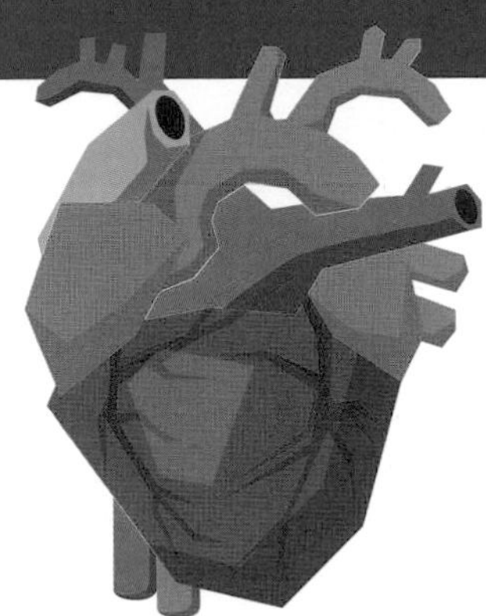

1967

Heart transplant

South African surgeon Christiaan Barnard and his team performed the first successful human-to-human heart transplant at the University of Cape Town, South Africa.

Born this day

1895 Anna Freud, Austrian psychoanalyst. She started the field of child psychoanalysis: using therapy to understand the minds of children.

1985 Amanda Seyfried, US actor. She starred in *Mean Girls, Mamma Mia!*, and voiced the role of Daphne in *Scoob!*

1926

Vanished!

British crime author Agatha Christie mysteriously disappeared from her home. A huge police search failed to locate her, but she reappeared 11 days later at a hotel. Christie said that she could not remember what had happened, and the mystery is still unsolved.

2001

Scooting about

The Segway Human Transporter – often called the Segway "scooter" – was unveiled by US inventor Dean Kamen. The original model could reach speeds of 13 kph (8 mph).

Also on this day

1689 The first successful surgery to separate conjoined twins finished in Basel, Switzerland. The surgery took nine days.

1992 The first International Day of Persons With Disabilities was held by the United Nations (UN).

1992 Neil Papworth, a British software whizz, sent the first text message.

December

2012 Early dinosaur

A *Nyasasaurus* fossil from Tanzania was dated at 245 million years old, making it the earliest known dinosaur by at least 10 million years. The fossil had been kept at London's Natural History Museum since the 1950s.

Also on this day

1676 The Battle of Lund was a bloody conflict fought between the Swedish army and Danish invaders.

1917 British psychiatrist W H Rivers presented his report on soldiers suffering the effects of shell shock after serving in World War I.

2019 A study found climate change to be the reason for North American birds becoming smaller over time.

Parker pen 1894

US inventor George Parker received a patent for his fountain pen with the unique Lucky Curve design, which fixed the problem of leaking ink. This was the first success for his Parker Pen Company.

Born this day

1973 Tyra Banks, Black American supermodel. The first Black woman to be featured on the cover of *GQ* magazine, she has been the face of many fashion and cosmetics campaigns, and has hosted her own TV talk show.

1872 Ghost ship

A mysteriously abandoned US ship, the *Mary Celeste*, was found drifting in the Atlantic Ocean. There was no sign of its crew on board, and they were never seen again. Theories explaining their disappearance range from underwater earthquakes to giant squid!

1935

Empowering Black women

The National Council for Negro Women was founded by Black American activist Mary McLeod Bethune to improve the lives of Black women in the USA.

Born this day

1901 Walt Disney, US animator and entrepreneur. He co-founded The Walt Disney Company and created many beloved cartoon characters, such as Mickey Mouse.

1916 Hilary Koprowski, Polish-American scientist. He developed the world's first polio vaccine that could be taken orally.

Lethal smog

1952

The Great Smog of London filled the city's air with pollution, mainly from burning coal. The foul smog lingered for four days, leading to the deaths of thousands. To prevent future smogs, the UK government introduced the Clean Air Act of 1956.

Battle of Leuthen

1757

Part of the Seven Years' War, the Battle of Leuthen saw King Frederick II of Prussia expand his empire by defeating a larger Austrian force.

Also on this day

1945 Flight 19, a group of five US military planes, went missing over the Bermuda Triangle, an area in the Atlantic Ocean known for the disappearance of aircraft and ships.

1955 The Montgomery bus boycott started when Black Americans refused to travel by bus in protest against racial segregation on public transport in the city of Montgomery, USA.

December 6

343 CE Saint Nicholas

The patron saint of children and sailors, Saint Nicholas, is believed to have died on this day. Christians celebrate this annual date as St Nicholas Day.

1913 Finding Nefertiti

More than 3,000 years after it was created, a bust of the Egyptian queen Nefertiti was found by German archaeologist Ludwig Borchardt in the city of Amarna, Egypt. It was buried under rubble at the site of the ancient workshop of the royal sculptor Thutmose.

Born this day

1977 Andrew Flintoff, British cricketer. A great player of the game, he won an MBE from Queen Elizabeth II for his services to cricket before retiring to become a television presenter.

Also on this day

1884 Construction of the Washington Monument was completed. It was built to honour George Washington, the first president of the USA.

1921 The Anglo-Irish Treaty was signed by the British government and Irish leaders to end the Irish War of Independence. It led to the establishment of the Irish Free State a year later.

2017 The discovery of the most distant supermassive black hole ever recorded, with a mass 800 million times greater than the Sun, was reported in the journal *Nature*.

1892 Nutcracker premiere

The first performance of the ballet *The Nutcracker,* created by Russian composer Pyotr Ilyich Tchaikovsky, was held in Saint Petersburg, Russia. The fairytale story was based on German author E T A Hoffmann's classic Christmas story for children.

December 7

1972

Blue Marble

While flying to the Moon, the *Apollo 17* crew took a picture of Earth from 29,000 km (18,000 miles) away. Called the Blue Marble, this photograph was shared around the world.

2019

Quadruple flip first

At the ISU Grand Prix of Figure Skating Final in Italy, teenage Russian figure skater Alexandra Trusova performed the first-ever quadruple flip jump by a female athlete in a figure skating competition.

Also on this day

1835 The first steam railway in Germany, the Bavarian Ludwig Railway, opened.

1909 The first synthetic plastic, named Bakelite, was patented by Belgian chemist Leo Baekeland. It was advertised as "the material of 1,000 uses".

1998 At the age of 17, German-Australian navigator Jesse Martin set sail on his solo trip around the globe and set a new world record 11 months later as the youngest person to do so.

Born this day

1942 Reginald F Lewis, Black American entrepreneur. He set up a food company that grew into a billion-dollar business, making him the first Black American to achieve this feat.

1941

Pearl Harbor

Without warning, Japanese military aircraft bombed the US naval base at Pearl Harbor in Hawaii, killing at least 2,000 people. The next day, the USA declared war on Japan, entering World War II.

December 8

Antarctic concert

2013

With a show called Freeze 'Em All in Antarctica, US heavy metal band Metallica became the first band to play a concert in all seven continents. Because of Antarctica's fragile ecosystem, the sound was transferred from amplifiers directly to headphones worn by the crowd.

Measuring Everest

2020

The height of Mount Everest was officially revised to 8,848.86 m (29,031.69 ft) following a survey conducted by researchers in Nepal and China, countries which share a border that passes over the mountain.

1881

Electric iron

US inventor Henry W Seely applied for a patent for the first electric iron. This early device used electricity to generate a constant amount of heat, which was a huge improvement on irons heated on a stove.

Also on this day

1987 At a summit in Washington, DC, USA, Soviet leader Mikhail Gorbachev and US president Ronald Reagan agreed to cut down on their nuclear weapons, signalling a thawing of the Cold War.

2010 With the successful Dragon mission, SpaceX became the first private company to launch a spacecraft into Earth's orbit and then recover it.

2020 Ninety-year-old Margaret Keenan from Coventry, UK, became the first person to receive the COVID-19 vaccine outside clinical trials.

Born this day

1935 Dharmendra, Indian actor and film producer. A popular actor in Bollywood, he has starred in more than 300 films.

1940 Infantry tanks

During World War II, the North African campaign of the Allied forces opened with shots fired by British infantry tanks called Matilda II. Although slow-moving, these tanks were heavily armoured, protecting the infantry.

Born this day

1934 Judi Dench, British actor. She started out as a theatre actor in 1957 and went on to star in a wide range of films. She is well known for playing the character M in the *James Bond* film series.

1824 Battle of Ayacucho

During Peru's War of Independence, military general Antonio José de Sucre led an army of rebels to victory against Spanish forces, effectively ending Spanish rule in the country.

1955 Euro flag

The flag of Europe was adopted by the Council of Europe. It features a dark blue background with a circle of 12 golden stars at the centre, symbolizing the union of the European nations.

Also on this day

1979 The World Health Organization (WHO) declared the eradication of the deadly smallpox virus.

1992 During the Somalian Civil War, the UN launched an international mission called Operation Restore Hope to rescue Somalian civilians from hunger and violence.

December 10

Also on this day

1823 British palaeontologist Mary Anning discovered the first complete skeleton of a *Plesiosaurus*, a prehistoric marine reptile, in the cliffs of Lyme Regis in Dorset, England.

1996 South African president Nelson Mandela signed the country's new constitution into effect, confirming that South Africa was now a democracy.

1911 Double winner

Polish physicist Marie Curie received her second Nobel Prize for discovering the elements radium and polonium, following her win for her research on radiation in 1903. This historic double win made her the first person to be awarded Nobel Prizes in different categories.

1901 Nobel Prize

To recognize outstanding achievements in chemistry, literature, medicine, peace, and physics, the first set of Nobel Prizes was given out. This fulfilled the last wishes of celebrated chemist Alfred Nobel and took place on the fifth anniversary of his death.

1868 Traffic lights

The world's first traffic lights were introduced outside the Palace of Westminster in London, UK. They made use of an adapted railway signal system, with semaphore arms and red and green gas lamps to indicate "stop" and "move with caution" for horse carriages and pedestrians.

Born this day

1815 Ada Lovelace, British mathematician. She worked on algorithms for an early computing machine, and is considered the world's first computer programmer.

December 11

1964 Revolutionary's speech

After leading the Cuban Revolution, Che Guevara gave a speech at the United Nations General Assembly in New York City, USA. He called on the USA to end its interference in Cuban affairs and to return occupied land.

Born this day

1843 Robert Koch, German physician. He discovered the bacteria that cause tuberculosis and cholera, winning a Nobel Prize for his work.

1911 Qian Xuesen, Chinese scientist. He made advances in aerodynamics that helped develop China's missile and space programmes.

Also on this day

1941 During World War II, Germany and Italy sided with Japan and declared war on the USA.

1946 The United Nations International Children's Emergency Fund (UNICEF) was set up by the UN after World War II to help vulnerable children in Europe and China.

1997 The Kyoto Protocol was signed in Kyoto, Japan, with many countries agreeing to reduce their greenhouse gas emissions.

1910 Neon lamp

The world's first neon lamp was presented to the public by French engineer Georges Claude at an exhibition in Paris, France. His glass tubes of neon gas gave off a glow similar to light bulbs.

2019 Prehistoric art

Dated at nearly 44,000 years old, cave paintings found in Sulawesi, Indonesia, were reported by science journal *Nature* to be the earliest examples of rock art showing animals and humans.

December

12

New national park

2001

Phong Nha-Ke Bang nature reserve in northern Vietnam was declared a national park to better protect the variety of rare animals and plants living there. The enormous park contains 300 caves, including the world's largest.

Born this day

1915 Frank Sinatra, US singer and actor. He sold more than 150 million albums and starred in a number of successful films.

Also on this day

1901 Italian inventor Guglielmo Marconi claimed to have sent the first radio transmission across the Atlantic Ocean.

1913 Leonardo da Vinci's painting *Mona Lisa* was found in an Italian hotel two years after it was stolen from the Louvre museum in France.

2015 The Paris Agreement, which set out goals to limit global warming to less than 2°C, was adopted by 196 countries.

2015

Votes for women

For the first time, Saudi Arabian women took to the polls, after they were granted the right to vote in local elections. They could stand as candidates, too. Saudi Arabia is the latest country to give women the vote.

December

13

2017 Acrobats on ice

The world-famous Cirque du Soleil performed its first circus show on ice, *Crystal*. Acrobats and ice skaters wowed the audience with their fearless stunts.

Born this day

1925 Dick Van Dyke, US actor and dancer. His 70-year career included film hits such as *Mary Poppins* and *Chitty Chitty Bang Bang*.

1967 Jamie Foxx, Black American actor and musician. His films include *The Amazing Spider-Man 2* and *Ray*. With four music albums to his name, he's also a Grammy winner.

2000

Plant DNA

Scientists decoded the first plant genome (set of genetic instructions), for a species known as *Arabidopsis thaliana*. This achievement made it possible to study which genes affect how a plant fights disease or survives with little water.

Also on this day

1545 At the Council of Trent, a group of Catholic bishops first met in Italy to discuss ways to reform the Catholic Church. This was in response to the rise of Protestantism, an alternative way to practise Christianity.

1939 World War II's first naval battle, the Battle of the River Plate, saw Germany fight the UK and New Zealand in the South Atlantic. It was a decisive victory for the Allies.

Snow in Egypt 2013

Egypt's capital city Cairo saw snow for the first time in 112 years as Storm Alexa battered countries in the Middle East with heavy snowfall and freezing temperatures.

December

14

1812

Retreat in the cold

The French invasion of Russia, led by Napoleon Bonaparte, ended after almost six months, with the last of the French forces leaving the country. The French were not prepared for the brutal Russian winter and left defeated.

Born this day

1918 BKS Iyengar, Indian yoga instructor. He introduced a version of yoga that focused on precision and alignment in postures.

1911

South Pole

In the race to reach the South Pole in Antarctica, Norwegian explorer Roald Amundsen and his team were victorious, planting their country's flag in celebration on arrival. They reached the pole 33 days before the British expedition led by Robert Falcon Scott.

1977

Saturday Night Fever

The world premiere of *Saturday Night Fever* took place in Los Angeles, USA. The film's dance sequences made a star of young actor John Travolta.

Also on this day

1962 NASA's robotic probe *Mariner 2* became the first spacecraft to fly by Venus.

1985 Wilma Mankiller was sworn in as the Principal Chief of the Cherokee Nation. She was the first woman to lead a major Indigenous American tribe.

1994 Work began on the Three Gorges Dam on the Yangtze River in China. It harnesses hydroelectric power from the river, and is now the world's largest power station.

December

15

2009

Clever octopus

Scientists in Indonesia reported seeing a veined octopus picking up coconut shells from the ocean bed and fitting them together to build a hideaway home. This was the first known example of an invertebrate (animal with no backbone) using tools in nature.

Also on this day

1612 German astronomer Simon Marius was the first to use a telescope to view the Andromeda galaxy (a system of millions of stars). Marius thought he was looking at a cloud of dust and gas within our own galaxy.

1929 Swiss pilot Walter Mittelholzer became the first to fly over Mount Kilimanjaro, the tallest mountain in Africa.

2011 The seven-year Iraq War ended when the USA announced the completion of its military mission in Iraq.

Born this day

37 CE Nero, Roman emperor. A cruel and ruthless ruler, he was rumoured to have caused the Great Fire of Rome, which left two-thirds of the city in ashes.

1832 Gustave Eiffel, French engineer. His most famous design is the Eiffel Tower in Paris, France.

1903

Ice-cream cups

Italian food vendor Italo Marchiony received the patent for his ice-cream cup machine, a moulding kit that created small pastry cups with handles for holding the sweet treat.

1989

Mount Redoubt

Ash from volcanic clouds spewed forth by the eruption of Mount Redoubt in Alaska, USA, caused an aircraft's engines to fail. The plane landed safely, but as a result of this event, the Alaska Volcano Observatory began closely monitoring volcanic activity in the region.

December

16

755

Chinese uprising

During the Chinese Tang Dynasty, rebellious military officer An Lushan staged a revolt against chancellor Yang Guozhong. This caused an uprising that spread throughout China and left the ruling Tang Dynasty weakened and in turmoil.

Also on this day

1707 Mount Fuji in Japan erupted, throwing volcanic rock and ash all over the city of Edo (modern-day Tokyo), 100 km (62 miles) away.

1850 British ships and settlers arrived in New Zealand, after the Canterbury Association in the UK decided to establish a colony there.

1944 The Battle of the Bulge began when Germany launched its final major attack of World War II, in the Ardennes, Belgium.

Born this day

1932 Quentin Blake, British artist. He created instantly recognizable illustrations for more than 300 books, including those by children's author Roald Dahl.

1773 Boston Tea Party

Angry at having to pay taxes to the British parliament, US colonists protested by climbing aboard British ships in Boston Harbor and dropping about 300 chests filled with tea leaves into the water. This event became known as the Boston Tea Party.

December 17

1903 Wright flight

US engineer Orville Wright piloted the first powered, heavier-than-air flight, lasting 12 seconds and covering 36 m (120 ft). Orville and his brother Wilbur continued testing the aircraft throughout the day.

Born this day

1945 Jacqueline Wilson, British author. She has written more than 100 children's books, often about young people experiencing big or challenging life events.

1973 Paula Radcliffe, British runner. She won the New York and London marathons three times each and was the world's fastest female marathon runner for 16 years.

Also on this day

1892 The first issue of weekly newspaper *Vogue* was published – it later became an iconic fashion magazine.

1989 The famous family of Homer, Marge, Bart, Lisa, and Maggie were introduced on US television in the first full episode of the cartoon *The Simpsons*.

2019 In Denmark, DNA taken from birch tar, which was used as chewing gum in ancient times, revealed details about a young female hunter-gatherer from 5,700 years ago.

1790 Sun stone

Commissioned by 15th-century Aztec ruler Axayacatl, the Sun Stone was rediscovered during renovations at Mexico City Cathedral. It had gone missing when Spain conquered the Aztec Empire.

Bike trip

In the city of Yokohama, Japan, British cyclist Thomas Stevens completed his round-the-world trip on a penny farthing, making history as the first person to travel the globe by bicycle.

December

18

Heroic "Tigers"

1941

Made up of former US Army pilots, The Flying Tigers engaged in combat for the first time in their distinctive aircraft. They were victorious in defending China against Japanese troops during World War II.

Born this day

1946 Steven Spielberg, US director. He has directed many acclaimed films, such as *Jurassic Park* and *E.T. the Extra-Terrestrial.*

1980 Christina Aguilera, US singer. Known for her four-octave vocal range, she has sold more than 75 million records worldwide.

Also on this day

1865 The Thirteenth Amendment was formally adopted, abolishing slavery in the USA.

1898 French racing car driver Gaston de Chasseloup-Laubat achieved the first land speed record, at 63.159 kph (39.245 mph).

1974 Soldier Teruo Nakamura of the Imperial Japanese Army was discovered hiding on the Indonesian island of Morotai, unaware that World War II had ended 29 years earlier.

A step for migrants

2000

To raise awareness of migration, the first International Migrants Day was recognized by the UN General Assembly (UNGA). Millions of people around the world choose to migrate, while others are forced to migrate due to war or persecution.

Tree dweller

1999

US activist Julia "Butterfly" Hill ended her protest against the extensive logging of California redwood trees. She had spent 738 days living in one of the trees, which she named "Luna".

December 19

1974

Mini computer

A pioneering do-it-yourself computer kit went on sale for the first time. The Altair 8800, produced by US company MITS, came with 256 bytes of memory – enough to store one sentence of text.

Also on this day

1843 The classic Christmas ghost story of redemption, *A Christmas Carol*, by British author Charles Dickens, was published.

1958 US president Dwight D Eisenhower sent a message into orbit. His voice became the first ever to be transmitted into space.

1983 The original football FIFA World Cup trophy, known as the Jules Rimet Trophy, was stolen in Brazil. It has never been recovered.

Born this day

1875 Carter G Woodson, Black American historian. In 1926 he launched the celebration of Negro History Week, which helped to inspire Black History Month.

Heating up

2019

Australia declared a state of national emergency as firefighters battled against nearly 100 bushfires. Caused by a record-breaking heatwave and extreme wind conditions, the raging fires spread from regions in South Australia to the east of the country.

2018

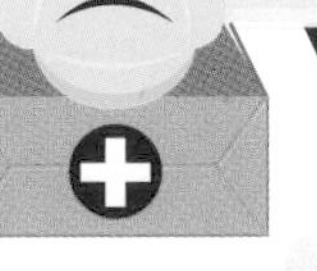

Drone delivery

A baby on an island in Vanuatu became the first to receive a vaccine delivered by a drone. This was part of the UNICEF charity's aim to immunize people living in remote communities.

December 20

Spymaster 1573

English diplomat Sir Francis Walsingham became Queen Elizabeth I's principal secretary. Using spies and secret agents, he protected the Protestant monarch from several Catholic plots, and executed her main rival, Mary, Queen of Scots.

1812 Grimm tales

German brothers Jacob and Wilhelm Grimm published their first volume of popular folk tales, *Children's and Household Tales* (later known as *Grimm's Fairy Tales*).

Born this day

1978 Geremi Sorele Njitap Fotso, Cameroonian footballer. He was famous for his ability to play in a number of different positions on the field.

Also on this day

1860 The US state of South Carolina broke away from the Union, which contributed to the outbreak of the US Civil War.

1951 The EBR-1 in Idaho, USA, became the first nuclear power plant in the world to generate electricity. The power it produced lit four light bulbs.

1999 Macau was handed over to China by Portugal, ending almost 600 years of colonial control.

Rowing feat

2015

A crew of disabled military personnel set off across the Atlantic Ocean to become the first physically disabled team of four to row any ocean. It took them 46 days, 6 hours and 49 minutes in their boat *Invictus*.

December 21

1913

The first crossword

The world's first modern crossword, by British-American journalist Arthur Wynne, was published in the *New York World* newspaper – although the idea can be traced back to ancient Rome.

Born this day

1914 Frank Fenner, Australian scientist. He helped to eradicate smallpox and to control Australia's rabbit plagues.

1948 Samuel L Jackson, Black American actor and producer. His films have made more than US $27 billion worldwide.

2012

Maya doomsday

The end of a cycle of the Maya calendar led to predictions that the world would end on this date, although scholars have never found evidence that the ancient Mayas actually believed this.

1968

Lift-off!

Apollo 8 was launched from the Kennedy Space Centre in Florida, USA. It was the first crewed spacecraft to leave Earth's orbit and reach another celestial object, the Moon, which it orbited 10 times.

Also on this day

1848 Ellen and William Craft escaped enslavement by daringly disguising themselves as a white man travelling with his servant.

1988 A bomb exploded on board Pan Am Flight 103 over Lockerbie, Scotland, killing 270 people – the UK's deadliest air disaster.

2020 Saturn and Jupiter appeared in a "great conjunction", the closest they had been when viewed from Earth since 1623.

December 22

1891

It's a rip off!

US inventor Seth Wheeler became the first person to sell perforated toilet paper in the USA. Though toilet paper was not new, his design allowed the user to easily tear off sheets.

1882

Christmas lights

Edward H Johnson, a US inventor, was the first person to use electric lights to decorate a Christmas tree. Before this, wax candles were used, which could be very dangerous.

Born this day

1960 Jean-Michel Basquiat, Black American artist. He mixed graffiti and painting to make unique artworks.

1962 Ralph Fiennes, British actor. He played the role of Voldemort in the *Harry Potter* films.

Also on this day

1788 Quang Trung proclaimed himself emperor of Vietnam.

1938 A coelacanth, a fish believed to have been extinct for 66 million years, was found in South Africa.

1971 Médecins Sans Frontières was founded. This humanitarian medical organization works globally to provide health care, particularly in regions with war and disease.

1989

Brandenburg Gate reopens

Closed for almost 30 years, the Brandenburg Gate reopened in Berlin, Germany. The landmark had become a symbol of the division of both the city and the country after World War II. Its reopening signalled the end of the Cold War, and Germany reunited a year later.

December

23

1897 Noche de Rábanos

The first *Noche de Rábanos* (Night of the Radishes) was held in Oaxaca, Mexico, to draw attention to the city's Christmas market. These days, revellers celebrate by carving radishes into figures and placing them together in scenes.

583 Maya queen

Yohl Ik'nal was crowned ruler of Palenque, a Maya city-state in modern-day Chiapas, Mexico. She was the first – and one of the only – female rulers that we know about in Maya history.

1997 Hanukkah in Vatican City

A Hanukkah candle – a symbol of the Jewish religion and the Jewish holiday of Hanukkah – was lit in celebration for the first time in the Vatican City, the centre of the Catholic Christian faith.

Also on this day

1952 Alain Bombard, a French biologist, completed a solo voyage across the Atlantic Ocean with no supplies of food or drink.

1970 The World Trade Center North Tower was finished. At 417 m (1,368 ft), it was the tallest building in the world at that time.

2007 Nepal became a federal republic, abolishing its monarchy.

Born this day

1867 Sarah Breedlove, Black American entrepreneur. Also known as Madam C J Walker, she was the first self-made female millionaire.

December 24

1818 Silent Night

Joseph Mohr and Franz Xaver Gruber gave the first performance of *Silent Night*, which has since become a favourite of Christmas carol singers around the world.

Also on this day

1801 British inventor Richard Trevithick showcased his steam-powered vehicle – the first of its kind that could carry passengers.

1893 Henry Ford – founder of the Ford car company – successfully tested his first engine invention.

1968 US astronauts aboard *Apollo 8* became the first humans to enter the Moon's orbit.

Born this day

1868 Emanuel Lasker, German chess player. He was the World Chess Champion from 1894 to 1921.

1956 Anil Kapoor, Indian actor. He has starred in many TV series and films, including *Mr India* and *Slumdog Millionaire*.

1943 Supreme commander

As World War II raged, US general Dwight D Eisenhower was put in charge of Operation Overlord – the planned Allied invasion of territory occupied by Germany. After the war, Eisenhower went on to be elected US president in 1953.

1878 Inventing the phonograph

US inventor Thomas Edison filed an application to patent his latest invention, the phonograph. This new device was capable of recording sound onto metal cylinders and playing it back.

December 25

Imperial coronation 800

Charlemagne was crowned the first Holy Roman Emperor. He united most of western Europe under his rule, earning him the title *Pater Europea*, or "Father of Europe".

Also on this day

336 CE Christmas was celebrated on 25 December for the first time in recorded history.

1776 George Washington crossed the Delaware River during the American Revolutionary War, surprising his British opponents.

1831 The Great Jamaican Slave Revolt saw thousands of enslaved Jamaicans rebel in an unsuccessful attempt to gain their freedom.

1223 First nativity scene

To celebrate the story of Christ's birth, St Francis of Assisi set up the first nativity scene. It is now an annual tradition among many Christians.

Born this day

1642 Isaac Newton, English mathematician and physicist. He developed theories about gravity and motion.

1971 Justin Trudeau, Canadian prime minister. As leader of the Liberal Party, he was elected to power in 2015.

Christmas truce 1914

In the midst of World War I, British and German soldiers called a brief truce, halting battle to meet in No Man's Land. Some even played football together before returning to the trenches.

December 26

1966 Kwanzaa celebration

The first *Kwanzaa*, meaning "first fruit" in Swahili, began in Los Angeles, USA. The seven-day annual festival is celebrated by Americans of African descent.

Ancient takeaway 2020

Almost 2,000 years after the city of Pompeii in Italy was buried during a volcanic eruption, archaeologists revealed they had uncovered a painted counter of an ancient street food shop, which sold fast food and drinks to hungry customers passing by.

Born this day

1791 Charles Babbage, British engineer. A pioneer of early computing, he designed the first mechanical computer, known as the Difference Engine, though he died before seeing his invention finished.

Feature film 1906

At 60 minutes long, *The Story of the Kelly Gang*, about the exploits of 19th-century outlaw Ned Kelly, became the world's first narrative feature film. Today only parts of the film survive.

Also on this day

1898 In France, scientists Marie and Pierre Curie declared they had discovered a new element – radium.

1991 The Soviet of the Republics (part of the Soviet Union's law-making body) voted to end the Soviet Union.

2004 An earthquake in Sumatra, Indonesia, caused a huge tsunami that devastated areas near to the coast.

Also on this day

1512 King Ferdinand II passed the Laws of Burgos to try to improve how Spanish settlers treated South American Indigenous Peoples.

1935 In Berlin, Germany, Regina Jonas became the first-ever female rabbi (Jewish religious leader).

2013 British adventurer Maria Leijerstam finished cycling from the Antarctic coast to the South Pole, becoming the first person to do so.

Huge pit find

1966

The world's largest cave shaft, named the Cave of Swallows, was found in Aquismón, Mexico. It measures 370 m (1,214 ft) in depth, deep enough for the Eiffel Tower to easily fit inside it.

Born this day

1995 Timothée Chalamet, US actor. He rose to fame in the film *Call Me By Your Name*, and has gone on to receive praise and award nominations for his work.

1722

Yongzheng's reign begins

The rule of Yongzheng Emperor began in China. He was one of the three great Qing Dynasty emperors, and helped to reduce corruption in the country during his peaceful 13-year reign.

Off to Neverland!

1904

Scottish author J M Barrie's play *Peter and Wendy*, about Peter Pan – a young boy from a place called Neverland who could fly – had its opening night.

December 28

1895 First picture show

French inventors the Lumière brothers set up the first-ever paid public screening of a film. The Cinématograph, a portable device patented by them, projected nine short films to an amazed audience.

Born this day

1922 Stan Lee, US comic book publisher. He co-created the superheroes Spider-Man, the X-Men, and many more.

1964 Denzel Washington, Black American actor. He has played the lead in many Hollywood thrillers and dramas.

1065 Medieval church

Westminster Abbey, in London, UK, was consecrated. A renovated monastery, it has been the setting of many coronations, and remains a burial place for famous figures – from warriors to poets.

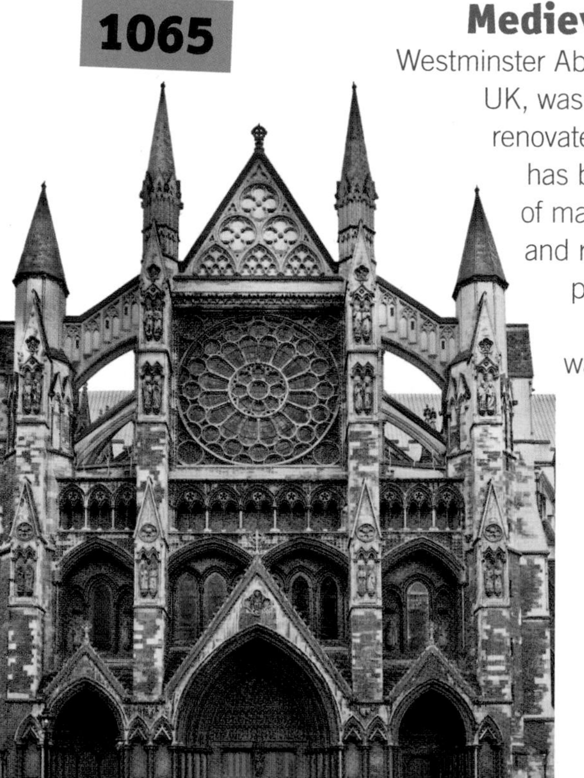

1912 Riding the rails

An estimated 50,000 people turned up to see the first public streetcars, the Municipal Railway No. 1, in San Francisco, USA. These vehicles are now part of the world's last manually operated cable car system.

Also on this day

1612 Neptune was seen for the first time by Italian astronomer Galileo Galilei, who mistook it for a star.

1886 The first automatic dishwasher, which was turned by hand, was patented by US inventor Josephine Cochran.

1973 The United States Endangered Species Act came into force to protect threatened species from becoming extinct.

December 29

1933
Dynamic duo

When *Flying Down to Rio* was released, it featured Fred Astaire and Ginger Rogers dancing together for the first time. The pair went on to star in some of the most glamorous Hollywood musicals of their time.

Born this day

1766 Charles Macintosh, Scottish inventor. He is known for inventing waterproof fabric and the Mackintosh raincoat is named after him.

1981 Shizuka Arakawa, Japanese figure skater. She was the first Japanese skater to win an Olympic gold medal.

2008
Worthy winners

In the USA, the Canadian Montreal Canadiens beat the US Florida Panthers, becoming the first ice hockey team in NHL history to win 3,000 regular-season games.

Also on this day

1860 Built for the British Royal Navy, the mighty HMS *Warrior* was launched – one of the first armour plated, iron-hulled warships.

1922 Canadian-American teenager Aloha Wanderwell set off to become the first woman to circle the globe in a Ford 1918 Model T.

1937 The Irish Free State was renamed Ireland with the adoption of a new constitution.

1653
Master of his craft

Dutch painter Johannes Vermeer registered as a master painter. Much of his artistic training remains a mystery. He would later go on to paint the famous *Girl with a Pearl Earring*.

December 30

534 Code of Justinian

A set of laws written down at the request of Byzantine emperor Justinian I came into effect throughout the Eastern Roman Empire. This law code forms the basis for many legal systems found in Europe today.

1986 Gas detectors

The British government announced plans to replace canaries in mines with electronic gas detectors. Canaries are more sensitive to poisonous gases than humans, so were taken down into mines as early warning systems.

Born this day

1975 Tiger Woods, US golfer. He has spent more weeks as the No. 1 golf player in the world than anyone else.

1984 LeBron James, Black American basketball player. Recognized as one of the greatest basketball players ever, he has had a long career, which includes NBA Championship and Olympic wins.

Also on this day

1922 The Soviet Union was formed when Russia, Ukraine, Belarus, and the Transcaucasus (Georgia, Armenia, and Azerbaijan) approved the Treaty on the Creation of the USSR.

1924 US astronomer Edwin Hubble shared proof that galaxies (systems of millions or billions of stars) exist beyond our own Milky Way.

1927 Ginza line

The first underground railway in Asia began service in Tokyo, Japan. It proved so popular that people waited in line for two hours just to make a short journey.

December 31

Also on this day

1935 The board game Monopoly was patented. It has since sold more than 250 million sets.

1999 Major celebrations were held all around the globe as the world marked the start of a new millennium.

2020 The UK formally left the European Union four years after the British public voted on whether to leave or remain.

1853

Dinosaur dinner

In the belly of a half-finished iguanodon sculpture, its creator Benjamin Waterhouse Hawkins held a dinner party for friends. The dinosaur was being built as a new attraction for Crystal Palace Park in London, UK.

1879

Incandescent light

US inventor Thomas Edison lit up his laboratory, as well as the surrounding area, in Menlo Park, USA. This was the first public demonstration of his incandescent light bulb.

Born this day

1948 Donna Summer, Black American singer and songwriter. Her 1977 single *I Feel Love* was a major hit in the disco genre, and laid the foundations for electronic dance music.

1995 Gabby Douglas, Black American gymnast. She was the first Black American to become all-round individual Olympic gymnastics champion, in 2012.

1907

Times Square tradition

New Year's Eve celebrations held in Longacre Square (now called Times Square) in New York City, USA, featured the first "ball drop" – a ball descending down a flagpole to count down to the new year. The tradition continues to this day.

Index

E

F

G

H

I

J K

Acknowledgments

The publisher would like to thank the following people for their help with making this book: Vikas Chauhan and Baibhav Parida for design assistancev Bandana Paul for illustrations; Avanika, Edward Aves, Kathakali Banerjee, Sreshtha Bhattacharya, Shaila Brown, Steven Carton, Ben Ffrancon Davies, Alexandra di Falco, Ian Fitzgerald, Ben Morgan, Rupa Rao, Neha Samuel, Anuroop Sanwalia, Pauline Savage, and Vatsal Verma for editorial assistance; Neeraj Bhatia, Mohd. Rizwan, and Vikram Singh for colour work; Vishal Bhatia for DTP assistance; Vagisha Pushp for picture research; Suhita Dharamjit, Priyanka Sharma, and Saloni Singh for the jacket; Victoria Pyke for proofreading; and Helen Peters for indexing.

Picture Credits

The publisher would like to thank the following for their kind permission to reproduce their photographs:

(Key: a-above; b-below/bottom; c-centre; f-far; l-left; r-right; t-top)

123RF.com: Maria Averburg 331tc, Corey A Ford 284cla, Godruma 343ca, kaowenhua 330tc, kchung 47bl, OLEKSII Kovtun 77cla, Krisztian Miklosy 12c, Frederic Prochasson 187br, tang90246 303tr, Marguerite Voisey 86br; **akg-images:** Africa Media Online 13cr; **Alamy Stock Photo:** 504 collection 172tc, Abaca Press 101br, 293cr, 366cla, Abaca Press / Hamilton / Pool 21ca, Abaca Press / Julien Poupart 221cra, Abaca Press / Laurent Zabulon 47tl, AF archive 117tl, agefotostock / Damian Davies 267ca, agefotostock / Historical Views 150br, Akademie / © ® The Nobel Foundation 350cr, Jerónimo Alba 311br, Album 30tr, 209ca, 317cla, Album / British Library 14c, Allstar Picture Library Ltd 127tl, Allstar Picture Library Ltd. 354tr, 369tl, Alpha Historica 22tc, 225cl, 351tl, Evan El-Amin 213cla, Sally Anderson 242cra, Antiqua Print Gallery 200b, Dzianis Apolka 193bc, Archive Images 108br, Art World 317cr, Arterra Picture Library / van der Meer Marica 21b, Artokoloro 124cla, 360cla, Aviation History Collection 277tc, Greg Balfour Evans 144br, 260bl, Holly Bickerton 359tl, BNA Photographic 52tr, Kevin Britland 147bl, Paul Brown 182tr, Bygone Collection 178b, Kristin Callahan / Everett Collection 306br, Chronicle 63br, 65cra, 98cla, 313tl, 341br, Amy Cicconi 267b, Classic Image 201bl, classicpaintings 48c, Cola Images 29tl, David Cole 300crb, Collection Christophel 249tl, Wendy Connett 321br, Dennis Cox 198ca, CPA Media Pte Ltd 297br, CPA Media Pte Ltd / Pictures From History 23cra, 74cra, 141ca, 155cra, 199bl, 213, 356tr, Ian Dagnall 103tl, 215cr, 239crb, Darling Archive 188t, REUTERS / David Gray 296cra, DE ROCKER 112tr, Design Pics Inc / Carrie McLain Museum / Alaska Stock 38bl, DOD Photo 316cla, dpa picture alliance 327cra, 335tl, Oscar Elias 346tr, Everett Collection Historical 35tl, 48br, 98br, 121br, 124b, 270cra, 273tl, Everett Collection Inc 169cr, Everett Collection Inc / © 20thCentFox 58tr, Everett Collection Inc / © Abramorama 151cra, Everett Collection Inc / © Warner Bros 214tr, Everett Collection Inc / CSU Archives 314tr, Everett Collection Inc / Ron Harvey 96tc, 368cr, Falkensteinfoto 326b, 354cla, Nicolas Fernandez 275br, FLHC 1 345cra, FLHC 40 298tr, FLHC1112 169clb, GL Archive 28br, 89tl, 95b, 119crb, 193cr, 248tr, 262tr, Glasshouse Images 197clb, graficart.net 227cr, Granger Historical Picture Archive 307cr, Granger Historical Picture Archive, NYC 23b, 31r, 37b, 42cl, 48cl, 79tl, 84cla, 155br, 156br, 159tl, 175ca, 176tr, 189cr, 246b, 271tc, 278tl, 279bl, 320tr, 324br, 328tr, 339crb, 341tl, The Granger Collection 332clb, Tom Grundy 348bl, Derek Harris 236tc, harry 314b, Hemis.fr / Jean-Marc Barrere 111tl, Paul Hennessy 258cla, Heritage Image Partnership Ltd / © Fine Art Images 166cla, 261cra, Heritage Image Partnership Ltd / Historic England 265tc, Heritage Image Partnership Ltd / Image / Index 91tl, Heritage Image Partnership Ltd / National Motor Museum 94b, Hi-Story 166bc, 223bl, Historic Collection 89cra, 295crb, 308br, Historic Images 221cla, History and Art Collection 77cr, 270bc, Horizon International Images Limited 190bl, Hum Images 81cr, IanDagnall Computing 126tc, 142cla, 144c, 164ca, 185tl, 266br, 296cl, 325cla, 326ca, imageBROKER / BAO 18tc, imageBROKER / Frank Sommariva 17cra, imageBROKER / Jochen Tack 249br, imageBROKER / Oleksiy Maksymenko 331br, Horizon Images / Motion 307b, incamerastock 298cla, incamerastock / ICP 51bc, 333bc, INTERFOTO / History 99cb, 102tc, 118br, 153bl, 283ca, INTERFOTO / Personalities 318ca, Ivy Close Images 162tc, Jimlop collection 206tc, Robert Kawka 137cra, Keystone Pictures USA 82tc, 2d Alan King 46b, Art Kowalsky 271cr, Lebrecht Music & Arts 10ca, 198tr, 240tr, 277br, Frans Lemmens 320b, Steve Lindridge 107tl, LOC Photo 357tl, Suzanne Long 223ca, Lordprice Collection 264tr, Malcolm Park editorial 310br, MARKA / Gustavo Tomsich 138bl, mauritius images GmbH / Jose Fuste Raga 247cra, mauritius images GmbH / Skaya 206b, MediaPunch Inc 233crb, MediaPunch Inc / John Palmer 334b, MediaPunch Inc / Mpi04 353tl, Mikołaj Michalak 352clb, David Morgan 143tl, movies 177tc, MPVHistory 90b, Mr.Black&White 166tc, MusicLive 212bl, Melinda Nagy 315tl, NASA Archive 56bl, National Geographic Image Collection / Tom Lovell 105tl, Nature Photographers Ltd / Paul R. Sterry 33tc, Sergey Nezhinkiy / © Canada Post Corporation 97cla, Niday Picture Library 60cla, 63tc, 255b, 300tr, 342b, NPS Photo 174tr, Old Paper Studios 235cl, Matteo Omied 328b, PA Images 139cra, PA Images / Anthony Devlin 310tr, PA Images / F. Stimpson 267tl, PA Images / Joe Giddens 112clb, PA Images / Lauren Hurley 360bl, PA Images / Neil Munns 87tl, Sean Pavone 65b, Photo 12 / Regency Enterprises 67tl, The Photo Access / Steven Bullock 318br, Photo12 / Archives Snark 26clb, Photo12 / Elk-Opid 295bc, Pictorial Press Ltd 5crb, 5bl, 8br, 59tr, 69cl, 114tr, 138tr, 141br, 147br, 155cla, 157ca, 186tr, 196tr, 224cla, 292ca, 307tl, 324ca, 332br, 354b, PictureLux / The Hollywood Archive 228tr, Ian Pilbeam 32tc, PJF Military Collection 50cla, Norman Pogson 146cla, PRiME Media Images / Andrew Rowland 154tr, Purepix 164b, Yao Qilin / Xinhua / Alamy Live News 80cla, Stefano Ravera 104cla, Realy Easy Star 370tc, Realy Easy Star / Toni Spagone 132cl, Reuters / Brendan Mcdermid 20bl, Reuters / Dondi Tawatao 60b, Reuters / Eddie Keogh 192tr, Reuters / Kieran Doherty 195br, Reuters / Leonhard Foeger 291bc, Reuters / Paul Darrow 219br, Reuters / Shamil Zhumatov 254bc, RGB Ventures / SuperStock / Natalie Fobes 89br, Riccardo Mancioli Archive & Historical 24t, Colin Rich 14bc, Peter Righteous 310cla, William Robinson 305b, Sam Rollinson 39tc, Sabena Jane Blackbird 334c, Tom Salyer 337cra, SBS Eclectic Images 108cla, Scherl / Süddeutsche Zeitung Photo 72br, 192b, Science History Images 106tr, 172tr, 201tl, Science History Images / Photo Researchers 8cla, 66clb, 181cla, 243cl, 326cr, 361cr, Separisa 168bl, Shawshots 128tr, Enrique Shore 27bl, Ian Skelton 145tl, Mark Smith 97br, Paul Souders 140b, SPUTNIK 32b, 173cb, State Archives of Florida / Florida Memory 345cla, Steve Davey Photography 255tl, Stock Imagery 240ca, Laurie Strachan 105bc, Todd Strand 239bc, Süddeutsche Zeitung Photo 34bl, Süddeutsche Zeitung Photo / Jose Giribas 319br, Phil Talbot 53bl, TAO Images Limited / Tianchun Zhu 274bl, TCD / Prod. DB / © BBC Studios 286cla, The History Collection 41cra, 85tl, 93cr, 205bc, 282br, The History Emporium 115cl, The Keasbury-Gordon Photograph Archive 364crb, The NASA Library 44tr, The Picture Art Collection 64bl, 117tr, 194bl, 251bl, 256tr, 281crb, 308tr, 346cl, 367cr, The Print Collector / Keystone Archives / Heritage Images 24bl, The Sports Dude 229clb, Trinity Mirror / Mirrorpix 15br, 45bc, 159cr, 177bl, 238br, U.S. Department of Defense Archive 187cb, Universal Art Archive 191br, UPI / Matthew Healey 231crb, UtCon Collection 125bl, V&A Images 87br, Marco Valentini 150cla, Lucas Vallecillos 4bl, 224b, 357cra, Ivan Vdovin 99br, Mike Veitch 355tc, Vintage_Space 152cla, WENN Rights Ltd 305cr, White House Photo 25tc, Milo Winter 121tl, World History Archive 57crb, 80tr, 163br, 183cla, 195cra, 214cla, 245cr, 259c, 286bl, 291tl, 304tr, 316bl, 366crb, YAY Media AS 148tl, ZUMA Press / © Joe Scarnici 91cr, ZUMA Press / © Scott A. Miller 36tc, ZUMA Press, Inc. / © Nancy Kaszerman 106bl, ZUMA Press, Inc. / © Richard Ellis 290b; **Archives Automobile Club de Monaco:** 26cr; **Avalon:** Zha Chunming 276tr, DPA Picture Alliance / DB Microsoft HO 100clb; **Bridgeman Images:** © Archives Charmet 195tl, © British Library Board. All Rights Reserved 137br, © Look and Learn 21cra, Look and Learn 297cra, Look and Learn / Peter Jackson Collection 98tr, National Trust Photographic Library 266cl, Peter Newark American Pictures 136bl, Peter Newark Military Pictures 130cra, © O. Vaering 288b; **© The Trustees of the British Museum. All rights reserved:** 43crb; **Eddie Clark:** 210br; **Courtesy of Smithsonian. ©2020 Smithsonian:** 66ca; **© Tim Davenport/WCS:** 146tr; **Dorling Kindersley:** Geoff Dann / Imperial War Museum, London 135c, Frank Greenaway / National Birds of Prey Centre, Gloucestershire 238tc, James Kuether 292br; **Dreamstime.com:** Albertoloyo 7tl, Alessandrozocc 22bl, Aleutie 149tl, Steve Allen 180cb, Altezza 368bl, Evgeny Babaylov 337cl, Pierre-yves Babelon 92b, Bargotiphotography 216crb, BiancoBlue 114b, Bouncy390 35b, Carolina K. Smith M.d. 127tc, Chiradech Chotchuang 50bl, Delstudio 36b, Destina156 349cra, Torian Dixon / Mrincredible 272tc, Viorel Dudau 19bc, Eastmanphoto 133clb, EPhotocorp 311tl, Artem Evdokimov 90tr, Alena Fayankova 186cla, Sheila Fitzgerald 237br, Svetlana Foote 336tr, Ed Francissen 153cr, Fredweiss 29bc, Benjamin Albiach Galan 6ca, Roberto Galan 291cra (man illo), Christos Georghiou 365cra, Godruma 85bc (Border Collie), 369br, Golasza 171b, Roxana Gonzalez 183r, Gordzam 43t, Igor Groshev 327b, Jon Helgason 276cla, Hobbitfoot 46cla, Hutchinsphoto 306cl, Vlad Ivantcov 282c, Jemastock 76cla, Jorisvo 293br, Jossdim 52cla, Raymond Kasprzak / Rkasprzak 283br, Wendy Kaveney 51br, Alexander Kirch 29crb, Alexander Kovalenko 370cla, Jesse Kraft 211b, Lexigel 35crb, Liskonogaleksey 45cla, Macrovector 357b, Martin Malchev 82cla, Markwaters 332cra, Dzianis Martynenka 86bc, Mast3r 311bl, Mcwilli1 62b, Anton Medvedev 71tc, Melica 42crb, Meowudesign 86bl, Microvone 170br, Krisztian Miklosy 158br, Minnystock 362b, Jaroslav Moravcik 52br, Mspoint 274cla, Pavel Naumov 83tl, Niky 002 369tc, Mykola Nisolovskyi 306tr, Stepanenko Oksana 15ca, Olgacov 148bl, Sean Pavone 71b, 132tr, Martin Pelanek 233bl, PixMarket 300cla, Olha Pohorielova 321clb, Pzaxe 69tc, Radevica 41b, Md. Mizanur Rahaman 85bc, Sabelskaya 22ca, Sborisov 323b, Ljubisa Sujica 359crb, Tartilastock 196bl, TasFoto 27c, Dmytro Tolda 225t, Tomas1111 84b, 232cla, 288tr, Travelling-light 134b, Typhoonski 104b, Vally 320cla, Vectomart 366tr, Hannu Viitanen 287cl, Wernerimages 291cra (girl illo), Xpdream 37tc, Yakub88 94tc, Yekaterinalimanova 319tl, Vladimir Yudin 13b, Andhi Yulianto 348cl, Yupiramos Group 362cla; ESA: Mars500 crew 160cr, NASA 251cr; **Getty Images:** © ABC / Contributor / Oscar Duarte 69b, AFP 122tr, AFP / - 137cla, 352br, AFP / Agence France Presse / Central Press 246tr, AFP / Alexander Blotnitsky 335bl, AFP / Brian Bahr 171cra, AFP / Carl Court 234cra, AFP / Denis Balibouse 218tr, AFP / Fabrice Coffrini 275tl, AFP / John D Mchugh 74bl, AFP / Kim Jae-Hwan 312br, AFP / Manjunath Kiran 329clb, AFP / Mike Fiala 175clb, AFP / Olle Lindeborg 102tr, AFP / Patricia Castellanos 363ca, AFP / Philippe Lopez 157tl, AFP / Prakash Singh 142br, AFP / Richard Juilliart 259tl, AFP / Rodrigo Buendia 16b, AFP / Tang Chhin Sothy 262br, AFP / Ted Aljibe 126bl, AFP / Trevor Samson 47cr, Allsport / Mike Powell 226br, Archive Photos 88cr, Archive Photos / Fotosearch 315cb, 358clb, Archive Photos / Graphic House 19cla, Archive Photos / Handout / Library of Congress 329tl, Archive Photos / Hulton Archive 253bc, Archive Photos / Library of Congress 161t, Archive Photos / MPI 130br, Archive Photos / New York Times Co. 45tc, Archive Photos / Robert Alexander 20tr, Archive Photos / Space Frontiers 322crb, Archive Photos / Stock Montage 365cl, Terje Bendiksby / AFP 309b, Bettmann 6br, 28bl, 57br, 61br, 73cra, 111cra, 115b, 129ca, 131bc, 156tr, 188bl, 199cla, 225br, 227b, 230br, 233cla, 253tl, 289cr, 302t, 324bl, 343bl, 350bl, Hamish Blair 181bl, Bloomberg 272br, Bloomberg / Mike Kane 167tl, Bongarts / Lutz Bongarts 214br, Andrew Burton 123br, Larry Busacca 119tc, Michael Campanella 238cra, CBS Photo Archive 257tl, Corbis / Ken Glaser 206cra, Corbis Historical 256b, Corbis Historical / adoc-photos 281bl, Corbis Historical / David Pollack 61tl, Corbis Historical / George Rinhart 31bl, Corbis Historical / Hulton Deutsch 209br, Corbis Historical / Leemage 279ca, Corbis Historical / Library of Congress / Eadweard Muybridge 172b, Corbis Historical / Micheline Pelletier 287tl, Corbis Historical / Stefano Bianchetti 136cla, Corbis Historical / VCG / David Turnley 122b, Corbis News / Ira L. Black 151b, Corbis Premium Historical / Ira Wyman 190cla, Corbis Sport / Tim Clayton 257cra, David Cannon Collection 179ca, De Agostini / DEA / A. DAGLI ORTI 163tr, 241tl, De Agostini / DEA / Biblioteca Ambrosiana 167bl, 226cla, De Agostini / DEA / G. Nimatallah 78bl, De Agostini Picture Library 92tr, 344br, 349clb, DigitalVision Vectors / ZU_09 50crb, Fairfax Media Archives / Miller 162bl, Fairfax Media Archives / Scott Whitehair 168br, Jonathan Ferrey 116c, Focus On Sport 294cra, Stu Forster 274cr, Future Publishing / James Sheppard 68tr, Gamma-Keystone / Keystone-France 107bl, Gamma-Rapho / Chip HIRES 342cl, David Gray 359cra, Jeff Gross 222tc, Handout / Predrag Vuckovic 184t, Handout / SpaceX 42tr, Matthias Hangst 229cra, Frazer Harrison 72cla, Hagen Hopkins 207br, Hulton Archive 189b, 196ca, 220cla, 285cr, 313br, Hulton Archive / Apic 325cb, Hulton Archive / Central Press 210cra, Hulton Archive / Culture Club 336br, Hulton Archive / Evening Standard 168tr, Hulton Archive / Fox Photos 250cra, Hulton Archive / Heritage Images 244br, 252bl, Hulton Archive / Keystone 239tl, Hulton Archive / Klemantaski Collection 152tr, Hulton Archive / Miller 287br, Hulton Archive / Print Collector 201tc, 202c, 284b, Hulton Archive / R. Knight 219tl, Hulton Archive / Sam Shere 132br, Hulton Archive / Tim Graham 259bl, Hulton Archive / Topical Press Agency 70tr, Hulton Royals Collection / London Stereoscopic Company 86tc, Hulton Royals Collection / Princess Diana Archive 216cla, Icon Sportswire / Cynthia Lum 203br, The Image Bank / Tuul & Bruno Morandi 208cra, Imperial War Museums / Fg. Off. S A Devon 337bl, IWM / Sgt. Chetwyn 321tl, Yunaidi Joepoet 351crb, Liu Kaiyou / Moment 302b, Kyodo News 170clb, 193tl, Mark Leech 301tc, Morris MacMatzen 128clb, Fred W. McDarrah 185br, David McNew 93tl, Michael Ochs Archives 162br, Manny Millan 49b, Mirrorpix 200cla, Mirrorpix / Monte Fresco 194tr, Jack Mitchell / Archive Photos 173cr, Moment / Geoff Livingston 169b, David Paul Morris 14tr, National Hockey League / Jeff Vinnick 135tl, New York Daily News Archive / Harry Warnecke 364bl, NordicPhotos / Lilja Kristjansdo 110b, NurPhoto / Mauro Ujetto 347tc, Paris Match Archive / Gamblin Yann 358br, Popperfoto 178cl, 263tl, 305clb, 340bl, Popperfoto / Bob Thomas 173cla, Rolls Press / Popperfoto 129br, Ross Land 18b, Science & Society Picture Library 66bc, 75tl, 120tc, 143cra, 144cra, 149crb, 228br, 230tr, 264bl, 301br, 322bl, 348tr, Cameron Spencer 282t, Sports Illustrated / George Long 313cra, Sports Illustrated / Jerry Cooke 205br, Sports Illustrated / Tony Triolo 269cra, Jamie Squire 227tl, SSPL / Daily Herald Archive 179bl, 338tr, Stocktrek Images 347bl, Sygma / Thierry Orban 268b, Sygma / William Nation 294b, Karwai Tang / WireImage 330bl, The Asahi Shimbun 76br, 208bl, 289bl, The Image Bank Unreleased / Ignacio Palacios 70cla, The LIFE Images Collection / Sahm Doherty 61cra, The LIFE Picture Collection / Loomis Dean 204tr, The LIFE Picture Collection / Time Life Pictures / Henry Groskinsky 17br, The LIFE Picture Collection / Time Life Pictures / J. R. Eyerman 336cla, Time Life Pictures / The LIFE Picture Collection 203tl, 240br, Toronto Star / Mike Slaughter 148tr, Toronto Star / Toronto Star 297clb, U.S. Coast Guard / Handout 116b, ullstein bild / Rudolf Dietrich 231tl, ullstein bild Dtl. 39cr, Photo12 / Universal Images 303br, Universal Images Group / Leemage 4tr, 220bc, Universal Images Group / Marka 198bl, Universal Images Group / PHAS 149bl, Universal Images Group / Photo 12 265cra, 277cl, Universal Images Group / Universal History Archive 15cl, 110cla, 365b, Ian Walton 232bl, WireImage / JAB Promotions 210cl; **Getty Images / iStock:** AlexPro9500 300bl, artisticco 211tl, Simon Dux 371bl, E+ / guenterguni 213b, E+ / JMichl 290tr, Givaga 353b, Srinivasan J 272cla, manpuku7 83c, Maurice Northrup 273b, pawel.gaul 96b, pictafolio 6crb, pseudodaemon 146b, Nicolas Tolstoï 292tr, ZU_09 75br; **Jorge Antonio Gonzalez:** 197ca; **Heritage Auctions, HA.com:** 184cb; **Library of Congress, Washington, D.C.:** LC-DIG-cwpbh-05089 252cla, LC-DIG-ds-00894 215bl, LC-DIG-ggbain-12476 / Bain News Service, publisher 68br, LC-DIG-ggbain-35680 130cl, LC-DIG-hec-16116 181cra, LC-DIG-npcc-17934 136tr, LC-DIG-ppmsca-02180 236cla, LC-DIG-ppmsca-03478 12tr, LC-DIG-ppmsca-54230 / Powelson, Benjamin F., 1823-1885 159bc, LC-USZ62-21222 280cla, LC-USZC4-1285 245tl; **Mary Evans Picture Library:** © The Royal Aeronautical Society (National Aerospace Library) 11t; **David L. Mearns / Blue Water Recoveries Ltd:** 134cla; **© The Metropolitan Museum of Art:** Bequest of Charles Allen Munn, 1924 312tr; **Marin Minamiya:** 109cr; **NASA:** 207tl, 248cla, 261tc, 312cla, DIGITAL 347tl, Brian Dunbar 108cr, ESA, NRAO / AUI / NSF and G. Dubner (University of Buenos Aires) 191tl, Aubrey Gemignani 154cla, JPL 55tc, JPL / Cornell University 30b, JPL-Caltech 223cr, NASAexplores 39bl, NSSDCA / Dr. David R. Williams 218b, Scientific Visualization Studio 286tr; **NAVY.mil:** 302cla; **Paul Cyr Photography:** 107cra; **Prosport International:** 81b; **Science Photo Library:** New Zealand American Submarine Ring Of Fire 2007 Exploration, Noaa Vents Program, The Institute Of Geological & Nuclear Sciences And Noaa-Oe 55br, Roman Uchytel 114cl, UIG / Dorling Kindersley 92cr; **Shutterstock.com:** 40tr, agencies 352tc, AlexAnton 59b, AP / Christian Palma 131cra, AP / Gene Smith 113bl, AP / Olivia Zhang 10b, AWI via ZUMA Wire / Stefan Hendricks 269br, Andrea Boohers 260cra, Samantha Crimmin 67b, Joshua Davenport 222bl, EPA / Kimimasa Mayama 117bl, EPA-EFE / Christian Bruna 291crb, James Fraser 58cl, Lukas Gojda 9, Kev Gregory 349tl, Dinesh Hukmani 158tr, J J Osuna Caballero 150crb, Kobal / National Geographic / J Chin 160l, Lukas Kovarik 299tl, melissamn 77b, myphotobank.com.au 299b, Paragon Space Dev Corp 303tl, S-F 258tr, spatuletail 99cra, Stacia020 250bl, Studio77 FX vector 273clb, Simon Tang 339tc, The Art Archive 49tl, Un Photo / Sipa 269cla, vectorOK 177r, Nickolas warner 367cl, Perla Berant Wilder 281cra, Kev Williams 82b; **SkyDrive:** 246cla; **Alexander Turnbull Library, Wellington, New Zealand:** Photograph of protesters on the Maori Land March, College Hill, Auckland. Heinegg, Christian F, 1940- :Photographs of the Maori Land March. Ref: PA7-15-17. Alexander Turnbull Library, Wellington, New Zealand. / records / 22898633 / photographer, Christian Heinegg 263bl; **V&A Images / Victoria and Albert Museum, London:** 83crb; **vanburenlegacy.com:** Dan Ruderman 257b; **Wellcome Collection:** Great War image from the Shahnameh. Attribution 4.0 International (CC BY 4.0) 73tl, Edward Jenner vaccinating a boy. Oil painting by E.-E. Hillemacher, 1884 140cla

26 8 11

2

13 10

5

31 17

24

23 16

28 25 22